Mary Meade's COUNTRY COOKBOOK

Mary Meade's
COUNTRY
COOKBOOK

By Ruth Ellen Church

Galahad Books · New York

Published in 1993 by

Galahad Books
A division of Budget Book Service, Inc.
386 Park Avenue South
New York, NY 10016

Galahad Books is a registered trademark of Budget Book Service, Inc.

This edition published by arrangement with Charles F. Church and Carter L. Church.

Library of Congress Catalog Card Number: 64-17448

ISBN: 0-88365-816-X

Printed in the United States of America.

To the Lovriens
Clark, Helen, Robin, and Frank
who make our country life
so much fun

Foreword

THIS IS a book about good, basic American cooking of the traditional kind. It is not a gourmet's cook book, and it is not a collection of short-cut recipes   longcut recipes often are better! It is just a carefully chosen, thoroughly tested assemblage of recipes for the kinds of food a family enjoys.

The recipes are those I use at home, both in the city and in the country cottage which all summer long—and sometimes in winter—is bursting its walls with humanity, usually young humanity. Humanity with big appetites.

Some of the recipes were $5.00 favorites of *Chicago Tribune* readers through the years. A few were very special $100 cook-of-the-month dishes. None is too difficult for a new cook and many are of the kind known as "old reliables." All have been tested many times, not only by me, but by members of the *Tribune's* Mary Meade staff, and some of them are family favorite recipes of my assistants.

I've tried to put into this book all of the recipes a homemaker will really need, although there have had to be numerous cuts and omissions simply because one book will not hold more than a few hundred. I hope it is a book which will be used until it is worn out, for that's the kind of cook book I've intended it to be.

Ruth Ellen Church

CONTENTS

BAKING

I'D LIKE to begin this book with a section on baking, for
here is where our greatest satisfactions and our greatest
rewards lie. Anybody with half a mind and ten minutes of
time can put together a casserole. But baking a loaf of
bread, a cake, a batch of cookies, or a pie takes a little time
and thought, and even a bit of skill. Not as much skill as
you may think, if you're a novice—it is easily acquired
skill. But enough to make it seem admirable to your friends.
Quite a lot of prestige goes with being able to bake something good. Quite a lot of joy in being creative. Quite a
lot of love and affection, when it's your family or your
friends you're baking for.

All Kinds of Breads

I WISH YOU COULD read some of the letters I receive from brides who have just discovered the joy of baking a loaf of bread. *Joy* is the very word. This girl has made a discovery: she has created something with her own hands that has pleased her husband and caused her mother-in-law to look upon her with greater satisfaction. As one young woman put it, "This is a way I can express my love for my family. I shall always give them homemade bread!"

I didn't tell her, but she'll soon find out that a woman can work off a good mad in a batch of yeast dough. When your husband or a child has caused your innards to tie themselves in knots and your brow to furrow with frustration, then, my dear, go get the yeast and the flour and the mixing bowl. Knead and beat and pummel away your anger. In that batch of bread you'll lose your desire to fling a plate at someone's head, or to have a good cry. This will be good for you, and OH! how good it will be for the family!

WHITE BREAD
Two LARGE LOAVES

Here's a beautiful bread you'll be proud to serve!

2 packages active dry or compressed yeast
1½ cups warm water (lukewarm for compressed yeast)
1½ cups milk, scalded
¼ cup sugar
1½ teaspoons salt
3 tablespoons shortening
7 cups flour (about)

Dissolve yeast in water. Add sugar, salt, and shortening to milk; let cool to lukewarm. Combine with yeast. Add 4 cups flour, beating until smooth, then work in about 3 cups more flour. At this stage the dough is somewhat sticky and rough looking. Turn out on a lightly floured board and knead until smooth and elastic, 8 to 10 minutes. Form into a ball and set in a large, greased bowl. Grease the top of the dough and cover the bowl with cloth. Let rise until doubled in bulk, about 1 to 1½ hours. Test by pressing finger deeply into dough; if indentation remains, the dough has risen sufficiently. Punch down, let rest 10 minutes, then cut in half and shape into 2 loaves. Place in greased pans, about 9x5 inches. Brush tops with melted fat and cover with clean towel. Again let rise until doubled, about 50 minutes. Bake at 425° F. for 40 to 45 minutes, or until browned. Remove from pans at once; let cool on racks away from draft.

SOME VARIATIONS OF WHITE BREAD

Apricot. Use 1 cup juice drained from cooked dried apricots in place of 1 cup milk or water in the recipe, and add 2 cups cooked apricots, cut fine, to dough.

Cheese. Add 1½ cups grated sharp cheese to dough.

Orange. Add 1 tablespoon grated orange rind, ½ cup sugar, 1 cup chopped candied orange peel to dough.

Prune or Raisin. Replace ½ cup milk or water with 2 beaten eggs and add 1 to 2 cups chopped cooked prunes, or raisins.

Rolled Cinnamon Loaf. Add 2 eggs and reduce liquid ½ cup. Make 3 cinnamon loaves, or 1 or 2 loaves and some pan rolls of the dough.

14

Roll one-third of the dough into rectangle for 1 loaf, brush with melted butter, sprinkle with 1 tablespoon cinnamon, ⅓ cup white or brown sugar, and raisins if you like. Roll as for jelly roll, place in greased pan for last rising. Bake at 400° F. for 10 minutes, then at 375° F. for 35 to 45 minutes.

Saffron. Steep ½ teaspoon saffron in 1½ cups boiling water 15 minutes, strain and cool water to warm or lukewarm for use in recipe. Add 1 cup currants, ¼ cup chopped citron to dough.

Pan Rolls from white bread dough. The kind mother used to make are ever so easy. Just butter your hands and roll pieces of dough into balls, place close together in buttered pans, let rise double, and bake 15 or 20 minutes, depending on size (they'll be brown and crusty when done), at 400° F. For cloverleaf rolls, put three tiny buttery balls of dough into each muffin cup and bake them individually.

WHOLE WHEAT BREAD   *Two* LARGE LOAVES

Use all whole wheat flour if you wish, but this combination makes a lighter-textured bread.

  2 packages active dry or compressed yeast
½ cup warm water (lukewarm for compressed yeast)
1½ cups hot water
  1 tablespoon salt
¼ cup shortening
⅓ cup molasses
3½ cups whole wheat flour (about)
2½ cups white flour

Soften yeast in warm water. Pour hot water over salt, shortening, and molasses; stir and cool. Add softened yeast and whole wheat flour, beating until smooth. Add remaining flour and work it in well with the hands. Turn onto floured board and knead until smooth and elastic. Place dough in a greased bowl, grease surface of dough, cover, and let rise until doubled in bulk, about 2 hours. Divide into 2 parts. Shape into loaves and place in greased loaf pans, about 8½x4½ inches. Cover and let rise about 30 minutes. Bake at 400° F. 50 to 60 minutes.

  Good with addition of nuts, raisins, or chopped prunes.

PUMPERNICKEL BREAD   *Two* LOAVES

Here's a bread you must eat with cheese and beer!

⅓ cup cornmeal	½ tablespoon caraway seed
¾ cup cold water	2 packages active dry or
¾ cup boiling water	compressed yeast
2½ teaspoons salt	¼ cup warm water (lukewarm
1 tablespoon sugar	for compressed yeast)
2 tablespoons butter or	3 cups rye meal or rye graham
margarine	flour
1 cup mashed potatoes	1 cup white flour

Stir the cold water into the cornmeal until smooth. Place over burner, add the boiling water and cook, stirring constantly, 2 minutes. Add salt, sugar, fat; cool to lukewarm. Add potatoes, caraway, and the yeast dissolved in the warm water. Add both flours. Mix and knead to a smooth, stiff dough, using white flour on the board. Cover, let rise until doubled. Shape into 2 loaves and place in greased pans (8½x4½ inches). Let rise until doubled. Bake at 375° F. for 1¼ hours.

FRENCH BREAD   *Two* LOAVES

These are long, narrow crusty loaves with soft insides, and they're so good!

1¼ cups warm water (lukewarm for compressed yeast)
  1 package dry granular or 1 ounce compressed yeast
1½ teaspoons salt
  1 tablespoon soft shortening
  1 tablespoon sugar
3½ cups sifted flour (about)

CORNSTARCH GLAZE: Blend 1 teaspoon cornstarch, 1 teaspoon cold water. Add ½ cup boiling water, cook and stir until clear. Cool slightly.

Measure water into a large mixing bowl. Add yeast and stir until dissolved. Add salt, shortening, and sugar. Stir in flour to make a soft dough.

16

Turn out on lightly floured board and knead 8 to 10 minutes or until dough is elastic and does not stick to board. Place in a greased bowl, grease surface of dough lightly, cover, and let rise in a warm place until doubled, about 1 hour. Punch down and let rise again until doubled, about 30 minutes.

Turn out on floured board and cut dough in 2 equal portions. Roll each into an oblong approximately 8x10 inches. Beginning with the wide side, roll each up tightly. Seal by pinching edges together. With a hand on each roll, roll gently back and forth to lengthen each loaf to about 16 inches, and taper ends. Place loaves on a greased baking sheet sprinkled lightly with yellow corn meal. Brush loaves with cornstarch glaze. Let rise, uncovered, for 1½ hours. Brush again with cornstarch glaze. With a sharp knife make ¼-inch slashes in dough at 2-inch intervals. Bake at 400° F. for 10 minutes. Remove from oven, brush again with glaze, and return to oven to bake about 30 minutes longer or until golden brown.

ORANGE CINNAMON LOAF *Two* LOAVES

A thin confectioners' sugar icing may be drizzled on top.

1 package active dry or compressed yeast
¼ cup warm water (lukewarm for compressed yeast)
1 cup milk, scalded
½ cup butter
½ cup sugar

1½ teaspoons salt
¼ cup undiluted frozen orange juice, room temperature
1 egg and 2 yolks, well beaten
5 cups flour (about)
1 cup sugar
1 tablespoon cinnamon

Dissolve yeast in water. Place milk, butter, sugar, and salt in a bowl. Cool. Add orange juice and eggs; mix thoroughly. Add yeast and half of flour and beat until smooth. Add remaining flour gradually and knead until smooth and elastic. Place in a greased bowl, cover, and let rise until doubled. Divide dough in half. Roll each piece into a rectangle about ½ inch thick. Sprinkle with half of sugar and cinnamon mixture. Roll like a jelly roll. Place in greased loaf pans and let rise until doubled in bulk. Bake at 400° F. for 15 minutes; lower heat to 375° F., and bake 30 minutes longer.

OATMEAL BREAD   *Two* LOAVES

My family could eat this as a steady diet. It's an excellent, nutritious bread.

2 cups rolled oats
½ cup dark molasses
2 teaspoons salt
2 tablespoons shortening
1 cup boiling water

1 package (1 oz.) active dry compressed yeast
¼ cup warm water (lukewarm for compressed)
¾ cup milk, scalded and cooled
5 cups flour (about)

Measure oats, molasses, salt, and shortening into a bowl. Add boiling water, blend, and let stand 1 hour. Soften yeast in water and stir into first mixture with the cooled milk. Work in half the flour, beating thoroughly. Knead in remaining flour gradually. When dough is smooth and elastic, round up, place in greased bowl, and brush top with melted fat. Cover with cloth and let rise in a warm place until doubled in bulk, about 1½ hours. Knead down, shape into 2 loaves, and place in greased bread pans, about 8½x4½ inches. Let rise again until doubled, about 1 hour. Bake at 375° F. approximately 45 minutes.

Nuts (1 cup) may be added, or part whole wheat flour may be used.

RYE BREAD   *Two* LOAVES

Here's bread with a personality of its own!

1 cup milk, scalded
2 tablespoons molasses or brown sugar
1 tablespoon each, sugar, salt, shortening
1 package active dry or compressed yeast

¾ cup warm water (lukewarm for compressed yeast)
3 cups rye flour
3 cups white flour
1 egg white plus 1 tablespoon water

Stir molasses, sugar, salt, and shortening into scalded milk. Cool to lukewarm. Soften yeast in the water, stirring to dissolve. Add lukewarm milk mixture to dissolved yeast. Combine rye and white flour and add half to yeast mixture, beating until smooth. Work in remaining flour. Turn dough out on lightly floured board and knead until smooth and elastic. Place dough in a greased bowl, brush lightly with melted shortening, and cover with a towel. Let rise in a warm place until doubled in bulk, about 1½ hours.

Punch down and let rise again until doubled, about 1 hour. Punch down and turn out on lightly floured board; divide into 2 equal portions. Round each into a smooth ball, cover with towel, and let rest 15 minutes on board. Flatten each portion slightly, then roll lightly to form loaves which are tapered at ends. Sprinkle a coating of cornmeal on greased baking sheet and place loaves on sheet. Cover with a towel and let rise a third time in a warm place until doubled in bulk, about 55 minutes. Brush tops with a mixture of unbeaten egg white and water. Slit top of each loaf diagonally in 3 places. Bake at 400° F. about 35 minutes.

For a tasty variation, use 2 cups whole wheat, 2 cups rye, 2 cups white flour.

POTATO BREAD
Two 1-POUND LOAVES

This flavorsome, crusty bread takes just one big potato.

2 packages active dry or compressed yeast
¼ cup warm water (lukewarm for compressed)
½ cup mashed potatoes
½ cup water in which potatoes were cooked

1½ cups scalded, cooled milk
1 tablespoon salt
2 tablespoons sugar
2 tablespoons melted shortening
5–6 cups flour

Soften yeast in warm water. Add potato water, milk, salt, sugar, and melted shortening to potatoes. Add softened yeast, then stir in flour. Mix thoroughly, using only enough flour to make a stiff, kneadable dough. Knead until smooth and elastic. Place in lightly greased bowl, cover, and let rise until doubled in bulk. Punch down and let rise again for about an hour (second rising may be omitted if you're short on time). Shape into 2 loaves and place in 2 greased 9x5-inch bread pans. Let rise once more until doubled in bulk. Bake at 400° F. for 50 to 60 minutes. Turn bread out on racks to cool.

SWEDISH LIMPA BREAD   *Two* LOAVES

A famous and delicious loaf. Only one "improvement" suggests itself—addition of 1 tablespoon grated orange rind.

2 cups water
½ cup brown sugar or honey
2 teaspoons caraway seeds
1 teaspoon anise seeds
2 tablespoons shortening
2 packages active dry or
     compressed yeast

¼ cup warm water (lukewarm
     for compressed yeast)
2 teaspoons salt
2 cups rye flour
4 cups white flour (about)

Combine water, sugar or honey, anise, caraway, and shortening in a saucepan. Bring to a boil; boil 5 minutes. Cool to lukewarm. Soften yeast in ¼ cup water, then add to lukewarm caraway mixture. Add salt, rye flour, and enough white flour to make a soft, kneadable dough. Turn out on a lightly floured board and knead until smooth and elastic. Round up, place in a large greased bowl, and grease surface of dough. Cover with cloth and let rise in a warm place until doubled in bulk, from 1 to 1½ hours. Knead down and divide dough in two portions. Shape each into a loaf and place in greased 5x9-inch pans. Cover and let rise again until doubled. Bake at 350° F. for 1 hour.

SOUR DOUGH BREAD   *One* LARGE LOAF

Easy to make—don't let anyone tell you otherwise—and beautiful bread!

STARTER

½ cake compressed yeast or ½ packet active dry yeast
2½ cups lukewarm water
1 tablespoon sugar
2 cups flour

Soften yeast in ½ cup water, add rest of water, sugar, and flour. Mix well. Let stand in a covered bowl for 3 days at room temperature, 78°–80° F. Stir down daily.

When you are ready to make bread, measure out 1 cup starter for the bread. To the remaining starter, add 1 cup water, ½ cup flour, and 1 teaspoon sugar. Cover and let stand again.

BREAD

1 cup starter	2 teaspoons melted
½ cup scalded milk	shortening
1 teaspoon salt	2½–3 cups flour
1 tablespoon sugar	

Cool milk to lukewarm and add to starter. Add salt, sugar, and shortening. Add flour and mix. Knead about 10 minutes. Place in greased bowl and let rise until doubled in bulk at 80°–85° F. Punch down and let rise a second time. Punch down and let dough rest for 10 minutes. Shape into 2 small loaves or 1 large one. Let rise in greased bread pan until double. Bake 40–45 minutes at 400° F.

APPLE KUCHEN   *One* LARGE or *Two* SMALL

With cream, this makes an excellent dessert.

1 cup scalded milk	2 well-beaten eggs
⅓ cup butter	3¾ cups flour (about)
⅓ cup sugar	5 apples, sliced
½ teaspoon salt	Sugar, cinnamon
1 package active dry or com-	1 egg yolk beaten with 3 table-
pressed yeast	spoons cream
¼ cup warm water (lukewarm	
for compressed yeast)	

Add butter, sugar, and salt to scalded milk. Cool to lukewarm and add yeast dissolved in warm water, eggs, and enough flour to make a stiff batter. Cover and let rise in a warm place until doubled in bulk. Punch down, beat thoroughly, and spread ½-inch thick in a buttered broiler pan or 2 buttered layer cake pans. Let rise until double. Lay sliced apples in parallel rows across the top of dough, pressing them slightly into it. Sprinkle thickly with sugar and cinnamon. Drip egg and cream around the apples. Bake 20 to 30 minutes at 400° F.

SWEDISH COFFEE BRAID   *Two* TWISTS

Everyone seems to like this coffee cake immensely.

1 package active dry or
    compressed yeast
¼ cup warm water (lukewarm
    for compressed yeast)
1 cup scalded milk

½ cup sugar
¼ teaspoon salt
½ cup butter or margarine
1 teaspoon ground cardamom
    About 4 cups flour

TOPPING: 2 egg yolks mixed with 4 tablespoons water, 6 tablespoons sugar, ⅔ cup slivered almonds.

Soften yeast in water. Pour scalded milk over sugar, salt, butter, and cardamom. Cool to lukewarm and stir in yeast mixture. Work in flour to make a soft dough. Knead until smooth. Place in greased bowl, brush with melted fat, and let rise until doubled, about 2 hours. Turn out on floured board, knead down, and divide dough in half. Cut each half into 3 parts. Roll each into a strip about 12 inches long. Braid 3 strips together for each coffee cake, tucking the ends underneath. Place on greased baking sheets, cover, and let rise about ½ hour, then brush each braid with half the beaten egg yolk mixture and sprinkle with half the sugar and almonds. Bake at 375° F. for 15 to 20 minutes.

CHRISTMAS STOLLEN   *One* LARGE or *Two* SMALL

Rich and fruited. One of the finest of holiday breads.

1 package active dry or
    compressed yeast
¼ cup warm water (lukewarm
    for compressed yeast)
½ cup scalded milk
¼ cup butter, softened
¼ cup sugar
1 teaspoon salt

3 cups flour (about)
1 egg, beaten
1 teaspoon grated lemon rind
1 cup white raisins
1 cup mixed candied fruit,
    chopped fine
½ cup chopped nuts

Soften yeast in warm water; add butter, sugar, and salt to hot milk, then cool to lukewarm. Beat in about 1 cup flour, or enough to make thick batter. Add yeast, egg, and lemon rind, mixing thoroughly. Add enough more flour to make a kneadable dough, then work in the fruits and nuts. Turn out on lightly floured board and knead until satiny. Place in greased bowl, cover, and let rise until doubled. Punch down; divide dough in half if 2 smaller cakes are wanted. Roll each half into an oval (approximately ¼-inch thick) and brush half of each oval with melted butter. Fold over other part of dough as for a large Parkerhouse roll. Place on greased baking sheets. Let rise until doubled. Bake at 375° F. for 25 to 30 minutes for 2 small cakes, 35 to 40 minutes for 1 large cake. When cool, ice with thin Confectioners' Sugar Icing (page 117) and decorate with halved candied cherries.

CHRISTMAS COFFEE CAKE   *One* LARGE CAKE

Ooh, what a delectable filling!

1 package active dry or
    compressed yeast
¼ cup warm water (lukewarm
    for compressed yeast)
¾ cup milk, scalded
¼ cup butter

¼ cup sugar
1½ teaspoons salt
3 egg yolks, well beaten
1 teaspoon vanilla
3½ cups flour (about)

FILLING: 9-ounce can crushed pineapple, ¼ cup sugar, 1 tablespoon cornstarch, 2 tablespoons butter, 1 cup chopped candied fruit, ½ cup white raisins, 1 cup chopped walnuts or pecans.

Dissolve yeast in water. Combine milk, butter, and sugar and stir until butter is melted. Cool to lukewarm. Add salt, egg yolks, vanilla, and yeast. Add about 2 cups flour and beat until smooth. Add remaining flour gradually. Turn out on a floured board and knead until smooth. Place in a buttered bowl, cover, and let rise until doubled.

Place pineapple in a saucepan. Mix sugar and cornstarch and add to pineapple. Cook, stirring constantly, until slightly thick. Add butter. Remove from heat, add fruit, and cool. Stir in nuts.

When dough has doubled in bulk, turn out on a floured board and roll into a rectangle about 15x18 inches. Spread filling on dough and roll like a jelly roll. Cut into 1-inch slices. Arrange cut side up in a buttered 10-inch tube pan. Let rise until light, about 1 hour. Bake at 350° F. for 50 minutes to 1 hour. Remove from pan and cool. Dribble on top a thin Confectioners' Sugar Icing (page 117).

CLUSTER COFFEE CAKE   *One* LARGE TUBE PAN

One of the most attractive of all coffee cakes. You just peel off a little roll for yourself.

    1 package active dry or compressed yeast
    ¼ cup warm water (lukewarm for compressed yeast)
    1¼ cups milk, scalded and cooled
    4 egg yolks, well beaten
    ½ cup sugar
    ½ cup butter, melted
    1 teaspoon salt
    4½–5 cups flour

COATING: ½ cup melted butter, ¾ cup sugar, 2 teaspoons cinnamon, ¾ cup finely chopped pecans or almonds.

Soften yeast in water 5 minutes. Add milk and 1 cup flour, beating thoroughly. Let mixture stand about 20 minutes, or until bubbly and light. Blend egg yolks, ½ cup sugar, ½ cup melted butter, and salt. Add to yeast mixture, mixing well. Then work in remaining flour and knead until smooth and elastic. Place in greased bowl, cover, and let rise until doubled in bulk. Turn out on well-floured board and divide in half. Form each half into a long roll and cut each roll into 24 pieces. Roll each piece into a ball. Dip in melted butter, then in sugar-cinnamon mixture and chopped nuts. Place in greased large tube pan, close together. Let stand in a warm place about 45 minutes, or until light. Bake at 350° F. for 45 minutes, or until done. Turn out of pan onto cake rack to cool.

VARIATIONS

Nut Rolls or Orange Rolls.   Just bake one layer of these coated little balls of dough. Raise the baking temperature to 375° F., and take a look after 15 minutes.

Orange Cluster Coffee Cake.   Omit cinnamon and dip balls into butter, then in sugar mixed with grated rind of 3 large oranges.

SWEDISH TEA RING *One* LARGE RING

This is one of the most highly regarded of coffee cakes—also one of the prettiest.

  1 package active dry or compressed yeast
¼ cup warm water (lukewarm for compressed yeast)
½ cup milk, scalded
¼ cup sugar
½ teaspoon salt
  1 egg, beaten
¼ cup butter or margarine
2¾ cups flour (about)

FILLING: ¼ cup melted butter, ½ cup packed brown sugar, 2 tea-spoons cinnamon, ½ cup raisins, ½ cup chopped candied cherries, ¼ cup chopped pecans or walnuts.

Mix yeast and water and let stand until softened, about 5 minutes. Pour scalded milk over sugar and salt; cool to lukewarm. Add yeast, beaten egg, and shortening, and beat until smooth. Add about 1½ cups flour, blending to make a soft batter. Then add enough more flour to make a soft, kneadable dough. Knead until smooth and satiny. Round up and place in greased bowl. Cover and let rise until doubled, about 1 hour.

Roll dough on lightly floured board into a rectangle, about ½-inch thick. Brush with melted butter, sprinkle with brown sugar and cinna-mon, and sprinkle on the raisins, cherries, and nuts. Roll up like a jelly roll. Join ends to make a circle, and place on greased baking sheet. With scissors, cut the ring at 1-inch intervals about ⅔ of the way through. Turn each slice partly on its side to expose filling, turning 1 slice out-ward, the next toward the center, so that a heart-shaped section is formed. Lightly press ring flat so that cake will be of even height. Cover and let rise again until doubled. Bake at 375° F. for 25 to 30 minutes. Frost while still slightly warm with a thin Confectioners' Sugar Icing (page 117).

PETAL COFFEE CAKE　　　　*Twelve* SERVINGS

A big, beautiful flower baked from light, soft dough.

1 package active dry or
　　compressed yeast
¼ cup warm water (lukewarm
　　for compressed yeast)
1 cup scalded milk, cooled
¼ cup butter or margarine

3 tablespoons sugar
1 egg, unbeaten
1 teaspoon salt
3½ cups flour (about)
　　Apricot-pineapple
　　　marmalade

Dissolve yeast in water. Add milk, butter, and sugar and beat in half of the flour. Add egg and salt, blending well. Work in enough flour to make a soft dough. Knead on lightly floured board until smooth and elastic. Place dough in greased bowl, cover, and let rise until doubled, about 1½ hours. Punch down and let rest 10 minutes.

Shape as follows: Divide dough into 12 equal pieces. Roll each piece under palm of hands until about 8 inches long. (Line pieces up to get them all the same length.) Twist 6 of the rolls into U-shaped pieces. Arrange side by side on a greased cooky sheet with ends toward center forming a scalloped circle. Twist remaining 6 rolls into oval-shaped pieces. Arrange on top of others so that ends meet in the center and each oval covers joining ends of 2 U-shaped pieces. Let rise until doubled, about 45 minutes. Bake at 375° F. for about 45 minutes. Remove from oven when done and spoon marmalade in indentations in top. Dribble with thin Confectioners' Sugar Icing (page 117).

STREUSEL COFFEE CAKE　　　　*Eight* SERVINGS

A combination of yeast and baking powder gives excellent results with a minimum of effort.

2 cups flour
¼ cup sugar
3 teaspoons baking powder
¾ teaspoon salt
⅓ cup butter
1 package active dry or
　　compressed yeast

¼ cup warm water (lukewarm
　　for compressed yeast)
½ cup milk, scalded
　　and cooled
1 egg plus 2 yolks,
　　slightly beaten

26

Streusel Topping: ¾ cup zwieback crumbs, 2 tablespoons flour, 2 tablespoons sugar, ½ teaspoon cinnamon, 3 tablespoons butter, 3 tablespoons chopped nuts.

Sift flour, sugar, baking powder, and salt together. Add butter and cut in as for pie crust. Dissolve yeast in water. Add milk. Add to dry ingredients with egg and yolks and beat well. Pour into buttered 9x9-inch pan. Work topping together with fingertips and sprinkle over dough. Let stand ½ hour. Bake at 375° F. for 30 minutes.

Streusel Topping No. 2, for this or almost any other coffee cake: Blend with fingertips ¼ cup butter, ¾ cup sugar, ½ cup flour, ½ cup ground almonds or fine dry bread crumbs, 1 teaspoon cinnamon.

CORNMEAL ROLLS   *Five* DOZEN

Cornmeal gives golden color and excellent flavor to these light-textured rolls.

1 cup boiling water	⅓ cup sugar
1½ cups yellow cornmeal	2 teaspoons salt
1 package active dry or	½ cup butter or margarine,
compressed yeast	melted
¼ cup warm water (lukewarm	2 egg yolks, well beaten
for compressed)	4 cups flour (about)
¾ cup milk, scalded	

Pour water over cornmeal in a large bowl and mix throughly. Cool. Dissolve yeast in water and let stand for 5 minutes. Add sugar, salt, butter, and egg yolks to milk, and cool. Add yeast and milk mixture gradually to cornmeal. Beat until smooth. Add about 2 cups flour and beat well. Gradually add remaining flour until a soft dough is formed. Knead until smooth and elastic. Place in a greased bowl. Brush dough with melted fat. Cover and let rise until doubled. Form into balls about 1 inch in diameter. Place close together in shallow pans. Let rise until doubled. Bake at 400° F. for 20 minutes.

ONE-HOUR KOLACHY   *Three* DOZEN

So tender, rich, and melt-in-the-mouth!

  2 packages active dry or compressed yeast
  ¼ cup warm water (lukewarm for compressed yeast)
  ¼ cup cream, scalded
  ¼ cup sugar
  ¾ pound butter
  3½ cups flour
  ½ teaspoon salt
  4 egg yolks, slightly beaten

Dissolve yeast in water. Dissolve sugar in cream and cool to lukewarm. Add to yeast. Cut butter into flour and salt as for pie crust. Add yeast mixture and egg yolks, stirring and beating to form smooth, soft dough. Cover tightly and let rise in a warm place for 1 hour. Turn out on lightly floured board and roll ¼-inch thick. Cut out with a round biscuit cutter, about 2¼ inches, and place on cooky sheet. Make wide, deep indentations in center and fill with any jam you like, or with prepared apricot, prune, poppyseed, or almond filling. Let rise 15 minutes and bake at 400° F. for 15 to 20 minutes.

ROSEBUD ROLLS   *One* DOZEN

Petal shaped, with delicious cranberry-pineapple centers.

  1 package active dry or compressed yeast
  ¼ cup warm water (lukewarm for compressed yeast)
  ½ cup milk, scalded
  1½ tablespoons sugar
  ½ teaspoon salt
  ¼ cup butter
  1 egg, slightly beaten
  3 cups flour (about)

FILLING: ½ cup cranberry sauce, ¼ cup drained crushed pineapple, ½ teaspoon grated orange rind.

Dissolve yeast in water. Mix milk, sugar, salt, and butter. Cool to luke-warm. Add yeast and egg and mix well. Add flour gradually. Turn out on a floured board and knead until smooth and elastic. Place in a greased bowl, cover, and let rise until doubled in bulk. Turn dough onto board and roll about 1/4-inch thick. Cut 72 circles with biscuit cutter about 1 1/4 inches in diameter. Place 5 circles around each buttered muffin pan, standing against sides. Place one in center. Let rise until light, about 30 minutes. Mix ingredients for filling. Press center of each roll down and place a spoonful of filling in each. Bake at 400° F. for 15 minutes.

SOUR CREAM FAN-TAN ROLLS   *Two* DOZEN

This has been a very popular recipe, and no wonder!

1 package active dry or compressed yeast	1/4 teaspoon soda
	2 teaspoons salt
1/4 cup warm water (lukewarm for compressed yeast)	1/4 cup sugar
	4 cups flour (about)
1 1/2 cups thick sour cream, scalded and cooled	Melted butter or margarine

Dissolve yeast in water and add cream. Add soda, salt, and sugar. Gradually work in flour. Place in greased bowl, brush with fat. Cover, let rise until doubled, about 1 1/2 hours. Knead lightly 1 minute. Divide dough in half and roll each half to 1/8-inch thickness. Brush with melted butter or margarine, cut into 1 1/2-inch strips, and place in stack of six strips. Cut into pieces 1 1/2 inches wide and place in greased muffin pans, cut edges up. Let rise in a warm place until doubled in size. Bake at 425° F. for 15 minutes, or until browned.

You can make these with 1 1/4 cups buttermilk instead of sour cream. Add 2 tablespoons fat to dough.

FEATHER BISCUITS   *Eighteen* BISCUITS

These can be made very quickly for breakfast, lunch, or dinner.

2 cups flour
2 teaspoons sugar
1 teaspoon salt
1 package active dry or compressed yeast
¾ cup warm water (lukewarm for compressed)
1½ tablespoons butter, melted.

Sift flour, sugar, and salt together. Dissolve yeast in water. Add to dry ingredients with butter. Mix thoroughly. Turn out on a floured board and knead until smooth and elastic. Roll ½ inch thick. Cut with a 2½-inch biscuit cutter. Let rise until doubled. Bake at 400° F. for 15 minutes.

CRUSTY ROLLS   *Eighteen* LARGE ROLLS

The pan of hot water in the oven does the trick. These are really crusty and very good.

1 package active dry or compressed yeast
1 cup warm water (lukewarm for compressed yeast)
1 tablespoon sugar
1 teaspoon salt
2 tablespoons melted shortening
2 egg whites, slightly beaten
3–4 cups flour

Soften yeast in half the water. To the remainder, add sugar, salt, and shortening. Add 1 cup flour, beating well. Add yeast and beaten egg whites. Mix thoroughly. Add enough more flour to make a soft dough. Knead until satiny. Round up in a greased bowl. Grease surface lightly. Cover dough and let rise until double in bulk. Punch down. Let rest 10 minutes, then divide into small portions for rolls. Place 2½ inches apart on a greased baking sheet, sprinkled with white cornmeal. Cover and let rise until double. Brush with egg yolk diluted with cold water. Bake at 450° F. for 20 minutes. Place large flat pan of hot water on the bottom of the oven to help give crustiness to the rolls.

Crusty Poppyseed Rolls. Sprinkle these lavishly with poppy seeds before baking and make 2 small cuts, forming an X, with sharp knife or scissors, on each roll.

HOT CROSS BUNS   *Two* DOZEN

Two snips of the scissors cut the cross on the traditional Good Friday breakfast buns.

> 1 package active dry or compressed yeast
> ¼ cup warm water (lukewarm for compressed yeast)
> 1 cup milk, scalded
> ¼ cup shortening
> ⅓ cup sugar
> 1 teaspoon salt
> 1 egg, well beaten
> ½ cup currants
> 1 teaspoon cinnamon
> ¼ teaspoon allspice
> 3½–4 cups flour

Soften yeast in warm water. Add shortening, sugar, and salt to scalded milk and cool to lukewarm. Then add softened yeast, currants, and egg. Blend well. Sift cinnamon and allspice with 3½ cups flour. Gradually add flour to yeast mixture, stirring gently until a soft dough is formed. Place in a greased bowl, cover with cloth, and let rise until doubled, about 1½ hours. Divide dough in half; shape each half into a roll about 2 inches in diameter. With a sharp knife cut each roll into 12 pieces. Shape pieces into buns, tucking edges of dough under. Place close together in greased jelly-roll pan, about 11x15 inches. Snip crosses on tops of buns with scissors. Brush buns with beaten egg white, let rise until light. Bake at 400° F. for 25 minutes. While still warm, fill cross on each with thin Confectioners' Sugar Icing (page 117).

CINNAMON ROLLS   *Two* DOZEN

These get a warm welcome in any family any time!

1 package active dry or compressed yeast	¼ cup butter
¼ cup warm water (lukewarm for compressed yeast)	3 tablespoons sugar
	1 egg, slightly beaten
1 cup scalded, cooled milk	1 teaspoon salt
3 cups flour (about)	½ cup raisins

FILLING: ¼ cup softened butter, ½ cup brown sugar, 1 teaspoon cinnamon.

Dissolve yeast in water. Stir in cooled milk and a cup of flour, beating until smooth; let stand until light and bubbly, about ½ hour. Cream together butter and sugar. Add egg and salt, blending well. Beat this mixture into sponge mixture. Work in remaining flour to make a soft dough. Add raisins. Knead until smooth and elastic. Place in a greased bowl, grease surface of dough, cover, and let rise in warm place until doubled, about 1 hour.

Roll dough out into a rectangle 12x18 inches. Spread with softened butter. Sprinkle on the brown sugar and cinnamon. Roll up dough tightly. Slice into 24 pieces. Place rolls close together in buttered 9x12-inch baking pan. Let rise again until light. Bake at 400° F. for 20 to 25 minutes. Remove from pan; turn out on cake rack. While still warm, dribble with thin Confectioners' Sugar Icing (page 117).

VARIATIONS

Rum Cinnamon Rolls. Mix 3 tablespoons rum, 1 tablespoon cream, 1¼ cups sifted confectioners' sugar. Dribble on rolls while warm.

Caramel Pecan Rolls. Make the Cinnamon Roll dough, but skip the raisins, and use a filling made of ¼ cup granulated sugar, 1 teaspoon cinnamon, and 3 tablespoons butter. Roll the dough as described for cinnamon rolls, but cut into only 16 pieces. In a 9x9x2-inch pan, melt ¼ cup (½ stick) butter, sprinkle with ½ cup dark brown sugar and 1 cup pecan halves. Place the rolls over this yummy mixture, let rise, and bake about 20 minutes at 375° F. These rolls may be baked in muffin pans, and then you'd probably want to cut two dozen of them. Depends on how big your muffin pans are.

32

TOP – *White Bread, page 14*
BOTTOM – *Strawberry Shortcake, page 164*

CRESCENT ROLLS   *Forty* ROLLS

Crescents are flaky dinner rolls which may be filled.

  1 cup scalded milk
  2 tablespoons butter or margarine
  2 tablespoons sugar
  ¾ teaspoon salt
  1 package active dry or compressed yeast
  ¼ cup warm water (lukewarm for compressed yeast)
  1 egg, slightly beaten
 3½–4 cups flour
  Melted butter or margarine
  ¾ cup soft butter or margarine

Pour scalded milk over 2 tablespoons butter, mixed with the sugar and salt. Cool. Add yeast dissolved in warm water. Add egg and flour (enough to make a soft dough). Turn out on board; knead slightly. Brush with melted butter or margarine; set aside to double in bulk. Roll dough out on a lightly floured board to a rectangle 10x20 inches, and spread with ¼ cup soft butter or margarine. Fold dough in thirds, roll out again to a rectangle 10x20 inches, and spread with another ¼ cup soft butter. Repeat process. Wrap dough in waxed paper, roll in dish towel, and chill several hours or overnight.

 Roll dough again to a rectangle 10x20 inches. Cut in half lengthwise. Mark the cut dough in 10 2-inch strips, then cut strips diagonally into wedges. Roll wedges from wide end, pressing the tip against the roll to keep it from unraveling, then shape into crescents. Place on ungreased cooky sheet, tip side down, and let rise until doubled. Brush with egg yolk mixed with 2 tablespoons milk. Bake at 450° F. for 15 minutes.

Filled Crescents. Beat 2 egg whites stiff. Beat in gradually ½ cup sugar. Add 1 cup ground nuts. Spread on rolled dough before shaping.

Orange Crescents. Brush rolled dough with butter, then with lukewarm frozen orange juice concentrate, and sprinkle with sugar.

33

Christmas Yeast Breads, pages 17–24

BAKING POWDER BISCUITS   One DOZEN

*Biscuits are not hard to make. They couldn't be simpler.
Every bride should know how to make them, for they are
basic to all kinds of other dishes such as strawberry shortcakes
and meat pies.*

    2 cups flour
    3 teaspoons (1 tablespoon) baking powder
    ½ teaspoon salt
    ¼ cup shortening (lard is great)
    ⅔ cup milk (about)

Put dry ingredients into sifter and sift into a medium-size bowl. Drop shortening into the dry mixture and blend with fingertips until mixture is in coarse crumbs. Add milk and stir to blend. You may need a little more milk for some flours, but not much. The dough is quite stiff. Turn it onto a lightly floured board and knead gently for 30 seconds. Do this by patting out the dough, giving it a quarter-turn and repeating the process several times. Roll out ½-inch thick, cut out biscuits with biscuit cutter, and bake on ungreased baking sheet 12 to 15 minutes at 450° F.

Space biscuits apart on the sheet for crusty ones; have them touching if you want soft sides. And be sure the oven is hot before you put them in if you want them to puff high.

Seconds saver: Pat out the dough, put it on the baking sheet, and cut squares or diamonds with a knife before baking.

SOME BISCUIT VARIATIONS TO GIVE YOU IDEAS OF YOUR OWN

Bacon Biscuits. Add 4 to 6 crumbled crisp slices bacon to dry ingredients; and if you like the idea, a tablespoon of minced green onions, too.

Buttermilk Biscuits. Use buttermilk in place of sweet milk, cut baking powder to 2 teaspoons, and add ¼ teaspoon soda with the dry ingredients. These are snowy white and tender as true love.

Cheese Biscuits. Add with the shortening ½ cup grated sharp Cheddar cheese. Or any other kind you like.

Ham and Cheese. Add also ¼ to ½ cup minced cooked ham.

Curry Biscuits. Nice for cocktail and salad accompaniment. Add ½ teaspoon curry powder and ½ teaspoon dry mustard to dry ingredients and use tomato juice instead of milk. Make the biscuits tiny.

Deviled Biscuits. Cut in ¼ cup deviled ham with the shortening and add 2 teaspoons prepared mustard with the milk.

Parsley or Watercress Biscuits. Pretty! Add ½ cup chopped parsley or cress to dry ingredients. And just try these with bacon and cheese too, for something super-delish!

Plopped Biscuits. More politely known as drop biscuits. Use 1 cup milk. Stir, don't knead. And plop in rough mounds on greased cooky sheet (you don't grease the sheets for the regulars). Try the variations also on the plopped biscuits.

SOUTHERN BEATEN BISCUITS *Three* DOZEN

> *Artist Becky Krehbiel's Mom gave me her cherished recipe, but wouldn't allow herself to be photographed with her bis-cuit machine*—she was afraid a horde of antique collectors would descend upon her!*

3 cups sifted flour
½ teaspoon salt
½ cup lard shortening
⅔ cup milk

Mix flour and salt, cut in shortening as for pastry, add milk, and mix until dough holds together. Now comes the fun and hard work!

Turn dough onto a board and beat the stuffing out of it with a small bat (ice crusher), a rolling pin, or an old-fashioned potato masher. Beat until smooth and velvety in texture. It will take a good 20 minutes, so you'd better get help from the youngsters on this. Roll out ½-inch thick and cut tiny biscuits. Prick each clear through with the tines of a fork, twice. Bake for half an hour at 350° F. Split and butter while hot. These delectable morsels are really worth the effort. Keep any unbaked ones in the refrigerator and bake them as you want them.

* It looks like an old-fashioned washing machine with a wringer. The biscuit dough is put through such a wringer again and again until its gluten structure breaks down. The beating is harder, but as effective.

ONION SQUARES   *Twelve* SERVINGS

Serve these with roast meat; they're a biscuit variation.

2 cups sliced onions
2 tablespoons butter or marga-
    rine
2 cups sifted flour
4 teaspoons baking powder

1 teaspoon salt
5 tablespoons shortening
¾ cup milk
1 egg, well beaten
¾ cup dairy sour cream

Cook onions in 2 tablespoons butter or margarine until delicately browned. Season with ½ teaspoon salt and ¼ teaspoon pepper. Sift flour, baking powder, and salt together. Cut in shortening until mixture resembles coarse crumbs. Add milk and mix to soft dough. Spread in a greased pan about 11x7 inches. Top dough with onions. Mix egg with sour cream and pour over onions. Bake at 450° F. for 20 minutes.

COTTAGE CHEESE BISCUITS   *Eighteen* BISCUITS

Very light-textured, and unusually good—you'll love them!

1 egg, slightly beaten
2 tablespoons milk, about
1 cup cottage cheese (cream style)
2 tablespoons melted butter or margarine
2 cups sifted flour
4 teaspoons baking powder
1 teaspoon salt

Combine egg, milk, cottage cheese, and butter. Mix well. Sift dry ingredients together and add to first mixture. Blend. Add more milk, a few drops at a time, if necessary to make dough hold together. Turn out on floured board and pat or roll out to ½-inch thickness. Cut with floured cutter and bake on greased baking sheet at 425° F., for about 12 minutes.

UPSIDE-DOWN ORANGE ROLLS   *Eighteen* ROLLS

What dainty, delicious little biscuits these are!

¼ cup butter
½ cup orange juice
½ cup sugar
2 teaspoons grated orange peel

1 recipe Baking Powder Biscuits (page 34)
Butter
¼ cup sugar
½ teaspoon cinnamon

Cook for 2 minutes butter, orange juice, ½ cup sugar, and orange peel. Pour into 18 greased medium-size muffin pans. Cool. Roll dough ¼ inch thick. Brush with butter. Sprinkle with ¼ cup sugar and cinnamon. Roll as for jelly roll. Cut into 18 slices, place cut side down over orange mixture. Bake at 400° F. for 25 minutes. You could put whole or chopped nuts into the orange sirup.

ORANGE TEA STRIPS   *Three* DOZEN

They're all so prettily glazed with honey.

2 cups sifted flour
3 teaspoons baking powder
¼ teaspoon nutmeg
½ teaspoon salt
2 tablespoons sugar

1 tablespoon grated orange rind
¼ cup butter or margarine
¼ cup orange juice
½ cup milk

TOPPING: Mix 2 tablespoons butter, ¼ cup honey, 1 tablespoon cream, ¼ teaspoon cinnamon.

Sift dry ingredients together, add rind; cut in butter. Add juice and milk and stir to soft dough. Pat out ½-inch thick on floured board and cut into strips ½x2 inches. Bake about 8 minutes at 450° F. Apply topping to baked strips while hot.

MUFFINS
One DOZEN

Spoil your family with a different muffin for breakfast every morning; sometimes plain, sometimes blueberry, then again jam-filled treats. This basic recipe should be in your head, if you're a serious-minded cook.

2 cups flour
3 teaspoons baking powder
2 tablespoons sugar
½ teaspoon salt
1 egg, beaten
1 cup milk
3 tablespoons oil or melted butter

Sift dry ingredients into a bowl. Beat egg in another small bowl and add milk and oil. Stir liquid ingredients into dry ones, just to blend. The batter should look lumpy. Fill well-greased muffin pans two-thirds full. Bake at 400° F. about 20 minutes. Serve hot.

SOME SIMPLE AND MIGHTY GOOD VARIATIONS

Blueberry. Ah, my favorite muffins! Increase the sugar to ¼ cup and fold into the batter 1 cup fresh or frozen blueberries. Sprinkle tops of muffins with cinnamon-sugar before baking, if you wish.

Buttermilk. Use buttermilk instead of milk, cut baking powder to 2½ teaspoons, and add ¼ teaspoon soda.

Cheese. Fold into the batter ½ cup grated sharp cheese.

Cherry. Fold in 1 cup drained fresh, canned, or frozen cherries. Chop sweet cherries first. Add 2 extra tablespoons sugar; for sour cherries, increase the sugar to ½ cup.

Cornmeal. Replace 1 cup flour with 1 cup cornmeal. Particularly good are cornmeal muffins with bacon drippings used for the fat and 3 or 4 crumbled crisp bacon strips folded into the batter.

Jam or Jelly Muffins. Spoon some batter into the muffin cups, add a teaspoon of jam, jelly, or preserves, then more batter. When you break these open, there's a surprise inside!

Oatmeal. Replace a cup of the flour with a cup of rolled oats. Add ½ cup raisins or chopped dates, too, if you like.

Pineapple or Strawberry. Use a cup of crushed pineapple including juice, or a cup of crushed sweetened strawberries to replace the milk. Um-mm, are THESE good!

Whole Wheat. Replace 1 cup flour with 1 cup whole wheat flour, and use brown sugar—¼ cup of it, if you wish.

APPLE MUFFINS Eighteen MUFFINS

That topping gets 'em every time. (Out of bed, I mean.)

2 cups flour
½ cup sugar
3 teaspoons baking powder
¼ teaspoon salt

1 cup coarsely chopped apples
1 egg, slightly beaten
1 cup milk
3 tablespoons butter, melted

TOPPING: ⅓ cup brown sugar, ½ teaspoon cinnamon, ⅓ cup chopped nuts.

Sift dry ingredients; add apples. Add combined liquid ingredients, mixing just enough to moisten. Turn into buttered muffin pans. Mix topping ingredients and sprinkle on top of muffins. Bake at 400° F. about 15 minutes.

BANANA BRAN MUFFINS Twelve to Fifteen

These have a nice banana flavor and tender texture.

1 egg, beaten
1½ cups mashed bananas
  (about 3)
¼ cup melted fat
1 cup bran

1½ cups flour
2½ teaspoons baking powder
½ teaspoon soda
½ teaspoon salt
½ cup sugar

Combine egg, banana, fat, and bran; mix well. Sift flour with remaining ingredients and add to first mixture. Mix only enough to dampen flour. Bake in greased muffin pans at 350° F. for 25 minutes.

SIX-WEEKS BRAN MUFFINS   *Five* DOZEN

I like this recipe, which was given to me by Pat O'Donnell, because it means instant muffins, any time, and it's great for country weekends when there's a mob of people getting up at different times.

You make the batter and store it away to bake in "takes" of any size—bake yourself just two muffins, if you wish!

2 cups whole bran cereal	5 cups flour
2 cups boiling water	4 cups bran flakes or raisin bran
1 cup shortening, melted	(use up all the breakfast
3 cups sugar	bran cereals)
4 eggs, beaten	5 teaspoons soda
1 quart buttermilk	2 teaspoons salt

Pour the boiling water over the whole bran and let stand. Mix sugar well with melted fat, beat in eggs and buttermilk. Add the wet bran mixture. Combine flour, rest of bran, soda and salt, and stir into the liquid combination. The mixture thickens as it stands.

Bake a dozen muffins now in greased pans (400° F. for about 20 minutes), and store the rest of the batter in a big covered jar in the refrigerator. (Don't fill jar too full—allow room for expansion.)

Dates, raisins, chopped prunes, or apples may be added.

CREOLE CORN MUFFINS   *Eighteen* MUFFINS

These won't go begging!

1½ cups sifted flour	1 cup milk
3 teaspoons baking powder	½ cup shortening, melted
1 teaspoon salt	1 tablespoon green pepper,
3 tablespoons sugar	chopped
¾ cup cornmeal	1 teaspoon onion, chopped fine
1 egg, well beaten	½ cup grated cheese

40

Sift flour with baking powder, salt, and sugar; add cornmeal and mix. Combine egg, milk, and shortening. Turn liquids into dry ingredients and stir vigorously until all flour is dampened. Add green pepper, onion, and cheese. Bake in greased muffin pans at 400° F. for 25 minutes.

CORN MUFFINS   One DOZEN

They're doubly corny, doubly good for lunch!

1½ cups sifted flour
3½ teaspoons baking powder
 1 teaspoon salt
 3 tablespoons sugar
 1 cup yellow cornmeal
 1 egg, beaten
1¼ cups milk
 3 tablespoons melted fat
 1 cup drained whole-kernel corn

Sift dry ingredients; combine liquids and corn and stir into dry mixture. Bake in greased pans at 400° F. about 25 minutes.

GINGER GEMS   Two DOZEN

Lightly spiced—you might want to add raisins.

¼ cup shortening
½ cup sugar
 1 egg
1¾ cups sifted flour
 1 teaspoon soda

¼ teaspoon salt
¼ teaspoon each, nutmeg, ginger, cinnamon
½ cup molasses
½ cup cold strong coffee

Cream shortening and sugar; add egg and beat well. Add sifted dry ingredients alternately with molasses and coffee in thirds, beating until smooth after each addition. Bake in greased pans at 375° F. for 20 minutes.

CRUMBLY-TOPPED CRANBERRY MUFFINS

One DOZEN

They're as appetizing as they look.

2 cups sifted flour
3 teaspoons baking powder
1 teaspoon salt
¼ cup sugar
1 teaspoon grated orange rind

⅓ cup shortening
1 egg, beaten
1 cup milk
1 cup chopped fresh cranberries

TOPPING: 1 egg white, 3 tablespoons flour, ⅓ cup brown sugar, 3 tablespoons butter or margarine.

Sift flour, baking powder, salt, and sugar into mixing bowl. Add orange rind. Cut in shortening. Combine egg and milk, add to flour mixture, and stir until just blended. Batter should be lumpy. Fold in berries. Fill greased muffin tins, brush with slightly beaten egg white, and sprinkle with a blend of other topping ingredients. Bake at 400° F. for 25 minutes.

PEACHY GOOD MUFFINS

One DOZEN

Out of season you might use canned or frozen sliced peaches, omitting the sugar for them.

1 recipe for Muffins (page 38)
1 teaspoon grated lemon rind
1½ cups sliced fresh peaches
¼ cup sugar
1 teaspoon cinnamon

Add lemon rind to muffin batter, spoon it into greased muffin cups, and top the muffins with the sliced peaches. Sprinkle the sugar and cinnamon on the peaches. Bake at 400° F. about 25 minutes.

APPLE-CHEESE BREAD *One* LOAF

Countless bake sales have featured this good loaf. If you have an electric blender, grate the apples in it, the easy way.

½ cup shortening
⅔ cup sugar
2 eggs, beaten
1½ cups grated or ground cook-
    ing apples (about 3) in-
    cluding juice

½ cup grated sharp
    Cheddar cheese
¼ cup chopped walnuts
2 cups flour
1½ teaspoons baking powder
½ teaspoon soda
½ teaspoon salt

Cream shortening and sugar; add eggs and mix well. Add apples, cheese and nuts. Add sifted dry ingredients and mix lightly. Bake in greased 9x5-inch loaf pan at 350° F. for 50 to 60 minutes.

APPLESAUCE-NUT BREAD *One* LOAF

Moist and delicious, it's a good keeper.

2 cups sifted flour
¾ cup sugar
3 teaspoons baking powder
1 teaspoon salt
½ teaspoon soda
½ teaspoon cinnamon

1 cup coarsely chopped walnuts
1 egg, well beaten
1 cup medium-thick, smooth
    applesauce
2 tablespoons melted shortening

Mix sifted dry ingredients and nuts together. Combine egg, applesauce, and shortening. Add to dry ingredients and stir just until blended. Bake in greased 9x5-inch pan at 350° F. 50 to 60 minutes.

Add a cupful of currants instead of, or along with, the nuts, for a really special loaf.

43

APRICOT BREAD   *One* LOAF

This loaf keeps moist and flavorsome for a week.

¼ cup butter or margarine
½ cup sugar
1 egg
1 cup chopped, cooked,
 drained, dried appricots
¼ cup apricot juice

1 cup sour milk or buttermilk
1½ cups sifted flour
½ teaspoon salt
1 teaspoon soda
1½ cups whole wheat flour
1 cup broken nuts

Cream shortening and sugar well. Beat in the egg, then blend in apricots and juice. Add the sifted dry ingredients alternately with sour milk, mixing just until blended. Stir in nuts. Bake in greased pan about 9x5 inches, at 350° F. 1¼ hours.

Prune Bread. Substitute chopped cooked prunes and juice for apricots and juice.

BANANA BREAD   *One* LOAF

This was the favorite of a half-dozen banana breads tested, time and again!

½ cup butter or margarine
1 cup sugar
2 eggs, beaten light
1 cup sieved bananas (about 3
 large)
1½ tablespoons sweet or
 sour milk

1 teaspoon lemon juice
2 cups sifted bread flour
1½ teaspoons baking powder
¼ teaspoon salt
½ teaspoon soda
1 cup chopped pecans or
 walnuts

Cream fat and sugar; add eggs. Add sour milk and lemon juice to sieved bananas and combine with fat and sugar. Add sifted flour, baking powder, salt and soda, and finally the nuts. Stir only enough to blend. Bake in a greased pan (8½x4½ inches) at 350° F. for 45 minutes.

ORANGE-DATE BREAD   *One* LOAF

This has been one of my favorites for years.

1 medium orange
1 cup pitted dates
2 tablespoons melted shortening
    or oil
1 teaspoon vanilla
1 egg, beaten

2 cups sifted flour
¼ teaspoon salt
1 teaspoon baking powder
½ teaspoon soda
¾ cup sugar
½ cup chopped nuts

Place unstrained juice and pulp of orange in a measuring cup and fill with water to make 1 cup. Pour into mixing bowl. Discard white part of orange peel and put peel and dates through food chopper. Together peel and dates should measure 1 cup. Add to mixing bowl. Blend in shortening, vanilla, egg. Sift flour with other dry ingredients and blend with other ingredients. Add nuts. Bake in well-greased 7½x4½-inch pan 1 hour and 20 minutes at 350° F.

PINEAPPLE-NUT BREAD   *One* LOAF

It's a good freezer, so better make 2 loaves.

1 cup white flour, sifted
1 cup whole wheat flour
½ cup sugar
½ teaspoon salt
1 teaspoon soda
1 cup raisins

1 cup coarsely chopped walnuts
1 egg, beaten
1 teaspoon vanilla
2 tablespoons oil or melted fat
1 cup crushed pineapple, not
    drained (No. 1 flat can)

Combine dry ingredients and add raisins and nuts. Combine egg, vanilla, and shortening. Add to mixture with pineapple. Stir until just blended. Bake in greased 7½x4½-inch loaf pan 1 hour at 350° F.

CORN BREAD or JOHNNY CAKE   Nine SERVINGS

I guess the kind of corn bread you think is the only one, or the very best one, is the one you had as a child. To me, corn bread must be made of yellow cornmeal. I like to split, toast, and butter any leftover squares for breakfast, or bake a double batch for that purpose.

1 cup flour	1 egg, beaten
1 cup yellow cornmeal	1 cup milk
2 tablespoons sugar	2 tablespoons bacon drippings or
1 teaspoon salt	other fat
3 teaspoons baking powder	

Sift the dry ingredients into a bowl. Add egg, milk, and fat. Stir to mix well. Spread in greased 9x9-inch pan and bake at 425° F. for 20 to 25 minutes.

Corn sticks may be made of the same batter. Bake in greased corn stick pans for 15 to 20 minutes at 425° F. Same thing for muffins.

Add crisp crumbled bacon to the batter, when you can.

Blueberry Corn Bread. Add 2 extra tablespoons of sugar and 2 of fat (make it butter). Then fold 1 cup blueberries into the batter. This is a New England treat.

SAUSAGE CORN BREAD   Six SERVINGS

An upside-down sausage pie, to serve as a main dish.

1 pound pork sausage meat	½ teaspoon soda
1½ cups cornmeal	1 egg
½ cup flour	1 cup sour milk or buttermilk
½ teaspoon salt	2 tablespoons drippings
2 teaspoons baking powder	

Break up sausage with a fork as you brown it thoroughly in a heavy skillet. Drain off drippings. Sift together cornmeal, flour, salt, baking powder, and soda. Combine egg and milk and beat until well mixed.

Add 2 tablespoons drippings to milk and egg mixture. Pour liquid into dry ingredients and stir just until well mixed. Pour batter over cooked sausage in heated skillet. Bake at 450° F. for 30 to 35 minutes. Turn out upside down on warm plate. Make gravy from drippings or serve with a canned soup sauce.

SOUTHERN SPOONBREAD   *Twelve* SERVINGS

Best you ever ate, and company size.

1 cup yellow cornmeal	½ cup milk
2 cups boiling water	½ cup flour
1 tablespoon butter	2 tablespoons sugar
1½ teaspoons salt	2 teaspoons baking powder
4 eggs, separated	

Add cornmeal to water with constant stirring and cook in top of double boiler with butter and salt until thick. Cool. Beat egg yolks with milk and beat into cooled mush. Add sifted dry ingredients and mix well. Fold in stiffly beaten egg whites. Turn mixture into 2-quart buttered baking dish and bake 35 to 40 minutes at 350° F. Serve from dish.

STEAMED BROWN BREAD   *Five* CANS

The recipe can be halved, but this good old-fashioned bread keeps well.

2 cups sifted white flour	1 teaspoon salt
2 cups whole wheat flour	2 cups molasses
2 cups cornmeal	2 cups thick sour milk
2 teaspoons soda	1 cup seeded raisins (optional)

Mix dry ingredients in large bowl and make a well in the center. Pour in molasses and sour milk. Add raisins (nuts too, if you wish), stir to blend, but do not beat. Pour into 5 greased baking-powder cans, 8-ounce walnut cans, or regular steamer cans, filling not more than two-thirds full. Cover cans tightly. Steam 2½ hours and dry out in a slow oven (300° F.) about 15 minutes. Or pressure cook for 50 minutes at 15 pounds and dry out 5 minutes in oven.

QUICK MUFFINY COFFEE CAKE   Nine SERVINGS

*Just look around your pantry—I'll bet you could make 25
coffee cake variations with things you have on hand: canned
fruits, pie fillings, jams, preserves, nuts, coconut, cheese,
dates, raisins, cereals.*

  1 batch Muffins (page 38)
  ¼ cup butter
  ¼ cup brown sugar
  1 teaspoon cinnamon
  1 cup fine dry bread, cake, or cooky crumbs, or crushed
      cereal flakes

Mix your muffin batter, following the basic recipe, and spread it in a
greased 9-inch square pan. Combine the other ingredients for a topping.
Spread over batter. Bake at 425° F. for about 25 minutes.

OTHER MUFFINY COFFEE CAKES

Apple or Peach or Plum.   Make neat rows of the sliced fruit on top of
the batter you've spread in the pan. Mix ½ cup brown sugar, ½ cup
flour, and ¼ cup butter (soft) with fingertips and scatter mixture over
fruit. Bake as specified.

Blueberry.   Add a cup of blueberries to the batter, spread in the pan
and sprinkle generously with white sugar and cinnamon. Dot with butter and bake.

Cherry.   Use fresh cherries in the same way as blueberries, only you'd
better sweeten them with 2 tablespoons sugar first, if they're the tart kind.

Pie-Filling Fruits.   Cherry, pineapple, peach, apple, and other pie fillings may be spread in the buttered baking pan before batter is added.
Thus you'll have upside-down coffee cake, and mighty delicious it is,
too.

Raisin or Currant.   Add 1 cup of the dried fruit to the batter, spread
in the pan, and sprinkle generously with brown sugar and cinnamon.
Dot with butter before baking.

Now YOU think up the next one!

UPSIDE-DOWN APPLE COFFEE CAKE

Six SERVINGS

If you haven't quite a cupful of sour cream, here's good use for it.

2 tablespoons butter	3 teaspoons baking powder
½ cup brown sugar	½ teaspoon soda
½ teaspoon each, cinnamon, nut- meg	½ teaspoon salt
2 medium apples, pared, cored	2 tablespoons shortening
2 cups sifted flour	2 eggs
¼ cup brown sugar	⅔ cup sour cream

Spread butter in bottom of pan. Mix brown sugar, cinnamon, and nut-meg and sprinkle half over butter. Arrange sliced apples on top and sprinkle remaining sugar over apples. Sift remaining dry ingredients to-gether, cut in shortening as for biscuits, then stir in combined beaten eggs and sour cream. Blend quickly just to moisten the flour mixture. Spread over apple topping and bake at 450° F. about 25 minutes.

CONTINENTAL TEA RING

Eight SERVINGS

Sour cream is one reason for the tremendous popularity of this ring.

½ cup butter	1 teaspoon baking powder
1 cup sugar	1 teaspoon soda
2 eggs, slightly beaten	1 teaspoon vanilla
1 cup sour cream	1 teaspoon cinnamon
2 cups flour	¼ cup sugar
¼ teaspoon salt	¼ cup chopped nuts

Cream butter and sugar. Add slightly beaten eggs. Blend. Stir in sour cream. Sift flour, salt, baking powder, and soda. Blend into sour-cream mixture. Stir in vanilla. Pour into well-greased 10-inch ring mold. Com-bine cinnamon, sugar, and nuts. Sprinkle over top of cake in pan. Bake at 350° F. for 45 to 50 minutes. Cool 10 minutes. Remove from pan.

QUICK STREUSEL COFFEE CAKE   Nine SERVINGS

This will get 'em up on Sunday morning!

¼ cup butter or margarine	½ teaspoon salt
½ cup sugar	½ cup milk
1 egg, well beaten	1 egg yolk, slightly beaten
1½ cups sifted flour	2 tablespoons cream
2 teaspoons baking powder	

STREUSEL TOPPING: ½ cup brown sugar, 3 tablespoons flour, 1 teaspoon cinnamon, 3 tablespoons butter, ½ cup chopped nuts.

Cream butter and sugar until light, add egg and beat well. Sift dry ingredients together and add alternately with milk, blending well after each addition. Turn into greased, floured 9-inch square pan. Blend egg yolk and cream together and pour over top of batter, tilting pan so mixture covers entire surface. Blend together the topping ingredients, using fingertips to make crumbly mixture. Sprinkle over surface of cake. Bake at 375° F. about 30 minutes. Serve warm.

ORANGE COFFEE CAKE   Eight SERVINGS

One of the most delectable of all—scrumptious!

2 cups sifted flour	¼ cup shortening
½ teaspoon salt	1 egg, beaten
½ cup sugar	½ cup orange juice
4 teaspoons baking powder	½ cup milk
1½ teaspoons grated orange rind (1 large orange)	

TOPPING: Combine with fork 1 cup flour, ¾ cup brown sugar, 2 tablespoons melted butter or margarine, 2 tablespoons orange juice, 1½ teaspoons grated orange rind, ½ teaspoon cinnamon, ¼ teaspoon salt.

Sift flour, salt, sugar, and baking powder; stir in orange rind; cut in shortening. Combine egg, orange juice, milk, and add to dry ingredients, stirring only enough to blend. Spread dough in well-greased 9-inch square pan. Sprinkle with topping. Bake 25 to 30 minutes at 400° F.

HARVEST COFFEE CAKE   *Six* SERVINGS

Use a mixture of fruits, if you'd like.

1 cup flour	2 cups sliced apples, plums,
¼ teaspoon salt	pears, or peaches
1 tablespoon sugar	1 cup sugar
1 teaspoon baking powder	1 teaspoon cornstarch
2 tablespoons shortening	1 egg, slightly beaten
¼ cup milk	½ cup milk

Sift flour, salt, sugar, baking powder. Cut in shortening with pastry blender. Add milk, mix well, and spread in bottom of greased baking dish about 10x6x2 inches. Arrange sliced fruit on top. Combine remaining ingredients and pour over fruit. Bake at 425° F. for 30 minutes.

ORANGE-CARAMEL SKILLET CAKE *Six* SERVINGS

This delightful sweet bread could be served for dessert.

1½ cups sifted flour	½ cup brown sugar
2 teaspoons baking powder	1 teaspoon cinnamon
½ cup sugar	1 tablespoon grated
½ teaspoon salt	orange rind
¼ cup butter or margarine	¼ cup chopped nuts
1 egg, well beaten	2 tablespoons butter
½ cup orange juice	

Sift flour, baking powder, sugar, and salt together. Cut in butter as for pie crust. Add egg and orange juice and mix thoroughly. Sprinkle brown sugar in bottom of a well-buttered 10-inch heavy frying pan. Top with cinnamon, orange rind, and nuts. Dot with butter. Spread batter over all. Bake at 375° for 30 minutes. Turn out on serving dish immediately.

For an interesting variation, slice an orange into the brown sugar before adding the batter.

POPOVERS
Six LARGE or *Twelve* SMALL

Big puffs with nothing but air inside!

2 eggs, well beaten
1 cup milk
1 cup sifted flour
¾ teaspoon salt
1 tablespoon melted shortening

Grease glass custard cups well. Add milk to beaten eggs and pour liquids into sifted dry ingredients, blending well. Stir in shortening and mix until batter is smooth. (Do not overbeat.)

Fill custard cups one-third full and bake at 375° F. for 50 to 60 minutes, or until popovers are puffy, browned, and crisp on top. Remove from cups at once and cut slit in side of each popover to let steam escape. Serve at once with butter and jelly. If muffin pans or popover pans are used, heat the greased pans in the hot oven, then add batter. An extra egg makes them even more gigantic and puffy!

SOME POPOVER VARIATIONS

Bacon.   Grease cups with bacon fat and use it as shortening. When you slit each popover, put a crumbled strip of crisp bacon inside.

Cheese.   Have pans very hot. Drop a tablespoonful of batter into each, sprinkle with grated cheese, add another spoonful of batter. Bake. Use 1 cup grated cheese altogether. They melt in your mouth!

Orange.   Add the grated rind of 1 orange and use orange juice for ½ the liquid.

Whole Wheat.   Use ⅔ cup whole wheat, ⅓ cup white flour.

DOUGHNUTS

Three DOZEN

These are the kind your grandmother made—so wonderful right out of the kettle!

1 cup sugar
2 eggs, beaten
1/4 teaspoon lemon extract
3 tablespoons melted fat
4 cups flour

4 teaspoons baking powder
1/2 teaspoon salt
1/2 teaspoon nutmeg
1 cup milk

Add sugar gradually to eggs, beating thoroughly. Add extract and shortening. Alternately add sifted dry ingredients and milk, mixing well after each addition. Knead lightly on a lightly floured board for 30 seconds. Roll out 1/2-inch thick and cut with a doughnut cutter. Drop into deep fat heated to 350° to 360° F. and fry until golden brown, turning once. Drain on soft paper. Roll in granulated or confectioners' sugar while warm, if you wish.

VARIATIONS OF PLAIN DOUGHNUTS

Baby Doughnuts. For a feminine party, cut miniature doughnuts, or make twists by tying strips of the dough in a knot, and fry these. Dust with confectioners' sugar while still warm.

Chocolate Doughnuts. Melt 2 squares chocolate and stir into the mixed dough. Cut the fat to 1 1/2 tablespoons.

Coconut or Nut Doughnuts. Frost lightly with vanilla-flavored Confectioners' Sugar Icing and sprinkle with coconut or chopped nuts.

Frosted Doughnuts. Frost on one side only. Use a thin frosting of confectioners' sugar and milk flavored with grated lemon or orange rind, with vanilla, or with 1/2 square melted chocolate.

Orange Doughnuts. Add the grated rind of 1 orange to batter.

Sour Milk or Buttermilk Doughnuts. Replace sweet milk with sour or buttermilk, reduce baking powder to 3 teaspoons, and add 1/4 teaspoon soda.

APPLESAUCE DOUGHNUTS   *Three to Four* DOZEN

They seem to stay fresh longer than most doughnuts. And they're "different."

1¼ cups sugar
 1 cup unsweetened applesauce
 3 tablespoons sour cream
 2 tablespoons melted butter
 2 eggs, well beaten
 1 teaspoon soda

 1 teaspoon baking powder
 1 teaspoon nutmeg
 2 teaspoons cinnamon
 ¼ teaspoon cloves
 ½ teaspoon salt
 4 cups flour (about)

Mix sugar, applesauce, cream, and butter. Add eggs, then sifted dry ingredients. Chill dough, then roll ½-inch thick, cut, and allow to dry slightly before frying in deep fat, 350° to 360° F., turning once.

Such Good Cookies!

THIS IS THE BEST spaghetti I ever ate!" I once said to my cousin Alice, after a meal with her and George.

"It ought to be. You gave me the recipe after I had it at *your* house and said I thought it was the best *I* ever ate!" she replied. "And you told me then it was your favorite recipe!"

Well, of course, it was at that time my favorite recipe. But anyone whose business is recipes is bound to change favorites when trying out not hundreds but thousands of new ideas. That's why I sometimes feel sorry for my children. They won't have enough memories of the dishes mother used to make, because she kept experimenting. She kept making different ones—and there were plenty that weren't too good and had to be discarded along the way, believe me! Merciful heavens, what if they remember only the failures!

Cookies are a little different. While one may change a favorite spaghetti recipe, one seldom abandons a good cooky. True, new recipes appear daily, but they are mostly new twists superimposed upon a classical butter cooky or oatmeal drop or brownie.

This group of cookies represents my real favorites over the years. I'd have to do a cooky cookbook to squeeze in as many recipes as I'd like. It hurts to eliminate even one old familiar formula, and I've had to, 'cause there just isn't room for any more. But those left are my pets, predominantly good, substantial cooky-jar fillers. I know that you and your family will love them.

ALMOND DROPS   *Four to Five* DOZEN

They are crisp, macaroon-like and professional looking.

¼ cup butter or margarine	1¼ teaspoons baking powder
½ cup shortening	¼ teaspoon each, mace, cinna-
1 cup sugar	mon
¼ teaspoon almond extract	¼ teaspoon salt
1 egg	⅓ cup finely chopped un-
1⅓ cups sifted flour	blanched almonds

Brown butter or margarine in a 1½-quart saucepan; remove from heat and add shortening, stirring to melt. Then blend in sugar and extract. Beat in egg with spoon. (Mixture will thicken and become smooth.) Mix in sifted dry ingredients and almonds. Use teaspoon measure to take out pieces of dough; form small balls and drop into a dish of sugar; roll to coat well. Sugar gives sparkle to the cookies, makes a crackly-crisp top.

Place sugared balls about 2 inches apart on greased cooky sheet. Bake at 375° F. about 10 minutes.

BUTTERSCOTCH-PECAN REFRIGERATOR COOKIES   *Six* DOZEN

Everybody likes these!

1½ cups butter or margarine	4 cups sifted flour
2 cups brown sugar	½ teaspoon soda
2 eggs	1 teaspoon baking powder
1 teaspoon vanilla or ½ tea-	½ teaspoon salt
spoon rum extract	1 cup chopped pecans

Cream butter or margarine and sugar until light; add eggs and vanilla. Beat well. Add sifted flour, soda, baking powder, and salt to creamed mixture. Add pecans and mix well. Shape into rolls and wrap in waxed paper or press into cooky molds. Chill until very firm, or freeze. Slice thin and bake on ungreased baking sheets in moderately hot oven, 400° F., for 8 to 10 minutes.

MARY BURNHAM'S BROWNIES   *Three* DOZEN

This is double the usual recipe—for the most obvious reasons!

> 1 cup butter or margarine
> 2 cups sugar
> 4 unbeaten eggs
> 4 squares unsweetened chocolate, melted
> 1 teaspoon vanilla
> 1¾ cups sifted flour
> ¼ teaspoon salt
> 1 cup chopped pecans or walnuts
> Chocolate Icing (see below)

Cream butter until soft and fluffy; gradually beat in sugar, creaming well. Add eggs, one at a time, and melted chocolate, mixing thoroughly. Add vanilla. Gradually beat in flour which has been sifted with salt. Stir in chopped nuts. Turn batter into greased jelly-roll pan. Bake at 350° F. for 25 minutes.

When cool, spread with Chocolate Icing made by mixing 1 square melted chocolate, 1 cup confectioners' sugar, 1 tablespoon soft butter, ½ teaspoon vanilla, and about 2 tablespoons water or milk.

We sometimes bake these brownies in tiny muffin pans lined with fluted paper baking cups. They're attractive that way.

SOME BROWNIE VARIATIONS

Black Walnut.   Use black walnuts in the recipe and flavor with brandy or sherry extract instead of vanilla.

Date-Nut Brownies.   Add 1 cup chopped dates.

Honey-Nut.   Substitute 1 cup honey for 1 cup sugar.

BROWNIES MADE IN YOUR BLENDER

This is an excellent blender-made cooky. Place eggs, vanilla, soft butter, sugar, and melted chocolate in blender container; cover, switch on the motor, and blend until smooth, using a rubber spatula in the top of the mixture. Pour over flour and salt in a pan, stir, add nuts, and bake.

BLONDE BROWNIES   *Four* DOZEN

The chewy kind are especially nice in a holiday assortment.

    3 eggs, beaten
    ¾ cup brown sugar
    1¾ cups light corn sirup
    1 teaspoon vanilla
    2 cups sifted flour
    ½ teaspoon salt
    1 cup chopped nuts
    ¾ cup chipped semi-sweet chocolate

Add sugar and corn sirup to eggs, gradually, beating until well mixed. Add vanilla. Add flour and salt; add nuts and blend well. Pour into greased 9x12x2-inch pan. Sprinkle chipped chocolate over batter. Bake at 350° F. for 25 minutes. Cut into bars.

MARASCHINO CHERRY COOKIES   *Four* DOZEN

Tender and delicately flavored with cherry, they're very pretty cookies for a holiday collection or for a tea party.

½ cup butter or shortening
½ cup sugar
1 egg
1 teaspoon grated lemon rind
1 teaspoon vanilla
1½ teaspoons maraschino
    cherry juice
1 cup sifted flour

¼ teaspoon soda
½ teaspoon baking powder
¼ teaspoon salt
½ cup chopped nuts
½ cup chopped raisins
½ cup crushed corn flakes
12 maraschino cherries,
    quartered

Cream butter and sugar, and beat in egg. Add lemon rind, vanilla, and cherry juice. Beat well. Sift dry ingredients together, and add to the first mixture with nuts and raisins. Mix well. Drop from a teaspoon onto crushed corn flakes, roll into balls, and place on ungreased cooky sheet. Top each cooky with a quarter maraschino cherry. Bake at 400° F. about 10 minutes, or until delicately browned.

CHERRY CRISPS   Five DOZEN

Roll these good cookies or shape them into balls and flatten them.

1 cup shortening	2 cups corn flakes,
1 cup brown sugar	crushed coarsely
3½ cups sifted flour	1 egg yolk, beaten, plus
2 teaspoons baking powder	1 tablespoon water
¼ teaspoon salt	Sugar
½ cup water	Sliced candied cherries

Cream shortening and sugar thoroughly. Add sifted flour, baking powder and salt alternately with water. Add corn flakes. Chill. Roll to ⅛-inch thickness and cut with floured cutters or shape into balls and flatten in greased cooky sheet. Brush cookies with egg yolk and water. Sprinkle with sugar and top with sliced candied cherries. Bake at 400° F. about 10 minutes.

CHOCOLATE ANGEL PUFFS   Three DOZEN

These dainty morsels that would melt in the mouth but for the coconut are favorites of Joyce Carlson, formerly a "Mary Meader," who helped with recipe tests for this book.

2 egg whites, unbeaten	1 teaspoon vanilla
1½ cups sugar	2 ounces unsweetened
5 tablespoons water	chocolate, melted
1½ teaspoons light corn sirup	2 cups shredded coconut

Combine egg whites, sugar, water, and corn sirup in top of double boiler, beating with rotary beater until thoroughly mixed. Place over rapidly boiling water and cook, beating constantly, for 7 minutes, or until mixture stands in peaks. Remove from hot water and add melted chocolate, vanilla and coconut. Drop from a teaspoon onto cooky sheet lined with waxed paper. Bake in moderately slow oven, 325° F., 20 minutes. Cool five minutes before removing from paper.

CHOCOLATE PEPPERMINT SANDWICHES

Three DOZEN

These cookies take a little fussing, but the results are rewarding.

3 squares unsweetened chocolate
½ cup butter
1 cup sugar
1 egg
2⅓ cups sifted flour
2 teaspoons baking powder
¼ cup evaporated milk or cream
Peppermint Filling (see below)

Melt chocolate; beat in butter, sugar, and egg. Add sifted flour and baking powder alternately with milk. Chill. Roll thin on a well-floured board; cut 2-inch rounds. Bake at 400° F. about 10 minutes. When cool, put 2 cookies together with peppermint filling.

Make Peppermint Filling by beating together 1 egg white, 1 tablespoon soft butter, 1½ cups confectioners' sugar, and 3 drops oil of peppermint.

CHOCOLATE NUT DROPS

Three DOZEN

This is a fine-flavored cooky with some tempting variations.

1 cup sugar
½ cup melted butter or
    margarine
1 egg, slightly beaten
1½ cups sifted flour
½ teaspoon soda
½ teaspoon salt
½ cup milk

3 squares chocolate, melted
    and cooled
1 teaspoon vanilla
½ cup chopped Brazil nuts or
    pecans
12 sliced Brazil nuts or
    pecan halves

Mix sugar, butter, and egg. Add sifted dry ingredients alternately with milk. Add chocolate, vanilla, and ½ cup nuts. Mix well and drop from a tablespoon on well-greased cooky sheets. Place piece of Brazil nut or half pecan in center of each cooky. Bake at 350° F. about 12 minutes.

VARIATIONS

Chocolate Black Walnut Drops. Use black walnuts in the cookies, and frost with plain Confectioners' Sugar Icing (page 117).

Frosted Fudge Drops. Omit the nut decoration and frost baked cookies with blend of 1 cup confectioners' sugar, 1 ounce chocolate, melted, ½ teaspoon vanilla, and hot coffee to make it spreadable.

COCONUT OATMEAL COOKIES

Three to Four DOZEN

Butterscotchy, crisp, ever so good. I usually bake a batch of these when I make Coconut Thinsies (page 63) as the recipe uses the extra half can of coconut so beautifully.

½ cup butter or margarine
1 cup firmly packed brown sugar
1 egg, well beaten
1 cup rolled oats
½ cup shredded coconut
1 cup sifted flour
½ teaspoon baking powder
½ teaspoon soda
½ teaspoon salt

Cream butter or margarine and sugar, beat in egg, and add oats and coconut. Add sifted flour mixture and blend. Shape dough into small balls, and place on greased cooky sheets. Flatten with a fork. Bake at 375° F. about 10 minutes.

COFFEE KISSES   Five DOZEN

Sweet sentiments, coffee flavored. They are not good keepers and I don't recommend them for freezing. They won't last to become a problem!

4 egg whites
3½ cups sugar
3 tablespoons instant coffee
⅛ teaspoon salt
1 cup crushed corn flakes

Beat egg whites until stiff enough to hold in peaks, but not dry. Sift sugar with powdered coffee and salt. Slowly beat in half of sugar mixture. Then fold in remaining sugar. Stir in crushed corn flakes. Drop from a spoon onto a well-greased cooky sheet. Bake at 275° F. from 15 to 30 minutes, depending upon size. Remove from pan while still warm.

COFFEE-OATMEAL COOKIES   Four DOZEN

This recipe makes thin, crisp cookies of good flavor.

2½ cups sifted flour
½ teaspoon salt
2 teaspoons baking powder
¼ teaspoon soda
2½ cups rolled oats

¾ cup shortening
2 cups firmly packed
   brown sugar
½ cup strong cold coffee

Mix and sift flour, salt, baking powder, and soda; add oats. Cream shortening with sugar, add dry ingredients and coffee alternately. Drop by tablespoonfuls at least 3 inches apart on a greased baking sheet. Flatten each cooky with a flat, wet cup or the bottom of a glass, patting until dough is about ⅛-inch thick. Bake about 10 minutes at 400° F.

COCONUT THINSIES   *Four* DOZEN

This is a good, crisp, coconut sugar cooky.

½ cup shortening
1 cup sugar
2 eggs, well beaten
½ teaspoon vanilla
½ teaspoon salt
2 teaspoons baking powder
2½ cups sifted cake flour
1½ cups shredded coconut

Cream shortening and sugar. Add eggs, then vanilla. Add sifted dry ingredients and coconut. Mix well. Chill for an hour. With the fingers, form dough into 48 balls about 1 inch in diameter. Place them on greased cooky sheets several inches apart, and press each into a flat cooky about 2¾ inches in diameter with the bottom of a tumbler covered with cheesecloth, or dampened and dipped in sugar. Bake 12 minutes at 375° F.

CORNFLAKE MACAROONS   *Three* DOZEN

Chewy, moist cookies, one of the best of their kind.

2 egg whites
⅛ teaspoon salt
1 cup granulated sugar
1 cup coconut or ½ cup nuts, finely chopped
2 cups crisp cornflakes
½ teaspoon vanilla

Let egg whites warm to room temperature. Beat with salt until stiff but not dry. Gradually beat in sugar, making a stiff meringue. Fold in coconut or nuts, cornflakes, and vanilla. Drop by spoonfuls onto a greased cooky sheet and bake at 350° F. about 12 to 15 minutes. Place pan on damp cloth and remove cookies immediately with spatula or knife. Makes 2 to 3 dozen macaroons, depending on size.

63

CHOCOLATE REFRIGERATOR COOKIES
Six DOZEN

A prize-winning recipe for the kind of cooky everybody dotes upon may become one of your favorites as it is one of mine.

1¼ cups butter	3 cups sifted cake flour
1½ cups confectioners' sugar	½ cup cocoa
1 egg	1½ cups chopped pecans
¼ teaspoon salt	4 ounces sweet chocolate

Cream butter and sugar, add egg and mix thoroughly. Add sifted salt, flour, and cocoa and blend well. Chill dough in refrigerator for about an hour. Mold into two long smooth rolls about 1½ inches in diameter. Roll in nuts, pressing them in on all sides. Wrap in waxed paper and chill overnight. Using thin, sharp knife, cut in slices ⅛-inch thick. Place on ungreased cooky sheets. Bake at 400° F. for about 10 minutes. Cool. Melt chocolate in double boiler and frost center of cookies.

CRISP REFRIGERATOR COOKIES
Eight DOZEN

Here's a rich, fine cooky you can vary with nuts and other flavorings.

1 pound butter or margarine	4 cups sifted flour
2 cups sugar	3 teaspoons baking powder
2 teaspoons vanilla	½ teaspoon salt
2 eggs, beaten	

Cream butter and sugar thoroughly. Add flavoring. Then beat in eggs and mix well. Sift flour, baking powder, and salt together and add gradually to creamed mixture. Pack cooky dough in refrigerator trays, or shape into bars and wrap in waxed paper. Chill overnight. If chilled in refrigerator trays, cut once lengthwise before slicing off cooky dough. Slice as thin as possible. Bake on cooky sheets at 350° F. about 15 minutes or until pale brown.

Lord Baltimore Cake (rear), page 99;
Cherry Angel Food, page 80; Chocolate Roll, page 85

VARIATIONS

Chocolate Refrigerator Cookies. Add 2 ounces chocolate, melted, to the dough.

Orange Refrigerator Cookies. Flavor with grated rind of 2 oranges instead of vanilla.

Rum Butter Cookies. Use 1 teaspoon rum extract instead of vanilla. Add 1 cup chopped nuts.

CRISP SUGAR COOKIES   *Seven* DOZEN

This is the perfect cooky of its kind, buttery, lemon-flavored, and freezable.

    1 pound butter
 1½ cups sugar
    2 eggs, slightly beaten
    2 tablespoons grated lemon rind
    3 tablespoons lemon juice
    5 cups sifted flour
    3 teaspoons baking powder
  ¼ teaspoon salt
  ½ cup milk

Cream butter until light; gradually beat in sugar. Beat in eggs, lemon rind, and juice. Sift flour, baking powder, and salt together and add alternately in thirds with the milk. Beat until smooth after each addition. Dough will be stiff. Round up dough, wrap in waxed paper, and chill several hours.

Roll out small portion of dough at a time until very thin. Use as little flour as possible on pastry cloth and rolling pin. Cut with small cooky cutters. Place on ungreased cooky sheets, sprinkle cookies with sugar, and bake in a hot oven, 400° F., until lightly browned, 8 to 10 minutes. The cookies are very thin, crisp, and fine-flavored. Use colored sugar at holiday time to decorate them.

65

TOP – *Pumpkin Pie, page 147*
BOTTOM – *One-Two-Three-Four Cake, page 102*

DATE-SLICE COOKIES   *Four* DOZEN (large)

These filled cookies are both good and beautiful. They are one of my pets.

FILLING
1¼ cups chopped pitted dates
½ cup water
½ cup sugar
½ cup nuts, chopped
    (optional)

DOUGH
½ cup shortening
1 cup brown sugar, packed
1 large egg, beaten
1 tablespoon cream
2 cups flour
¼ teaspoon salt
¼ teaspoon soda

Mix filling first. Combine dates, sugar, and water, and cook until thick. Add nuts and cool.

Cream shortening for dough, add sugar, and cream well. Beat in egg; add cream. Add sifted dry ingredients. Mix well and chill dough. Roll between 2 sheets of waxed paper into a rectangle ¼-inch thick. Cut into 2 equal parts.

Spread ⅔ of the date filling on one part and sandwich with the other. Cut lengthwise in two again. Spread rest of date filling on one part and top with second. Then cut into lengthwise bars the width of the cookies you like, and wrap these bars in waxed paper for refrigerator storage. When ready to bake, slice thin and bake on greased cooky sheets at 400° F., about 10 to 12 minutes.

DATE DROPS   *Four* DOZEN

Want a rich, fruity cooky with some variations? Here it is!

1 cup butter or margarine
1½ cups brown sugar,
    well packed
3 eggs, well beaten
2¼ cups sifted flour
¼ teaspoon salt

1 teaspoon soda
½ cup water
1 teaspoon vanilla
1 cup chopped pecans
1 pound dates, chopped

Cream butter and sugar until light; add eggs and beat well. Add sifted flour, salt, and soda alternately with water and vanilla, beating until smooth after each addition. Stir in nuts and dates and let mixture stand for 15 minutes. Drop from a teaspoon on greased cooky sheets. Bake at 400° F. for about 12 to 15 minutes.

Spiced Date Drops. Add ¼ teaspoon each of cinnamon, cloves, nutmeg, ginger. Omit vanilla.

Orange Date Drops. Use orange juice instead of water; omit vanilla and add grated rind of 1 orange.

DATE BARS   Two DOZEN

A favorite with the Mary Meade staff. We usually make these bars for our annual cooky-and-eggnog Christmas party —these and a dozen other kinds of cookies!

    3 eggs, separated
    ¾ cup sugar
    1 teaspoon vanilla
    2 cups fine-cut dates
    ¾ cup chopped nuts
    ⅓ cup sifted flour
    1 teaspoon baking powder
    ½ teaspoon salt

Beat egg yolks until thick and lemon colored. Add sugar gradually. Add vanilla. Fold yolk mixture into stiffly beaten egg whites, using an egg whisk or spatula. Fold in dates and nuts mixed with sifted flour, baking powder, and salt. Spread in greased pan about 9x12 inches. Bake at 350° F. for 25 minutes. Cut while hot; roll in confectioners' sugar when cool.

DATE CHEWS   *Two* DOZEN

Date Chews are perfect to send away—they improve with age.

    1 8-ounce package pitted dates
    1 cup walnuts or pecans
    1 can moist coconut (1 cup)
   1/2 cup brown sugar, firmly packed
    1 egg

Force dates and nuts through food chopper, using coarse blade. Add half of coconut, brown sugar, egg; mix well. Shape into 2-inch fingers and roll in remaining coconut. Bake on greased cooky sheet at 350° F. for 15 minutes.

These are really ambrosial with black walnuts!

DREAM BARS   *Three* DOZEN

Dream Bars are one of the most popular cookies ever invented, and no wonder! They're YUMMY!

 1/2 cup shortening
 1/2 cup brown sugar
   2 cups flour

TOPPING: 2 cups brown sugar, 1 tablespoon flour, 1/4 teaspoon baking powder, 2 eggs, well beaten, 1 cup coconut, 1 cup chopped nuts.

Cream shortening. Blend in brown sugar and flour, stirring until well mixed. Pat out about 1/4-inch thick on greased cooky sheet (with sides). Bake for 10 minutes at 325° F.

To make topping, combine brown sugar, flour, and baking powder, and add eggs, beating well. Stir in coconut and nuts. Spread this mixture over crumbs in pan and bake at 325° F. for 30 minutes longer. Remove from oven and cut into bars.

VARIATIONS

1. Add ½ cup chopped dates or crushed pineapple (well drained) to the topping.

2. Ice the hot, baked bars with a blend of 1½ cups confectioners' sugar, 2 tablespoons melted butter, 2 tablespoons orange juice, 1 teaspoon each of grated lemon and orange rind.

FIVE-IN-ONE COOKIES   *Five* DOZEN

Keep the frozen dough on hand and you'll think of many more variations.

1 pound butter or margarine	2 tablespoons cocoa
3 cups sugar	¼ cup chopped pecans
2 eggs, beaten	3 tablespoons poppy seeds
2 teaspoons vanilla	Sliced candied cherries
5 cups sifted flour	Colored sugar
3 teaspoons baking powder	2 tablespoons brandy or rum
1 teaspoon salt	

Cream butter or margarine and sugar until light, add eggs and mix well. Add vanilla. Sift flour, baking powder, and salt, and mix into dough. Divide dough into five portions. To the first, add the cocoa and finely chopped pecans. Shape into a roll, wrap in waxed paper, and chill. To the second portion add the poppy seeds. Shape into tiny balls and place on cooky sheet. Place third and fourth portions in cooky press and shape into two forms, decorating one with sliced cherries, sprinkling the tops of the others with colored sugar. To the last portion add 2 tablespoons brandy or rum and shape into tiny rolls. Slice the chilled chocolate-nut dough thin. Bake all cookies at 375° F. until lightly browned, about 10 minutes. Coat the little rolls with confectioners' sugar after removing them from the oven.

There are other possibilities with a batch of dough like this. Part could be flavored with grated orange peel or lemon peel. Anise seeds could be added to another part. Cinnamon, cloves, and nutmeg might spice a third portion.

DROP SUGAR COOKIES   *Five* DOZEN

So easy to make, you can be getting lunch at the same time.

1 cup butter or margarine	1 teaspoon salt
1 cup sugar	2 tablespoons vinegar
1 egg	1 teaspoon vanilla
2½ cups sifted flour	1½ teaspoons grated lemon rind
½ teaspoon baking soda	

Cream butter and sugar until light and fluffy. Add egg and beat thoroughly. Add sifted dry ingredients, vinegar, and flavoring, and mix well. Drop teaspoonfuls on greased cooky sheets. Sprinkle a little granulated sugar on each cooky. Bake in a moderately hot oven, 400° F., for about 12 minutes or until delicately browned.

GRACE F'S DROP COOKIES   *Six* DOZEN

I treasure this recipe which I got from a favorite Sunday school teacher, years ago.

1 cup shortening	1 cup sour milk
2 cups sugar	4 cups sifted flour
3 eggs	2 teaspoons soda
2 teaspoons vanilla	1 cup coconut
½ teaspoon salt	1 cup raisins
⅔ cup dark corn sirup	2 cups rolled oats

Cream shortening and sugar, beat in eggs, and add vanilla, salt, and corn sirup. Mix well. Add sifted flour and soda alternately with sour milk. Mix in coconut, raisins, and oats. Drop from a spoon onto a greased baking sheet, flatten a little with a spatula, and bake at 400° F. about 15 minutes.

No sour milk? Add 1 teaspoon vinegar to 1 cup sweet milk.

FRUITED OATMEAL DROPS   *Four to Five* DOZEN

A fine keeper—know someone to send them to?

¾ cup shortening
1 cup sugar
2 eggs
1 cup mashed bananas
2 cups sifted flour
½ teaspoon soda
2 teaspoons baking powder
½ teaspoon salt
1 teaspoon cinnamon

¼ teaspoon allspice
¼ teaspoon cloves
2 cups quick-cooking oats
1 cup raisins, plumped in boil-
    ing water
1 cup chopped nuts
½ cup candied red cherries,
    chopped

Cream shortening and sugar, beat in eggs, one at a time. Add bananas.
Add sifted dry ingredients; stir in oats. Add raisins, nuts, and cherries,
mixing well. Drop from a teaspoon onto a greased baking sheet. Bake
12 to 15 minutes at 375° F.

LEMON DROPS   *Five* DOZEN

A really lemon-flavored cooky—so good!

2 cups sifted flour
3 teaspoons baking powder
¾ teaspoon salt
1 tablespoon grated lemon rind
½ cup shortening
1 cup sugar
1 egg
¼ cup lemon juice
¼ cup cold water

Sift flour, baking powder, and salt. Blend rind and shortening; add
sugar gradually, creaming well. Add egg, beat well, and add lemon
juice and water. Add dry ingredients and mix. Drop by level tablespoonfuls onto greased cooky sheet. Bake at 375° F. for 10 to 12 minutes

FROSTED CREAMS   *Twenty-eight* COOKIES

It's a very good spice bar; I've eaten these cookies from childhood.

⅓ cup hot water or coffee
½ cup shortening
¾ cup molasses
2½ cups sifted flour
1 cup sugar
1½ teaspoons baking powder

1 teaspoon salt
½ teaspoon soda
½ teaspoon each, cinnamon,
    ginger, and cloves
2 eggs

Pour hot water over shortening. Stir until melted. Add molasses. Sift dry ingredients into mixing bowl. Add molasses mixture and eggs. Mix well. Spread in greased jelly-roll pan. Bake at 350° F. until cookies spring back when touched gently with fingertips, 25 to 30 minutes. Cool and frost with Seven-Minute Icing (page 120). Cut into bars.

FROSTED DELIGHTS   *Three* DOZEN

The caramel-nut topping makes this cooky.

½ cup butter
1 cup sugar
2 eggs
½ teaspoon salt

1 teaspoon baking powder
1½ cups sifted flour
½ teaspoon vanilla
    Topping (see below)

Cream butter and sugar until light and fluffy. Add well-beaten eggs and sifted dry ingredients. Add vanilla and mix well. Spread as thin as possible on a buttered baking sheet. Spread topping on the dough.

Make topping by beating 1 egg white until stiff and folding in 1 cup light brown sugar gradually. Sprinkle 1 cup chopped nuts over this frosting. Bake at 325° F. for 30 minutes. Cool and cut into squares.

GINGER COOKIES or   *One hundred* COOKIES or
GINGERBREAD MEN   *Forty-eight* GINGERBREAD MEN

*The dough keeps for weeks, so make the big batch; even
if you don't need them all at once.*

1 cup shortening	1 teaspoon salt
1 cup sugar	1½ teaspoons cinnamon
1 egg	2 tablespoons ginger
2 cups molasses	¼ teaspoon nutmeg
2 tablespoons vinegar	3 teaspoons soda
6–8 cups sifted flour	1 cup boiling water

Cream fat and sugar thoroughly, beat in egg, and add molasses and
vinegar. Mix well. Sift flour with salt and spices. Dissolve soda in boiling
water and add alternately with flour, stirring well. Dough should be
soft but rollable. Chill and roll out a portion of the dough at a time,
keeping the rest chilled. Cut with cutters into shapes you like, or make
gingerbread boys. Bake cookies 12–15 minutes at 350° F. Decorate with
tinted Confectioners' Sugar Icing (page 117).

I make these cookies often and sometimes cut them 6 inches in
diameter with a canister top, to the delight of all the big and little boys
on hand.

OLD-FASHIONED GINGERSNAPS   *Four* DOZEN

Love at first bite! I usually make a double batch.

½ cup shortening	2¼ cups sifted flour
1 cup sugar	1 teaspoon soda
1 beaten egg	½ tablespoon ginger (1½ tps.)
½ cup molasses	½ teaspoon salt

Cream sugar and shortening until light and fluffy. Stir in egg, then
molasses. Sift flour with soda, ginger, and salt and add. Shape into
small balls in the hands and roll in sugar. Place on a lightly greased
cooky sheet, from 2 to 3 inches apart. Bake at 375° F. for about 15
minutes. Cookies flatten and crackle in the baking.

MARG McCARTHY'S OATMEAL COOKIES

Ten DOZEN

When we were budding journalists together at Iowa State, my friend Margaret McCarthy (then McDonough) said she'd rather have eight children than a career. She careered for awhile and now has ten children. Marg finds she has to double her mother's recipe for oatmeal cookies to keep anything in the cooky jars.

2 cups shortening	1 teaspoon cloves
2 cups sugar	1/2 teaspoon nutmeg
2 eggs	4 cups rolled oats
1 cup sour milk (or buttermilk)	4 cups flour
2 teaspoons soda	2 cups raisins
2 teaspoons cinnamon	1 1/2 cups chopped nuts

Cream shortening and sugar, beat in eggs, and add sour milk with soda dissolved in it. Combine dry ingredients, add raisins and nuts and mix with the first mixture. Drop by teaspoonfuls on ungreased baking sheets and bake at 350° F. about 15 minutes.

OLD-FASHIONED SOUR CREAM COOKIES

Four DOZEN

Here's a cherished childhood memory come true!

1 cup butter or margarine	4 1/2 cups sifted flour
1/4 teaspoon salt	1 teaspoon baking powder
2 cups brown or white sugar	1/2 teaspoon soda
1 egg	1 teaspoon vanilla or
1 cup sour cream	1/2 teaspoon lemon
(dairy-made kind)	extract

Cream butter or margarine with salt and sugar. Add egg and cream. Add sifted flour, baking powder, soda, and vanilla. Chill dough, then roll out on lightly floured and sugared board, sprinkle with sugar, roll in very lightly, and cut your cookies. Bake in a 375° F. oven about 10 to 12 minutes, or until lightly browned. Sour cream cookies should be big, according to Granny, so I use my biggest cooky cutter. But neat little cookies also are nice for tea.

Two old-time variations: A seeded raisin in the middle of each big cooky; a bit of jam or jelly in a hollow poked with your finger before baking.

OATMEAL-FILLED COOKIES   *Five* DOZEN

These are fine for church suppers, picnics, after-school snacks.

    1 cup shortening
    1 cup brown sugar
    ½ cup water
    2½ cups rolled oats
    2½ cups sifted flour
    1 teaspoon soda
    1 teaspoon salt

DATE, PRUNE, OR APRICOT FILLING: 2 cups pitted prunes, dates, or dried apricots; 1 cup white or brown sugar; ½ cup water or orange juice; ¼ cup chopped nuts, if you wish.

Cream shortening and sugar; add water and oats. Mix well, and add sifted flour, soda, and salt. Divide dough in half, and pat one half out to fit a 12x15-inch cooky sheet. Spread with filling. Pat out pieces of remaining dough to cover filling. Bake at 350° F. about 30 minutes. Cut into bars. Cookies may be rolled, cut in rounds, and sandwiched together with the filling.

To make the filling, use the moist kind of prunes or apricots, or else partly cooked fruit. Combine ingredients, except nuts, and cook until thick, stirring to keep from scorching. Add nuts. Grated orange rind can also be added, if you like.

Mincemeat may also be used as filling.

SOFT MOLASSES COOKIES   *Four* DOZEN

It's often the hairy arm that plunges into the cooky jar for these!

3 cups sifted flour	½ cup shortening
2 teaspoons soda	½ cup sugar
1 teaspoon each, cinnamon, ginger, nutmeg	1 egg, well beaten
	1 cup molasses
¼ teaspoon cloves	1 tablespoon vinegar
¾ teaspoon salt	½ cup boiling water

Sift together the flour, soda, spices, and salt. Cream shortening with sugar until light; add egg, then molasses, and beat thoroughly. Add sifted dry ingredients to creamed mixture alternately with vinegar and boiling water. Mix thoroughly and drop by spoonfuls 2 inches apart on well-greased cooky sheet. This is a very soft dough. Sprinkle with sugar. Bake 12 to 15 minutes or until firm to touch, at 375° F. Sometimes I frost these very spicy drops, a family favorite.

ORANGE OATMEAL COOKIES   *Four* DOZEN

This is a treasure of a recipe! Use it when you're asked to make cookies for a bake sale or church social.

1 cup butter, margarine or shortening	2 cups sifted flour
	1 teaspoon soda
2 cups brown sugar, firmly packed	½ teaspoon salt
	2 cups rolled oats
2 eggs, beaten	1 cup raisins or dates, chopped
2 tablespoons grated orange rind	
Juice of 1 orange	½ cup chopped nuts

Cream shortening and sugar. Beat in eggs until light. Add orange rind and juice. Sift flour, soda, and salt and add to creamed mixture. Add oats, raisins, and nuts; mix to blend. Drop from teaspoon onto greased baking sheet and bake in a moderately hot oven, 375° F., for 12 to 15 minutes, or until browned. These are family favorites at our house.

76

RASPBERRY JAM BARS *Two* DOZEN

*Apricot jam and cherry preserves are good alternates for this
cooky sandwich.*

½ cup shortening	½ teaspoon salt
1 teaspoon almond extract	½ teaspoon cinnamon
½ cup sugar	½ teaspoon cloves
1½ cups flour	1 egg
1 teaspoon baking powder	¾ cup raspberry or other jam

Combine shortening, flavoring, and sugar. Add sifted dry ingredients,
and mix until crumbly. Add beaten egg, blending well. Spread half the
dough in bottom of greased pan about 7x11 inches. Spread jam over
batter and cover with remaining dough. Bake at 400° F. for 25 to 30
minutes. Cut in bars.

RAISIN COFFEE COOKIES *Five* DOZEN

*These rate A plus! The blend of brown sugar, coffee, and
spice flavors is marvelous.*

¾ cup shortening	1 teaspoon nutmeg
2 cups brown sugar	½ teaspoon cloves
2 eggs	1 cup warm coffee
1 teaspoon soda	1 cup raisins (softened by
3½ cups sifted flour	heating in small amount
1 teaspoon baking powder	of water)
1 teaspoon salt	1 cup nuts (pecans or black
1 teaspoon cinnamon	walnuts)

Cream fat and sugar. Add eggs one at a time, beating after each addition. Sift flour, soda, baking powder, salt, and spices. Add coffee to
creamed mixture alternately with flour, beating after each addition. Add
drained raisins and nuts. Drop from teaspoon onto greased baking sheet.
Bake at 375° F. for 12 to 15 minutes, or until cookies spring back when
touched lightly with a fingertip.

RAISIN DROP COOKIES (ROCKS) Three DOZEN

It's a fruited drop cooky of excellent flavor.

2¾ cups sifted flour
1 teaspoon soda
1 teaspoon salt
½ teaspoon cloves
1 teaspoon cinnamon
½ teaspoon nutmeg
½ cup butter or
     other shortening

½ cup sugar
1 egg
½ cup sour milk
½ cup molasses
1 cup raisins
½ cup chopped nuts

Sift flour with soda, salt, and spices. Cream butter and sugar until light, add egg, and beat well. Combine sour milk and molasses. Add alternately with dry ingredients to creamed mixture. Mix well. Add raisins and nuts. Drop by teaspoonfuls on greased baking sheet and bake at 400° F. for 10 to 12 minutes.

RIBBON COOKIES Six DOZEN

One of the prettiest cookies of all—and a favorite of mine.

1 cup shortening
1¼ cups sugar
1 egg, beaten
1 teaspoon vanilla
2½ cups sifted flour
1½ teaspoons baking powder
½ teaspoon salt

¼ cup candied cherries,
     cut in small pieces
1 square unsweetened
     chocolate
¼ cup pecans
2 tablespoons poppy seed

Cream shortening and sugar; add egg and vanilla. Sift flour, baking powder, and salt. Add to creamed mixture. Mix well. Divide in three parts. Add cherries to one part, chocolate and pecans to another, poppy seed to the third part. Line a 12½x4½-inch pan with waxed paper. Place dough with cherries on bottom, then the chocolate dough and nut mixture, and then the poppy seed. Cover with waxed paper. Chill in refrigerator overnight. Cut loaf in half lengthwise. Slice thin cookies. Bake on ungreased cooky sheet in a 375° F. oven 10 to 12 minutes.

78

Good
Old-Fashioned
Cakes

OH, YES, WE DO! We still make cakes from scratch!" So chorus readers of my daily food column whenever I publicly mourn the olden days when cake was cake and women were proud of their reputations as cake makers.

There are many excellent cake mixes. But they make tenderer cakes, fluffier cakes, cakes with less substance and often less flavor than those we used to make. And I, for one, like a cake you can sink your teeth into, not one that crumbles away at the first bite!

Here are cakes "with meat on their bones." Some—like the Lord and Lady Baltimore cakes—are old and steeped in tradition. Others have been popular favorites with my readers. Many are my own pets which I make at home as often as I can.

All of these recipes have been carefully chosen, and among them you'll find birthday cakes, church supper and picnic cakes, and traditional holiday fruit cakes. Have fun with them!

The best cake maker I have ever known is Mary Burnham, director of the Mary Meade Test Kitchen at the *Chicago Tribune*. Mary (who is Mrs. Norbert Burnham, Jr., mother of Maryann, Bill and Bonnie), prepares our cakes and other foods for their photographs, and she has such a reputation about Tribune Tower that blissful smiles break out all over when the word gets out there's a "Mary Burnham cake" to sample. Mary has made many, if not most, of these cakes, and I think I shall dedicate this chapter to her, as a kind of benison for the cooks who bake them.

ANGEL FOOD CAKE   *Twelve to Sixteen* SERVINGS

Angel Food is the Queen of Cakes; beautiful, tall, and tender.

1½ cups egg whites (12-14 eggs)
½ teaspoon salt
2 teaspoons cream of tartar
2 tablespoons water
1 teaspoon vanilla
1 teaspoon almond extract
2 cups less 2 tablespoons sugar
1½ cups sifted cake flour

Beat egg whites and salt until frothy; sprinkle on the cream of tartar. Continue beating until whites are in soft, moist peaks. Gradually beat in water and flavorings. Fold in half the sugar, sifting 2 tablespoons at a time over the surface. Beat until egg whites are stiff and glossy, but not dry. Using a wire whisk, carefully fold in mixture of remaining sugar and flour, which have been sifted together 4 times. Add about ¼ cup at a time, scattering it over the meringue as you fold. When batter is blended, pour into ungreased 10-inch tube pan and bake at 375° F. for 40 minutes. Invert pan and let the cake hang until it is perfectly cold. Loosen it carefully with a slim, sharp knife when turning it out of the pan. Ice with a thin Butter Icing (page 113) if you wish, or serve with whipped cream or fruit sauce.

SOME DELECTABLE ANGEL FOOD VARIATIONS

Cherry Angel Food. Measure ½ cup finely cut, drained (on paper toweling) maraschino cherries. Turn a third of the Angel Food batter into the pan and sprinkle with half the cherries. Add another third of the batter, and scatter the rest of the cherries. Top with remaining batter. Run a knife up and down through the batter several times to distribute the cherries. You could pinken the batter by using cherry juice instead of water, but I think the cherry specks in the snow-white cake are prettier.

Cocoa Angel Food. Sift ½ cup cocoa with sugar and flour mixture as directed in Angel Food Cake.

Cocoa-Pecan or Black Walnut Angel Food. Fold into the cocoa batter above 1 cup broken pecans or 1 cup finely chopped black walnuts.

Mocha Angel Food. Sift with the sugar and flour mixture ⅓ cup cocoa and 2 tablespoons instant coffee.

Orange Angel Food. Replace water with orange juice or orange concentrate, and add 2 tablespoons grated orange rind to batter. Ice with thin Orange Butter Frosting (page 113).

Angel Food in Layers or Loaves. Angel Food batter may be baked in two 9x9x2-inch square pans at 325° F. about 40 minutes. Hang upside down to cool. Loaf pans or cupcake pans may be used. Don't grease them.

LEMON REFRIGERATOR CAKE   *Sixteen* SERVINGS

Here's the last word in luscious desserts; it has been extremely popular.

> 1 10-inch Angel Food cake (or sponge or chiffon)
> 1 tablespoon plain gelatin softened in ¼ cup
>   cold water
> 6 eggs, separated
> 1½ cups sugar
> ¾ cup lemon juice
> 1½ teaspoons grated lemon rind
> 1 cup cream, whipped

Combine slightly beaten egg yolks, ¾ cup sugar, lemon juice, and rind and cook over hot, not boiling, water until mixture coats a spoon. Remove from heat and stir in gelatin. Beat egg whites until stiff and gradually add remaining sugar, beating constantly. Fold into custard. Tear cake into small pieces and arrange a layer in bottom of oiled Angel Food pan. Pour custard over cake and alternate layers of cake and filling until all is used. Chill until firm. Unmold and ice with whipped cream and decorate with cherries or nuts, if you wish. You may prefer to slice the cake into 3 layers, using the lemon mixture as filling.

SUNSHINE CAKE
Sixteen SERVINGS

A huge beauty that deserves its name; this is a true sponge cake.

12 eggs, separated
 2 teaspoons cream of tartar
1¼ cups sugar

1 cup sifted cake flour
1 teaspoon vanilla
1 teaspoon almond flavoring

Beat egg whites until frothy; add cream of tartar and beat until stiff but not dry. Add ¾ cup sugar very gradually, folding in thoroughly. Sift flour with remaining ½ cup sugar 4 times. Sift over egg white mixture, a little at a time, and fold in lightly. Add flavoring to yolks beaten thick and yellow and fold into white mixture. Bake in an ungreased 10-inch tube pan at 325° F. for 1 hour and 10 minutes. Invert pan to cool. All you need is a thin Butter Icing (page 113). This is also *wonderful* prepared as Lemon Refrigerator Cake (page 81).

GOLD CAKE
Twelve SERVINGS

Only the yolks are used in this sponge-type cake of exceptional tenderness. Why not make Angel Food (page 80) with the whites, and freeze it for later use?

 12 egg yolks
 ¼ teaspoon salt
 ¾ cup warm water
  1 cup sugar
1¾ cups sifted cake flour
 ½ teaspoon lemon extract
 ½ teaspoon vanilla
  2 teaspoons baking powder

Beat yolks until thick and lemon colored; add water and salt and beat until thick. Add sugar gradually; continue to beat until all sugar is dissolved. Fold in flour. Add flavoring, and then fold in baking powder. Bake in ungreased 10-inch tube pan at 325° F. about 50 minutes.

JELLY ROLL

Eight to *Ten* SERVINGS

Here's an old-fashioned dessert we should serve more often.

      4 eggs, separated
      1 cup sugar
      3 tablespoons cold water
      1 teaspoon vanilla
      1 cup sifted cake flour
   1¼ teaspoons baking powder
      ¼ teaspoon salt
      1 cup currant jelly or raspberry jam

Beat egg whites until stiff but not dry. Gradually beat in ½ cup sugar. Beat egg yolks, water, and vanilla together until thick; slowly blend in remaining ½ cup sugar. Sift together flour, baking powder, and salt; fold into yellow mixture. Now carefully fold yellow mixture into whites. Pour into a 10x15-inch jelly roll pan lined with greased waxed paper. Bake at 425° F. for 12 to 15 minutes, or until cake springs back when lightly pressed with fingers. Immediately turn hot cake onto warm, slightly damp towel. Remove paper and cut off all crusty edges of cake. Spread with jelly or jam. Roll lengthwise, cover with towel, and let stand a few minutes. Remove towel and sift confectioners' sugar lightly over the top.

A good way to cut Jelly Roll: Place center of a 15-inch length of white thread under roll where you want to cut, bring ends together over the top, cross them and pull down quickly, making a clean, quick cut through the roll.

Lemon Roll.   Fill with ½ recipe for filling used with Lemon Refrigerator Cake (page 81), and top each slice with whipped cream.

Strawberry Cream Roll.   Whip 1 cup cream, fold in ¼ cup sugar, ½ teaspoon vanilla, and 1 pint sliced strawberries. Use as filling instead of jelly.

Pudding-filled Roll.   Use any kind of pudding mix or pie filling for the "jelly."

LEMON-ORANGE SPONGE CAKE

Twelve to Sixteen SERVINGS

A tender, golden dessert to frost or top with berries and whipped cream.

8 eggs, separated
¼ cup lemon juice
¼ cup orange juice
1½ cups sugar
1½ cups sifted cake flour

1½ teaspoons baking powder
½ teaspoon salt
1 teaspoon each of grated
      lemon and orange rind

Beat egg yolks until thick and lemon colored. Add fruit juices. Gradually add half the sugar, beating well until sugar is dissolved. Fold in sifted flour, baking powder, and salt. Beat egg whites until stiff but not dry, add remaining sugar, and continue beating until well blended. Fold yolk mixture into egg whites with grated rind. Bake in ungreased 10-inch tube pan at 350° F. for 1 hour and 15 minutes. Ice with Orange Butter Frosting (page 113) or serve with strawberries or raspberries and whipped cream.

Spring Orange Cake. Split in three layers; fill and frost with whipped cream, slightly sweetened and flavored with grated orange rind.

BURNT SUGAR CHIFFON CAKE

Twelve to Sixteen SERVINGS

One of the most delicate and delicious of the chiffons— you'll love it!

¾ cup sugar
1 cup boiling water
2¼ cups sifted cake flour
1¼ cups sugar
3 teaspoons baking powder
1 teaspoon salt

½ cup salad oil
5 unbeaten egg yolks
⅓ cup water
1 teaspoon vanilla
1 cup egg whites (8-10 eggs)
½ teaspoon cream of tartar

Melt sugar in heavy skillet over low heat; add water and stir over low heat until lumps dissolve. Sift dry ingredients into a bowl; make a well in them. Add salad oil, egg yolks, water, vanilla, and 6 tablespoons cool sugar sirup. Beat until satin smooth. Combine egg whites and cream of tartar. Beat until they form very stiff peaks. Fold egg-yolk mixture into whites. Bake in ungreased 10-inch tube pan at 325° F. for 55 minutes, then in moderate oven, 350° F., 10 to 15 minutes. Invert pan until cool. Frost with Burnt Sugar Frosting (page 120).

CHOCOLATE ROLL (COCOA LOG) *Eight* SERVINGS

A luxury dessert with some wonderful variations, this roll came out on top in a comparison of 4 recipes.

6 tablespoons cake flour	¾ cup sugar
6 tablespoons cocoa	4 eggs, separated
½ teaspoon baking powder	1 teaspoon vanilla
¼ teaspoon salt	1 cup cream, whipped

Sift flour, cocoa, baking powder, and salt together 3 times. Fold sugar into stiff-beaten egg whites gradually, about 2 tablespoons at a time. Fold well-beaten yolks and vanilla into whites. Fold dry ingredients in carefully, about 2 tablespoons at a time. Pour into a shallow 10x15-inch pan lined with greased waxed paper. Bake at 400° F. for 13 minutes. Turn out immediately onto warm, slightly damp towel. Remove paper and cut off all crusty edges of cake. Roll lengthwise and cover with towel. Cool. Unroll, spread plain or sweetened cream on cake and re-roll. Serve plain, or cover with a thin chocolate Confectioners' Sugar Icing (page 117) and nuts.

Use chocolate instead of cocoa, if you'd rather. Fold in 2 ounces, melted, last.

Double Chocolate Roll. Fill with any good chocolate pudding made from a mix.

Peppermint Ice Cream Roll. Fill roll with 1 quart peppermint ice cream, and keep frozen until you want to eat it.

Peppermint Whipped Cream Roll. Fold into the whipped cream 1 cup crushed peppermint candy.

DE LUXE STRAWBERRY CHEESE CAKE

Sixteen SERVINGS

Awfully, awfully rich and expensive, but simply divine! Make it when you want a smash hit!

COOKY CRUST

>   1 cup flour
> 1/4 cup sugar
>   1 teaspoon grated lemon rind
> 1/2 teaspoon vanilla
>   1 egg yolk
> 1/2 cup butter

Combine flour, sugar, lemon rind, and vanilla. Make well in center and add egg yolk and butter; blend. Wrap in waxed paper and chill an hour. Roll about a third of the dough between floured pieces of waxed paper into a circle 9 1/2 inches in diameter and 1/8-inch thick. Place on bottom of 9-inch spring form pan and trim to fit. Roll remaining dough into rectangle 4 inches wide and 15 inches long; cut in half lengthwise. Line side of pan with cooky strips, making a rim on your cooky base. Bake at 400° F. about 10 minutes. If rim slips during baking, press in place with a spoon.

FILLING

> 2 1/2 pounds cream cheese
> 1 3/4 cups sugar
>   3 tablespoons flour
> 1/4 teaspoon salt
> 1/2 teaspoon each, grated orange and lemon rind
> 1/4 teaspoon vanilla
>   5 eggs, plus 2 yolks
> 1/4 cup heavy cream

Combine sugar, flour, salt, orange and lemon rinds, and vanilla and blend gradually into softened cream cheese, keeping mixture smooth. Add eggs and egg yolks, one at a time, blending well after each addition. Gently stir in cream. Turn into lined pan. Bake in very hot oven, 500° F., for 12 to 15 minutes. Reduce temperature to 200° F. and continue baking 1 hour. Cool away from drafts. Remove side of pan and chill. If you use strawberry glaze, add it after cake has cooled, before chilling.

STRAWBERRY GLAZE

Wash and hull 1 quart strawberries. Crush enough berries to make ½ cup; keep rest whole. Put crushed berries, ½ cup sugar, ¼ cup water, and 4 teaspoons cornstarch into saucepan; bring to boil and boil 2 minutes. Stir in 1 teaspoon butter and a few drops of red food coloring. Strain and cool slightly. Arrange whole or halved berries on cheese cake, pour sauce over berries, and chill.

LEMON CHEESE CAKE   *Eight* SERVINGS

This is a good, plain "cakey" cheese cake, such as you'll find in good restaurants.

¼ cup butter or margarine
¾ cup sugar
4 eggs, separated
   Grated rind of 1 lemon
1 tablespoon lemon juice
2 cups cottage cheese, sieved
½ cup cream
¾ cup flour
3 tablespoons fine dry bread crumbs

Cream butter and sugar until light, add egg yolks, one at a time, and beat well after each addition. Add lemon rind and juice. Add cheese and cream alternately with flour, mixing until smooth after each addition. Fold in stiff-beaten egg whites. Sprinkle bread crumbs in well-buttered pan, 8x8x2 inches. Add filling and bake at 325° F. for 1 hour and 15 minutes.

APPLESAUCE CAKE   *Twelve* SERVINGS

This is the kind of cake I like to take on a picnic. It is my favorite applesauce cake.

2½ cups flour
1½ cups sugar
  1 teaspoon baking powder
  1 teaspoon soda
  1 teaspoon salt
  1 teaspoon cinnamon
½ teaspoon each, cloves, nut-
    meg, allspice

½ cup shortening
  1 No. 303 can (1 lb.)
    applesauce
  2 eggs
  1 cup chopped dates or raisins
  1 cup chopped nuts
    (optional)

Put flour sifter in mixer bowl and place the flour, sugar, baking powder, soda, salt, and spices in it. Sift into bowl, then add shortening and apple-sauce. Mix 2 minutes at medium mixer speed, scraping the bowl down once or twice. Add unbeaten eggs and mix 2 minutes longer. Fold in dates and nuts and turn into greased pan, 9½x13½ inches. Bake 50 minutes, or until done, at 350°F. Cool in the pan, on a rack, and frost cake with any Butter Frosting (page 113) or sprinkle with sifted con-fectioners' sugar.

BANANA LAYER CAKE   *Ten* SERVINGS

A very popular, very delicious cake—moist and tender.

2¼ cups sifted cake flour
1¼ cups sugar
2½ teaspoons baking powder
½ teaspoon soda
½ teaspoon salt

½ cup shortening
1½ cups mashed ripe bananas
    (4-5 bananas)
  2 eggs
  1 teaspoon vanilla

Sift dry ingredients into a large mixing bowl. Add shortening, ½ cup bananas, and the eggs. Beat 2 minutes at slow to medium speed with electric mixer or 2 minutes by hand. Scrape down bowl and beater or

88

spoon frequently during mixing. Add rest of bananas and vanilla. Beat 1 minute longer, scraping down bowl and beater frequently. Turn into two well-greased 9-inch round pans and bake at 375° F. about 25 minutes. Fill and frost with whipped cream, Seven-Minute Frosting (page 120) or a variation of Basic Butter Frosting (page 113).

BOSTON CREAM CAKE $\quad$ *Ten* SERVINGS

We called this Boston Cream Pie at home. My mother made it with a single layer of one-egg cake, splitting it for the delicious cream filling. It was the delight of my childhood.

½ cup butter or margarine
1 cup sugar
2 eggs, beaten
2 cups sifted cake flour
2½ teaspoons baking powder

½ teaspoon salt
½ cup milk
1 teaspoon vanilla
Cream Filling (see below)

Cream shortening and sugar until light, add eggs and mix well. Add sifted dry ingredients alternately with milk. Add vanilla and bake in two 9-inch greased layer pans lined with waxed paper at 375° F. about 25 minutes. Put together with Cream Filling, sprinkle with confectioners' sugar, and serve in wedges.

CREAM FILLING: Mix ¾ cup sugar, ⅓ cup flour, ¼ teaspoon salt. Pour over the mixture 2 cups scalded milk. Stir and cook until thickened. Mix in quickly 2 eggs, slightly beaten, and stir over low heat 2 minutes more. Add 1 tablespoon butter and 1 teaspoon vanilla. Cool.

You can also use any prepared pudding or pie-filling mix. The custard and cream ones are especially suitable.

BLACK WALNUT CAKE   *Twelve* SERVINGS

Oh, the flavor in these rich nuts!

⅔ cup butter
1½ cups sugar
3 eggs, well beaten
2 cups sifted cake flour
2¾ teaspoons baking powder
¼ teaspoon salt
¾ cup milk
1 teaspoon vanilla
1½ cups ground black walnuts

Cream butter and sugar until light, add eggs, and beat well. Add sifted dry ingredients alternately with milk and vanilla, mixing thoroughly. Fold in nuts and bake in two greased, floured 9-inch round cake pans at 375° F. for 30 minutes. Use ½ recipe Butter Cream Frosting (page 115) or full recipe Seven-Minute Frosting (page 120).

BURNT SUGAR CAKE   *Sixteen* SERVINGS

Palomino color, marvelous flavor, and perfect texture. What more can you ask?

¾ cup butter or margarine
1¼ cups sugar
3 eggs, separated
3 tablespoons Burnt Sugar Sirup (see below)

3 cups sifted cake flour
3 teaspoons baking powder
¾ teaspoon salt
1 cup milk
1 teaspoon vanilla

Cream butter and sugar until fluffy. Add egg yolks, one at a time, beating well after each. Blend in Burnt Sugar Sirup. Now add sifted dry mixture alternately with milk, beating after each addition. Add vanilla. Fold in stiffly beaten egg whites. Bake in two greased pans (8x8x2 inches) at 375° F., 25 to 30 minutes. Cool thoroughly on cake rack. Fill and frost layers with Burnt Sugar Seven-Minute Frosting (page 120). Arrange salted pecans around sides of cake.

BURNT SUGAR SIRUP: Melt ½ cup granulated sugar in a heavy skillet, stirring constantly. When dark in color, remove from heat and slowly add ⅓ cup hot water, stirring until dissolved.

CHECKERBOARD CAKE   *Twelve* SERVINGS

You can buy special pans for such a cake, but they aren't necessary if you follow this recipe.

¾ cup butter or margarine
1½ cups sugar
3 eggs
3 cups sifted cake flour
3½ teaspoons baking powder

½ teaspoon salt
¾ cup milk
1½ teaspoons vanilla
1½ ounces unsweetened chocolate, melted and cooled

Grease 3 round 8-inch layer pans, and cut a circle of waxed paper to fit the bottom of each. Draw a circle 2⅔ inches in diameter in the center of each piece of waxed paper and another circle 1⅓ inches outside this. This is a guide for pouring the batter, dividing the pan into three equal rings, from center out.

To mix batter, cream butter and sugar thoroughly; add eggs, one at a time, beating until smooth after each. Add sifted dry ingredients to creamed mixture alternately with milk. Add vanilla. To a third of the batter, which is rather thick, add the cooled chocolate.

Make outside ring and center of 2 layers, using the yellow batter. Pour chocolate batter in the remaining ring of these 2 layers and in the outside ring and center of the third layer, filling in with yellow batter. Bake at 375° F. about 30 minutes. Fill and frost with double recipe of Chocolate Butter Frosting (page 113) putting the chocolate-bordered layer between the 2 yellow-bordered layers.

BLUEBERRY CAKE   *Eight* SERVINGS

"This is the blueberry cake everyone around here makes,"
says my friend, Jule Wilkinson, who summers in Maine.
That's where "around here" is, Maine.

1 cup blueberries
¼ cup flour
¼ cup butter
1 cup sugar
1 egg, beaten
1¾ cups flour
2 teaspoons baking powder
½ teaspoon salt
½ cup milk
⅓ cup sugar
1 teaspoon cinnamon

Mix blueberries with the ¼ cup flour. Cream sugar and butter well and add the egg. Sift flour with baking powder and salt and add alternately with milk. Beat well after each addition. Fold in berries. Pour into buttered 8x8-inch square pan and top with mixture of sugar and cinnamon. Bake at 350° F. for 40 minutes.

Blueberry Cupcakes.   Prepare same batter and bake in buttered cupcake pans for 25 minutes.

BUTTERMILK   *Eighteen* SERVINGS
PRALINE CAKE

You'll be glad it's such a big cake when you see how greedy
it makes your guests!

1 cup butter or vegetable
   shortening
2 cups sugar
4 eggs, separated

3 cups sifted cake flour
1 teaspoon cream of tartar
1 teaspoon soda
1 cup buttermilk

Cream shortening and sugar until light. Add egg yolks, one at a time, and beat until fluffy. Sift dry ingredients together and add alternately with the buttermilk. Fold in stiffly beaten egg whites. Bake in a 9x13-inch greased, floured pan at 350° F. for 50 minutes. Remove from oven and spread with topping. Place under broiler 3 inches from unit for 1 or 2 minutes.

PRALINE TOPPING: Mix ½ cup brown sugar, 1 cup chopped nuts, ¼ cup melted butter, and 3 tablespoons cream.

CHURCH SUPPER CHOCOLATE CAKE   *Forty-eight* SERVINGS

Everybody loves chocolate cake and this may be just what you need when there's going to be a crowd. It will make two large pans.

1¾ pounds cake flour (7¾ cups)
  4 teaspoons baking powder
  2 teaspoons soda
2½ cups butter or margarine
  6 cups sugar
1½ teaspoons salt
1½ tablespoons vanilla
2⅛ cups cocoa (⅛ cup = 2 tablespoons)
  2 cups eggs (9 or 10)
  3 cups sour milk or buttermilk

Have ingredients at room temperature. Sift flour, baking powder, and soda twice. Cream butter 10 minutes at medium mixer speed; add sugar, salt, vanilla, and cocoa gradually and continue beating until very light and fluffy. Beat eggs separately until light and add to batter. Mix 2 minutes on medium speed. Add all of the sifted dry ingredients, then all of the milk; mix for 1½ minutes at high speed, then 45 seconds at medium. Bake in 2 well-greased 10x14-inch pans at 350° F. for 40 to 50 minutes. Cool and frost with two recipes of Peppermint Candy Frosting (page 115). Cut each cake, when cooled, into 24 portions.

CHOCOLATE MOCHA CAKE   *Twelve* SERVINGS

The touch of spice is ever so nice! A perfect party cake.

¾ cup shortening
2¼ cups sugar
3 eggs
3 cups sifted cake flour
¾ teaspoon baking powder
1½ teaspoons soda
1 teaspoon salt
1½ teaspoons cinnamon

2 tablespoons instant coffee
¾ cup cocoa
1 cup sour milk or
    buttermilk
1½ teaspoons vanilla
¾ cup water
¾ cup chopped pecans
    (optional)

Cream shortening and sugar well, add eggs one at a time, and beat well after each. Add sifted mixture of dry ingredients alternately with sour milk and flavoring, beating well after each addition. Add water; stir smooth. Fold in nuts if you use them. Bake in 3 greased 9-inch layer pans at 350° F. for 30 minutes. Fill and frost with Chocolate Butter Frosting (page 113) or Marshmallow Seven-Minute Frosting (page 121).

DOUBLE FUDGE CAKE   *Twelve* SERVINGS

A dark, tender beauty! It makes a fine birthday cake for chocolate-loving kids.

4 squares unsweetened
    chocolate, melted
1¼ cups milk
¾ cup firmly packed brown
    sugar
⅔ cup butter

¾ teaspoon salt
1 teaspoon vanilla
1 cup granulated sugar
3 unbeaten eggs
1 teaspoon soda
2¼ cups sifted cake flour

Melt chocolate in milk over hot water and blend with rotary beater. Add brown sugar and stir until smooth. Cool. Cream shortening, salt, vanilla; beat in granulated sugar gradually. Beat in eggs thoroughly, one at a time. Add small amounts of sifted soda and flour alternately with chocolate mixture, beating after each addition until smooth. Bake in 2 greased 9-inch layer pans at 375° F. 25 to 30 minutes. When cool, put together and frost with Butter Fudge Frosting (page 116).

CRUMB CAKE *Twelve* SERVINGS

So easy you can't believe it can be so delicious! Serve it plain.
Some people call it coffee cake and serve it for breakfast.

> 2 cups flour
> 2 cups packed brown sugar
> ½ cup butter or margarine
> 1 egg
> 1 cup sour milk or buttermilk
> 1 teaspoon soda

Mix and sift flour and sugar. Cut in butter as for pastry. Remove a cup of crumbs and save for topping. Drop egg into remainder and add sour milk in which soda has been dissolved. Beat to mix (there may be some tiny lumps, but that's all right) and pour into greased 9x13-inch pan. Sprinkle reserved crumbs on top. Bake about 30 minutes at 350° F.

Add a teaspoonful of nutmeg to the crumb mixture, if you like. Dates and nuts may be added, 1 cup of each.

DANISH LAYER CAKE *Eight to Ten* SERVINGS

Fill this delicate cake with whipped cream and strawberries.

> ¾ cup milk
> ⅓ cup butter
> 3 eggs, beaten until thick and yellow
> 1½ cups sugar
> 1½ cups sifted cake flour
> 1½ teaspoons baking powder
> ¼ teaspoon salt
> 1 teaspoon vanilla
> 1 cup cream, whipped
> 1 pint strawberries, sliced, sweetened

Heat milk and butter to boiling point. Beat sugar gradually into eggs, and beat until very thick and light. Add sifted flour, baking powder, and salt, mixing thoroughly with mixer at low speed. Add hot milk and butter mixture and beat well. Batter will be bubbly and quite thin. Pour into 2 greased, floured 8-inch layer pans. Bake at 375° F. for 25 minutes.

Cool layers on racks, split, and put together with whipped cream and strawberries. Frost top with whipped cream and garnish with halved strawberries.

PLAIN GINGERBREAD
AND SOME VARIATIONS

Nine SERVINGS

This is the gingerbread most families prefer, I think. We always ate ours at home as bread, and with butter. But it is really cake!

⅓ cup butter, margarine, or shortening
½ cup sugar
1 egg, unbeaten
⅔ cup molasses
2 cups sifted cake flour

2 teaspoons baking powder
¼ teaspoon soda
2 teaspoons ginger
1 teaspoon cinnamon
½ teaspoon salt
¾ cup sour milk or buttermilk

Cream butter and sugar well, beat in egg, add molasses, and beat thoroughly. Sift dry ingredients together and add alternately with sour milk, beating well after each addition. Bake in greased pan (8x8x2 inches) at 350° F. about 50 minutes.

This batter will make 24 cupcakes. Bake 20 minutes at 375° F. Serve warm or cold.

VARIATIONS

Apple Gingerbread. Add 1½ cups chopped apples to the batter before baking.

Chocolate Gingerbread. Add 1 ounce melted chocolate or ¼ cup cocoa to the batter. If you use cocoa, take out ¼ cup of the flour.

Fruited Gingerbread. Fold in 1 cup raisins or chopped dates, 1 cup mincemeat, or 1 cup chopped prunes. Nuts might also be added.

Cream Cheese Topped Gingerbread. Whip 4 to 6 ounces cream cheese fluffy with 2 or 3 tablespoons milk, cream, or orange juice. Add a teaspoon of grated rind if you use orange juice. Spread over gingerbread before serving.

Gingerbread Shortcake. Split your loaf while warm, and fill with sliced sweetened fresh peaches, or canned peach slices, or with banana slices or applesauce. Top with whipped cream.

96

Gingerbread with Sauce. Soft Custard (page 158), any pudding sauce (lemon, orange, or vanilla), and softened ice cream make fine sauces for this spice cake.

Orange Gingerbread. Use orange juice as the liquid and add a teaspoon of grated rind.

Upside-Down Gingerbread. Melt ¼ cup butter in the bottom of the baking pan, add 1 cup brown sugar, and arrange 3 sliced apples in the mixture. Then add your batter and bake as usual. Or use 3 tablespoons butter, ½ cup brown sugar, and 3 or 4 slices pineapple in the same way. Both upside-down versions are best hot, and with a little whipped cream on top of each portion.

Ginger Tea Cakes. When you bake this batter as cupcakes, an excellent way to make them even more spicy is to fold into the batter 2 or 3 tablespoons of chopped crystalized ginger. Makes 'em really hot! Or you can add the ginger to the whipped cream or cream cheese topping.

FEATHER NUTMEG CAKE   *Twelve* SERVINGS

It's marvelous with a lemon filling and boiled icing.

½ cup butter or margarine	1 teaspoon baking powder
1½ cups sugar	1 teaspoon soda
3 eggs, well beaten	2 teaspoons nutmeg
2 cups sifted cake flour	1 cup buttermilk
¼ teaspoon salt	½ teaspoon vanilla

Cream butter and sugar until fluffy, add eggs and beat well. Add sifted dry ingredients alternately with milk and flavoring, beating until smooth after each addition. Bake in 2 greased and floured 9-inch pans at 375° F. for 30 minutes. Fill with Lemon Filling (page 117) and top with Boiled Frosting (page 115). Or fill and frost with good old whipped cream (page 121).

Variation. Bake the cake in three 8-inch layers, adding mixture of 1 tablespoon cocoa and 1 tablespoon water to batter for second layer. Put together with Coffee Butter Frosting (page 113).

HONEY SPICE CAKE   *Eight to Ten* SERVINGS

*This batter makes nice cupcakes, too. Bake them for the same
length of time.*

½ cup shortening
½ cup brown sugar
1 egg
1 cup honey
1 cup sour milk or buttermilk
2½ cups sifted cake flour
1½ teaspoons baking powder

½ teaspoon soda
½ teaspoon salt
1 teaspoon ginger
1 teaspoon cinnamon
¼ teaspoon cloves
½ cup raisins

Cream shortening and beat in brown sugar. Add beaten egg, and blend
thoroughly. Add honey. Alternately add sifted flour mixed with baking
powder and spices, and sour milk, beating batter smooth. Add raisins.
Bake in two greased 8-inch pans at 350° F. for 35 minutes. Cool, fill,
and frost with a Lemon Butter Frosting (page 113) or Honey Frosting
(page 117).

LADY BALTIMORE CAKE   *Twelve* SERVINGS

*An extravagant white cake with a rich, fruity filling—one of
the traditional cakes. The left-over egg yolks can be used for
a Lord Baltimore Cake.*

1 cup butter or margarine
1½ cups sugar
3½ cups sifted cake flour
4 teaspoons baking powder
½ teaspoon salt
1 cup milk

1 teaspoon vanilla
8 egg whites
½ cup sugar
⅛ teaspoon salt
Boiled Frosting (page 115)

Cream butter and sugar until fluffy. Add sifted dry ingredients alternately with milk and vanilla. Beat egg whites until stiff; gradually beat
in remaining ½ cup sugar and salt. Carefully fold beaten whites into
batter. Pour into 3 greased, waxed-paper lined, and again-greased 8-inch

layer pans. Bake at 375° F. about 25 minutes. Cool. Spread filling between layers and frost top and sides with Boiled Frosting. Sprinkle shredded coconut on top of cake.

FILLING: To half of Boiled Frosting, add ½ cup chopped nuts, ½ cup chopped dates, and ½ cup chopped candied cherries.

LORD BALTIMORE CAKE   *Twelve* SERVINGS

A traditional cake, companion to Lady Baltimore and equally delectable.

CAKE BATTER

¾ cup butter or margarine
1¼ cups sugar
8 egg yolks, beaten until
    very thick
2½ cups sifted cake flour

2½ teaspoons baking powder
¼ teaspoon salt
¾ cup milk
1 teaspoon lemon extract
1 teaspoon orange extract

Cream butter and sugar until light. Add egg yolks. Beat well. Add sifted dry ingredients alternately with milk and flavorings, beating after each addition. Bake in 2 greased, waxed-paper-lined 9-inch pans at 375° F. for 25 minutes. Cool. Put layers together with Lord Baltimore Filling and Frosting. Garnish top and sides of cake with pecan halves.

FILLING AND FROSTING

1½ cups sugar
½ teaspoon cream of tartar
    Dash salt
½ cup hot water
3 egg whites, beaten stiff
½ teaspoon vanilla

2 teaspoons lemon juice
½ cup macaroon crumbs
12 candied cherries, chopped
½ cup chopped blanched
    almonds
¼ cup chopped pecans

Cook sugar, cream of tartar, salt, and hot water without stirring to soft ball stage, 240° F. Pour sirup in a fine stream over beaten egg whites, beating constantly. Add vanilla. Add lemon juice to crumbs. Now fold crumbs, cherries, and nuts into 1½ cups of frosting and use this for filling. Frost cake with remainder.

LEMON CRUNCH CAKE   *Sixteen* SERVINGS

*After this appeared in my newspaper food column as a
"Cake of the Week," it was adapted for large-quantity
baking by the test kitchen staff of the Chicago Public Schools
and has since become a favorite dessert in school lunchrooms.*

¾ cup butter or margarine
1½ cups sugar
  3 eggs, well beaten
  3 cups sifted cake flour
  3 teaspoons baking powder

½ teaspoon salt
1 cup milk
Juice and grated rind of 1
  lemon
1 cup chopped pecans

Cream butter and sugar until fluffy. Add eggs; blend well. Add sifted
dry ingredients alternately with milk. Stir in lemon juice and rind. Generously grease a 10-inch tube pan with butter and cover bottom with
chopped nuts. Pour in batter. Bake at 375° F. for 1 hour and 15
minutes.

LEMONADE CAKE WITH RAISINS *Nine* SERVINGS

*Moist and very lemony in flavor—a simple and delicious
dessert.*

½ cup shortening
1 cup sugar
2 eggs, beaten
1⅔ cups sifted flour
1 teaspoon baking powder
½ teaspoon soda
¾ teaspoon salt

½ teaspoon nutmeg
½ cup sour milk or buttermilk
1 cup seedless raisins, ground
Rind of ½ lemon, ground
Lemonade Topping (see be-
  low)

TOPPING: Combine ½ cup sugar, 3 tablespoons lemon juice, ½ teaspoon grated lemon rind, and 1 tablespoon water.

Cream shortening and sugar well, blend in eggs, and beat thoroughly.
Add sifted dry ingredients alternately with sour milk. Add raisin and
lemon-rind mixture and mix well. Bake in greased 9x9x2-inch pan at
350° F. for 50 to 60 minutes. Allow cake to cool about 10 minutes, then
spoon Lemon Topping over it slowly, allowing it to soak into cake.

ORANGE VELVET CAKE   *Eight* SERVINGS

*Dates or prunes may be used instead of raisins. This is a
love of a cake.*

⅓ cup butter
2 teaspoons grated orange rind
1 cup sugar
1 egg
2 cups sifted cake flour

2 teaspoons baking powder
¼ teaspoon salt
½ cup finely chopped raisins
¾ cup milk

BASTING MIX: ½ cup orange juice, ½ cup sugar

Cream butter, orange rind, and sugar until fluffy. Add egg, beating it in
well. Alternately add sifted dry ingredients with raisins, and milk, beating well after each addition. Bake in a greased 8x8x2-inch pan at
350° F. for 50 minutes.

Cool cake 20 minutes in the pan. Then cover with the basting mix,
spooning it over the cake a little at a time. Repeat at intervals until all
of the mixture has been used. Serve the cake with a sprinkling of confectioners' sugar or topping of whipped cream.

Secret: You can use this orange sirup basting mix with any plain
cake. Try it when you've baked a cake that seems a little dry.

PEPPERMINT CANDY CAKE   *Eight* SERVINGS

It's easy to make, family-sized, pink, and pleasing.

½ cup butter or margarine
½ cup sugar
1½ cups sifted cake flour
1½ teaspoons baking powder
¼ teaspoon salt

½ cup milk
½ teaspoon vanilla
½ cup fine crushed peppermint
    candy
3 egg whites, beaten stiff

Cream butter or margarine and sugar until light and fluffy. Add sifted
flour mixture alternately with milk, beating until smooth after each addition. Add vanilla and candy. Fold in stiffly beaten egg whites. Bake in
greased 8x8x2-inch pan at 350° F. for 30 to 35 minutes. Use Peppermint Candy Frosting (page 115), or sprinkle crushed candy over cake
frosted with Basic Butter Frosting (page 113).

ONE-TWO-THREE-FOUR CAKE

Sixteen SERVINGS

Except for the years when the boys refused to have anything but chocolate cake with chocolate filling and frosting, this has always been our family's birthday cake.

1 cup shortening (butter or margarine)
2 cups sugar
½ teaspoon salt
1½ teaspoons vanilla
4 eggs, separated
3 cups sifted cake flour
3 teaspoons baking powder
1 cup milk

Cream the shortening, 1½ cups of the sugar, salt, and vanilla very well together. Add the egg yolks, one at a time, and beat well. Sift the flour and baking powder together several times. Add the dry mixture and the milk in alternate portions to the creamed blend. Beat smooth. Whip egg whites until they hold soft peaks. Beat in gradually the other ½ cup sugar. Beat until egg whites form a shiny meringue with stiff peaks. Fold carefully into batter.

To make 3 9-inch layers, bake in greased, waxed-paper-lined pans 25 minutes at 350° F. or bake 2 9-inch square layers at the same temperature for 35 minutes. Bake cupcakes about 25 minutes.

I must confess that I often make this cake without separating the eggs, just beating them into the batter one at a time. It works fine!

VARIATIONS

Old-Fashioned Chocolate Layer Cake. Fill and frost with Chocolate Butter Frosting (page 113) or Butter Fudge Frosting (page 116).

Coconut Cream Cake. Fill this cake with Coconut Cream Filling (page 119) frost with Seven-Minute Frosting (page 120) and sprinkle with coconut.

Lemon or Orange Cake. Substitute 1 teaspoon lemon or orange extract for vanilla and add some grated lemon or orange rind, if you can. Fill with Prize Lemon Filling (page 120) or Orange Custard Filling (page 121) and flavor Seven-Minute Frosting (page 120) with lemon or orange to frost cake.

Pineapple Cake. Fill with Pineapple Filling (page 122) and use pineapple juice as liquid in Seven-Minute Frosting (page 120).

Ribbon Cake. Add an ounce (square) of chocolate, melted, to a third of the batter for the middle layer. Tint another layer pink. Fill and frost with Chocolate Filling and Frosting (page 116).

Rose Cake. Ah, here's something lovely! Flavor the batter with 1 tablespoon rose water (from the drug store) and ½ teaspoon almond extract instead of vanilla, and tint light pink. Tint Boiled Frosting (page 115) light pink, too, to fill and frost. You might decorate the cake with Crystallized Rose Petals (page 122).

PINEAPPLE LAYER CAKE *Twelve* SERVINGS

I've heard many testimonials to the goodness of this cake.

½ cup butter	¼ teaspoon salt
1½ cups sugar	1 cup canned pineapple juice
3 eggs, separated	½ teaspoon almond extract
2½ cups sifted cake flour	Pineapple Custard Filling
2 teaspoons baking powder	(see below)
½ teaspoon soda	

Cream butter and 1 cup sugar until very light; add beaten egg yolks. Alternately add sifted dry ingredients with pineapple juice and almond extract, beating thoroughly after each addition. Beat egg whites until stiff and beat in remaining ½ cup sugar gradually, beating until whites are stiff and glossy. Fold into batter. Bake in 3 greased, waxed-paper-lined 9-inch layer pans at 375° F. for 25 to 30 minutes. Cool and put together with Pineapple Custard Filling. Frost with Pineapple Butter Frosting (page 113).

PINEAPPLE CUSTARD FILLING: Combine in top of double boiler ¼ cup flour, ¾ cup sugar, ⅛ teaspoon salt. Add ½ cup plus 2 tablespoons pineapple juice, and 2 tablespoons lemon juice. Cook over direct heat, stirring constantly, until thickened. Remove from heat, stir in 1 beaten egg quickly, place over hot water, and stir for 2 minutes. Add 2 tablespoons butter and ½ teaspoon grated lemon rind. Cool.

LEMON JELLY CAKE   *Twelve* SERVINGS

Topped with whipped cream or butter frosting, this dessert is one you'll be proud to serve.

BATTER

1 cup butter	3 cups sifted cake flour
2 cups sugar	4 teaspoons baking powder
1 teaspoon lemon extract	1 teaspoon salt
6 eggs, separated	1 cup milk

LEMON JELLY FILLING

6 eggs, well beaten	Grated rind of 1 lemon
2 cups sugar	Juice of 3 lemons
1/4 teaspoon salt	1 tablespoon butter

Cream butter and sugar until very fluffy; add lemon extract and egg yolks; beat well. Add sifted dry ingredients alternately with milk in thirds, beating until smooth after each addition. Fold in egg whites, beaten stiff. Spread in greased, waxed-paper lined, again-greased 9-inch layer pans and bake at 375° F. for 25 to 30 minutes. Turn out on cake racks. When cold, split layers and fill, putting cake together with the Lemon Jelly Filling.

To prepare filling, mix eggs, sugar, salt, lemon rind, and juice in top of double boiler. Cook, stirring frequently, until thick. Add butter and cool.

PINEAPPLESAUCE CAKE   *Eight* SERVINGS

A most delectable cake, easy to make, you'll find.

1/2 cup shortening	2/3 cup crushed pineapple
1 cup sugar	(not drained)
2 eggs, separated	1 3/4 cups sifted flour
1/2 teaspoon vanilla	1/4 teaspoon soda
1/4 teaspoon lemon extract	1 1/2 teaspoons baking powder
1/4 teaspoon almond extract	1/4 teaspoon salt

Cream shortening and sugar until light; add egg yolks and flavorings and beat well. Add pineapple. Stir in sifted dry ingredients, beating until smoothly blended. Add salt to egg whites and beat stiff; fold into batter. Bake in a greased 8x8x2-inch pan at 350° F., about 40 minutes. Cool and frost with Pineapple Butter Frosting (page 113).

PINEAPPLE UPSIDE-DOWN CAKE

Twelve SERVINGS

Use pineapple rings, peaches, or other fruit with the same cake batter, if you wish.

TOPPING

    ½ cup butter
    1 cup brown sugar
    1 can (1 lb. 4½ ozs.) crushed pineapple, well drained
    12 maraschino cherries

Melt ½ cup butter in a saucepan; stir in brown sugar until it dissolves. Pour mixture into a 9x12x2-inch pan. Top with crushed pineapple. Arrange cherries in three rows of four, so that a cherry will be centered in each serving piece.

BATTER

½ cup butter	2½ teaspoons baking powder
1 cup sugar	¼ teaspoon salt
2 eggs	½ cup milk
2 cups sifted cake flour	1 teaspoon vanilla

Cream butter until light and fluffy, gradually adding sugar. Add eggs one at a time, blending well after each addition. Sift dry ingredients, then add them alternately with milk and vanilla to the creamed mixture. Pour batter over pineapple and cherries. Bake at 375° F. for 45 to 50 minutes, or until cake tests done. Then loosen cake from sides of pan with spatula and invert on large cake platter. Serve cake warm. Top with whipped cream, if you wish.

SNOW CAKE
Sixteen SERVINGS

One of my favorites, with several glamorous variations.

1 cup butter or margarine	1½ teaspoons vanilla
1¼ cups sugar	6 egg whites
3 cups sifted cake flour	¾ cup more sugar for egg
½ teaspoon salt	whites
3 teaspoons baking powder	
1 cup milk	Eggnog Filling (see below)

Cream butter and sugar until light and fluffy. Add sifted dry ingredients alternately with milk. Add flavoring. Beat egg whites until foamy; gradually add the ¾ cup sugar, beating constantly until stiff. Fold into batter. To make 3 layers, bake 25 minutes in greased, waxed-paper-lined 9-inch round pans. (For 2 square layers, bake about 40 minutes in 9x9-inch square pans). Turn out, cool on racks, fill with Eggnog Filling, and frost with Boiled Frosting (page 115).

EGGNOG FILLING: Mix ½ cup sugar, 3 tablespoons cornstarch, and a pinch of salt. Stir in 1 egg yolk and ½ cup milk. Cook 10 minutes in a double boiler, stirring constantly. Add ¼ cup brandy and cook 5 minutes more, until thick. Add 1 tablespoon butter, 1 cup chopped nuts, ¼ cup chopped citron, and ¼ cup chopped candied cherries. Cool.

Coconut Cream Cake. Put together with Coconut Cream Filling (page 119). Sprinkle lavishly with coconut—fresh, grated coconut, if possible. The easy way to grate fresh coconut is in your electric blender.

Christmas Snow Cake. Rub 1 cup coconut bright green with food color, and use it to make a Christmas tree on the top of the frosted cake. If you aren't good at free-hand decorating, cut a pattern. Do this by first tracing around the cake pan on a piece of plain paper. Now trace a Christmas tree in the center of your paper. Cut out the tree. Lay the paper circle with its stencil pattern on the frosted cake. Sprinkle the green coconut in the pattern, carefully following the design. Fill in base of tree with shaved chocolate. (Shave it with a potato peeler.) Carefully remove circle of paper. Sprinkle a few balls of silver candy on the tree to resemble ornaments, and place tiny red candles in holders on the branches.

POUND CAKE   *Two* LOAVES

*This is the old-fashioned, close-textured cake your grand-
mother loved so well.*

1 pound butter (2 cups)
1 pound sugar (2¼ cups)
9 eggs
4 cups sifted cake flour
1 tablespoon grated lemon rind
1 tablespoon lemon juice

Cream butter and sugar until very light and creamy. Beat in eggs, one
at a time, beating well after each. Gradually add cake flour, blending
thoroughly. (Use moderate speed on electric mixer.) Add lemon rind
and juice. Bake in two greased, waxed-paper-lined 9x5-inch pans at
350° F., about 1 hour and 15 minutes. Frost or leave plain. Slice thin.

Half-Pound Cake. Use half the recipe (5 eggs) for one loaf.

Honey Pound Cake. Use half honey, half sugar.

PUMPKIN SPICE CAKE   *Twelve* SERVINGS

*A most pleasing cake that really tastes of pumpkin—you'll
enjoy it.*

½ cup shortening
1½ cups sugar
3 eggs
1¼ cups canned pumpkin
½ cup milk
3 cups sifted cake flour

5 teaspoons baking powder
1 teaspoon salt
1 teaspoon cinnamon
¼ teaspoon each, ground cloves
    and cardamom

Cream shortening and sugar until light; add eggs, one at a time, beating
thoroughly after each. Mix pumpkin and milk. Add sifted dry ingredients alternately with pumpkin-milk mixture, a small amount at a time.
Beat until smooth after each addition. Turn into 2 greased, floured
9-inch layer pans. Bake at 375° F. for 35 minutes. Fill and frost with
Maple Nut Frosting (page 118) or Cream Cheese Frosting (page 118).

HOLIDAY FRUIT CAKE   *Three* LOAVES (11 pounds)

"Best I ever made" many women have told me of this 12-egg, wine-flavored cake.

½ pound chopped citron
½ pound candied cherries
½ pound candied pineapple
2 pounds seeded raisins
1 pound currants
1 pound mixed candied fruits
1 cup wine, any kind
⅔ cup honey
⅔ cup molasses

1 pound chopped walnuts or pecans
1 pound butter or margarine
1 pound brown sugar
12 eggs, beaten
4½ cups sifted cake flour
1 teaspoon soda
1 teaspoon cinnamon
1 teaspoon nutmeg
½ teaspoon cloves

Combine candied fruits, raisins, currants, and wine and let stand overnight. Add honey, molasses, and nuts. Make the cake batter by creaming butter or margarine and brown sugar until mixture is light, then beating in eggs, and stirring in sifted dry ingredients. Add fruits and nuts and mix well. Pour into 3 well-greased 9x5-inch loaf pans lined with greased heavy brown paper. Place a pan of water in the oven with the cakes and bake at 250° F. for 2 to 3 hours, depending on size. Cool cakes thoroughly before storing. Peel off brown paper, wrap in wine-moistened cloth, then in waxed paper.

MOTHER CHURCH'S DARK FRUIT CAKE   *Thirty-six* SERVINGS

Everybody in the family thinks this cake is the ONLY true fruit cake, and I must say that it is both very good and inexpensive. It seems to be a pound cake of sorts, with no nonsense about cherries or pineapple, or even nuts. Mother thought she had lost her battered old recipe, and she had— but luckily I had copied it for my own use a good twenty years ago! It's a family treasure we are glad to share.

108

1 pound butter
1 pound brown sugar
1 tablespoon each of nutmeg, cloves, allspice
⅔ cup molasses
1 pound eggs (about 9) separated
1 pound flour (4 cups) sifted
2 teaspoons baking powder
2 pounds seeded raisins, rinsed in hot water, dried
2 pounds currants, rinsed, dried
½ pound citron, cut fine

Cream butter and sugar well, add spices and molasses; beat well. Beat egg yolks until light and stir into mixture. Fold in flour sifted with baking powder, after mixing some of the flour with the fruits. Fold in egg whites, beaten stiff. Add floured fruit last. Mix well and turn into greased 10-inch tube pan lined with heavy brown paper, well oiled. For the first 2 hours in the oven, cover cake with a cap of brown paper (more modern: aluminum foil). Bake at 275° F. for 3½ to 4 hours.

Be sure to use *seeded*, not *seedless* raisins. They are the fat ones and they have much more flavor.

MAYWOOD FRUIT CAKE   Two LOAVES

This is one of the finest of all light fruit cakes—you'll make it year after year.

1 pound mixed fruits, cut in
    fairly large pieces
½ pound candied cherries
½ pound candied pineapple,
    sliced
1 pound white raisins
1 cup any kind of wine
1 pound butter or margarine

¾ pound powdered sugar
    (2½ cups)
7 eggs, separated
1 pound pecans
4 cups sifted flour
1 teaspoon baking powder
½ teaspoon salt
½ teaspoon cinnamon

Mix fruits, add wine; let stand overnight. Cream butter and sugar, add well-beaten egg yolks and whip until light. Add fruit and nuts. Gradually add sifted flour, baking powder, salt, and cinnamon. Stir lightly. Fold in the stiffly beaten egg whites. Bake in greased paper-lined fruit cake or loaf pans (9x5 inches), filling about ⅔ full. Bake at 250° F. about 3 hours.

SCRIPTURE CAKE *Twenty-eight* SERVINGS

This old recipe, originally from England, I believe, was in my files as a curiosity for a long time before I made it, not really expecting it to work. But it does! I have given the directions to many church groups which have made and sold the cakes as a money-making project.. There's a translation below for checking, after you've searched the Scriptures.

  ½ cup Judges 5:25, last clause
  2 cups Jeremiah 6:20
  2 tablespoons I Samuel 14:25
  6 Jeremiah 17:11
1½ cups I Kings 4:22
  2 teaspoons Amos 4:5
  II Chronicles 9:9, to taste
    Pinch of Leviticus 2:13
  ½ cup Judges 4:19, last clause
  2 cups Nahum 3:12
  2 cups Numbers 17:8
  2 cups I Samuel 30:12

Whip the Judges, Jeremiah, and I Samuel until light. Beat the 6 Jeremiah yolks and add. Add Kings, Amos, Chronicles, and Leviticus alternately with Judges. Fold in Nahum, Numbers, and Samuel, then also the 6 Jeremiah whites, beaten stiff. Bake 2 hours in greased 10-inch tube pan at 300° F.

INTERPRETATION OF SCRIPTURE CAKE

Beat together until light and fluffy ½ cup butter, 2 cups sugar, and 2 tablespoons honey. Beat 6 egg yolks until light and add. Add sifted mixture of 1½ cups sifted flour, 2 teaspoons baking powder, 2 teaspoons cinnamon, ½ teaspoon ginger, 1 teaspoon nutmeg, ½ teaspoon cloves, and a pinch of salt, in alternate portions with ½ cup milk. Stir in 2 cups chopped figs, 2 cups raisins, and 2 cups chopped almonds. Fold in 6 egg whites, beaten stiff. Bake the cake in well-greased 10-inch tube pan (line it with greased brown paper for extra protection in the oven) 2 hours at 300° F.

LAURINE'S CHRISTMAS CAKE   Five POUNDS

When Pat O'Donnell sent me this cake for Christmas, I demanded the recipe. It came from her mother-in-law's personal file. The cake is mighty good.

1 cup shortening	3 cups seedless raisins
1½ cups brown sugar	1 cup currants
6 eggs, separated	½ cup citron, cut finely
¼ cup fruit juice	½ cup candied orange peel, cut
¾ teaspoon soda	½ cup candied lemon peel, cut
½ cup molasses, heated	¾ cup dates, cut
½ cup drained maraschino cherries	1½ cups blanched and toasted almond halves
½ cup candied pineapple, chopped	2 cups sifted flour
3 cups seeded raisins, finely cut	½ teaspoon cloves
	¼ teaspoon nutmeg
	½ teaspoon cinnamon

Cream shortening and sugar, add beaten egg yolks and fruit juice and mix well. Dissolve soda in heated molasses and add to shortening mixture. Combine fruits and almonds with 2 tablespoons flour, then add with rest of flour and spices to creamed mixture and mix thoroughly. Fold in beaten egg whites. Bake in 9x5-inch loaf pans lined with greased brown paper, in 300° F. oven from 2 to 2½ hours.

FRUIT CAKE GLAZES

A glaze makes a fruit cake more attractive, gives it finish, and helps to hold fruit and nut decorations in place. Do the glazing after your cakes have ripened, usually not more than a few days before you wish to serve them or give them as gifts.

Apply the glaze hot, brushing it well over the surfaces of the cake. Stick your fruit and nut decorations in a pattern on the glaze, then brush more glaze over them, when the first coat has dried. When the final glaze has dried, wrap your cakes in transparent plastic. They'll look pretty until you want them.

Clear Glaze. Boil for 10 minutes ½ cup light corn sirup, ½ cup sugar, ¼ cup water. Coats 2 cakes.

Orange Glaze. Boil until thickened and clear 1 tablespoon cornstarch mixed with ¼ cup cold water, *then* mixed with 1 cup sugar and 1 cup orange juice. Coats the tops and sides of 3 or 4 cakes.

Apricot Glaze. Purée cooked dried apricots or canned ones and measure 1 cup pulp and juice. Cook with 1½ cups sugar to a thick, sticky consistency, being careful not to scorch. Apply hot to 3 or 4 cakes. This coating is opaque but shiny. The puréeing is done easily in an electric blender.

BASIC BUTTER FROSTING

One EIGHT-INCH CAKE
OR *Two* LAYERS

Use your electric mixer for a very fluffy frosting, easily made.

¼ cup butter or margarine
2 cups sifted confectioners' sugar
⅛ teaspoon salt
3 tablespoons milk, cream, coffee, water or fruit juice
1 teaspoon vanilla or other flavoring

Cream butter until fluffy; gradually work in 1 cup of the sugar. Add salt, liquid, and vanilla, then work in remainder of sugar, or enough to make a spreadable frosting.

For thin frosting to coat a coffee cake, add more liquid and beat smooth. To fill and frost a 3-layer cake, double the recipe.

VARIATIONS

Chocolate Butter Frosting. Add 2 ounces melted chocolate or ⅓ cup cocoa.

Coffee Butter Frosting. Use strong, freshly brewed coffee for the liquid. Or use cream and 1 teaspoon instant coffee.

Mocha Butter Frosting. Add chocolate plus coffee.

Lemon Butter Frosting. Use lemon juice for the liquid and add 1 teaspoon grated lemon rind instead of vanilla. Or substitute lemon extract for vanilla, if you haven't any lemon juice on hand.

Orange Butter Frosting. Use orange juice as liquid; add 2 tablespoons grated rind. Omit vanilla.

Pineapple Butter Frosting. Make the liquid pineapple juice and flavor with lemon.

CREAMY BUTTER FROSTING   *Two* LAYERS

A larger batch with more butter.

⅓ cup soft butter
3 cups sifted confectioners' sugar
¼ teaspoon salt
3 tablespoons cream
1½ teaspoons vanilla

Cream the butter until fluffy, then gradually beat in the sugar. Add salt, cream, and vanilla and beat until fluffy.

All the variations of Basic Butter Frosting also apply here.

VANILLA BUTTER FROSTING   *Three* LAYERS

This is a rich, fluffy, beautiful finish for a fine cake such as a birthday, anniversary, or wedding cake. I have made it with 1 cup butter for a little less rich cake filling and topping, and like it just about as well.

1½ cups milk
6 tablespoons flour
1½ cups butter or margarine
1½ cups sugar
1 tablespoon vanilla

Blend milk and flour until smooth. Cook, stirring constantly, until thick and smooth. Cool. Cream the butter and sugar until light and fluffy. Add milk-flour mixture and vanilla. Beat smooth.

For a smaller cake, use two-thirds of the recipe: 1 cup milk, 4 tablespoons flour, 1 cup butter, 1 cup sugar, 2 teaspoons vanilla.

Chocolate-Vanilla Butter Frosting.   Add 2 ounces unsweetened chocolate, melted and cooled, to the full-sized recipe.

BUTTER CREAM FROSTING   *Three* LAYERS

*A rather thick, fluffy icing which holds up beautifully. Good
for a tiered special-occasion cake.*

4 egg whites
2 cups granulated sugar
6 tablespoons cold water

¼ teaspoon cream of tartar
1 pound sweet butter, softened
2 teaspoons vanilla

Combine egg whites, sugar, water, and cream of tartar in upper part
of double boiler. Have water boiling vigorously in lower part; set
upper part over it, and remove double boiler from heat immediately.
Beat mixture 8 minutes, or until thick and light. Cover with damp cloth,
and allow to cool. Beat softened butter until creamy. Add cooled egg-
white mixture to butter, a small amount at a time, blending well.
Stir in vanilla.

BOILED FROSTING   *Two* LAYERS

A wonderful snowy frosting for any kind of cake.

1½ cups sugar
½ cup water
1 tablespoon light corn sirup
2 egg whites

¼ teaspoon cream of tartar
⅛ teaspoon salt
1 teaspoon vanilla

Put sugar, water, and corn sirup in saucepan and stir over low heat
until sugar is dissolved. Boil, covered, about 3 minutes, then boil uncovered and without stirring until a small amount of sirup forms a
soft ball when dropped into cold water (238°–240° F.) Remove sirup
from heat; quickly beat egg whites with cream of tartar until stiff
but not dry, then pour sirup in fine stream over egg whites, beating
constantly; add salt and flavoring, and continue beating until frosting
is cool and of spreading consistency. If frosting threatens to harden
before you spread it, add a few drops of hot water.

Peppermint Candy Frosting. Before spreading, add ½ cup crushed
peppermint candy. A few drops red food coloring also might be added.

BUTTER FUDGE FROSTING Two LAYERS

Chopped nuts could be sprinkled over this fine frosting.

2½ cups sugar
1 cup milk
2 ounces unsweetened chocolate, cut in pieces
2 tablespoons light corn sirup
Dash of salt
½ cup butter
1 teaspoon vanilla

Heat sugar, milk, chocolate, corn sirup, and salt to boiling, stirring until smooth and blended; then boil to 234–236° F. Add butter and cool to lukewarm without stirring. Add vanilla and beat until creamy and thick enough to spread on cake.

CHOCOLATE FROSTING AND FILLING Three LAYERS

A good general-purpose cake frosting. This recipe will frost an 8-layer torte made from split quarters of a jelly roll.

4½ ounces unsweetened chocolate
½ cup (1 stick) butter
3 cups confectioners' sugar
⅓ cup milk
2 egg whites, unbeaten
1 teaspoon vanilla

Melt chocolate and butter together and add sugar, milk, egg whites, and vanilla. Place over ice cubes and beat until mixture is spreadable.

Flavor, if you'd rather, with ½ teaspoon brandy or rum extract, or with 2 tablespoons real brandy or rum, crème de cacao, crème de menthe, Cointreau, or other liqueur.

116

CONFECTIONERS' SUGAR ICING

This is the kind you drip over coffee cake, cookies, brownies and other goodies.

2 cups sifted confectioners' sugar
½ cup milk
 Few drops vanilla or lemon extract

Mix ingredients and drip from a spoon. If icing seems thick, add a little more milk; if thin, add a little more sugar.
 Add 1 ounce chocolate for Chocolate Icing.

HONEY FROSTING   *Two* LAYERS

This frosting stays creamy and soft. Use it on spice cakes.

1½ cups honey
 ⅛ teaspoon salt
 2 egg whites, beaten stiff
 ½ teaspoon vanilla

Cook honey and salt to 238° F. or until it spins a thread. Pour in a thin stream over beaten whites, continuing to beat until frosting stands in peaks. Add vanilla.

EASY LEMON FROSTING   *Two* LAYERS

One grandmother never made!

½ cup frozen concentrate for lemonade
 1 pound confectioners' sugar
 Dash salt
 2 egg whites

Combine ingredients and whip with rotary or electric beater until mix-ture reaches spreading consistency.

117

CREAM CHEESE FROSTING   *Two* LAYERS

Awfully good on chocolate cake.

3 ounces cream cheese (room temperature)
2 tablespoons milk or cream
2 cups sifted confectioners' sugar
  Dash of salt
1 teaspoon vanilla

Mix cheese and milk; work in sugar. Add salt and vanilla. Beat until creamy. More milk may be added if mixture seems thick.

Chocolate Cream Cheese Frosting. Add 2 ounces melted, cooled chocolate.

Pineapple Cheese Frosting. Cream 2 tablespoons butter with the cheese, use pineapple juice in place of milk, add 2 teaspoons lemon juice in place of vanilla, and work in ½ cup drained, crushed pineapple, and whatever extra confectioners' sugar (about 1 cup) you need.

MAPLE BUTTER FROSTING   *One* SQUARE CAKE

Try it on any plain or white cake, maple cake, spice cake, or gingerbread.

½ cup maple sirup
 3 tablespoons butter
 2 cups sifted confectioners' sugar
   Few grains salt

Cook the sirup slowly for 3 minutes. Cool. Cream the butter, and add part of the sugar gradually, blending well. Add sirup alternately with the remaining sugar until frosting is of spreading consistency. Beat well, add salt, and spread over cake.

Maple Nut Frosting. Sprinkle chopped nuts over frosted cake.

ORNAMENTAL FROSTING (ROYAL ICING)

Use to make decorations on cakes or to frost an 8-inch square cake. Double the recipe for decorating a wedding cake.

> 2 egg whites
> 1¾ cups sifted confectioners' sugar
> ½ tablespoon lemon juice
> ½ teaspoon vanilla

Beat egg whites with 2 tablespoons sugar for 3 or 4 minutes with rotary beater. Add 2 tablespoons more sugar, beat again, and continue adding sugar and beating until half the sugar has been used. Add lemon juice gradually as mixture thickens. Continue adding sugar, a tablespoon at a time, beating several minutes between additions, until you can cut the frosting with a knife. Add vanilla. This frosting is most easily made with an electric mixer, of course.

The mixture may be piped through a pastry tube to make rosettes and other ornamentations when stiff enough. Less beating is required if it's for frosting. This mixture dries out readily and should be kept cool and covered with a damp cloth while you work with it.

COCONUT CREAM FILLING   *Three* LAYERS

Best for a 3-layer white cake with Seven-Minute Frosting and coconut topping.

3 tablespoons flour	2 cups scalded milk
3 tablespoons cornstarch	6 egg yolks
⅔ cup sugar	1½ teaspoons vanilla
¼ teaspoon salt	½ cup coconut

Mix flour, cornstarch, sugar, and salt, add a little of the scalded milk, and stir vigorously. Add rest of milk and cook in top of double boiler until thickened and smooth, stirring constantly. Cover and cook 15 to 20 minutes longer, stirring occasionally. Beat egg yolks, add a portion of the hot mixture to them, and stir vigorously. Turn into double boiler, stir hard, and cook and stir 2 minutes longer. Cool slightly, add vanilla, and chill. Stir in coconut and fill cake.

119

PRIZE LEMON FILLING   *Two* LAYERS

For white or yellow cake, split angel food, or sponge.

> Grated rind of 1 lemon
> 1/2 cup sugar
> 1 teaspoon flour
> 1/4 cup lemon juice
> 1 egg, slightly beaten
> 1/4 cup cold water
> 1 teaspoon butter

Mix lemon rind, sugar, and flour. Add lemon juice, egg, water, and butter. Cook until thick, stirring constantly. Cool.

SEVEN-MINUTE FROSTING

A popular frosting with several variations. This recipe will frost the top and sides of a 3- or 4-layer cake, or can be used as filling and frosting for a 2-layer.

> 2 egg whites
> 1 1/2 cups sugar
> 1 1/2 teaspoons light corn sirup or
> 1/4 teaspoon cream of tartar

> 1/3 cup cold water
> Few grains salt
> 1 teaspoon vanilla

Place ingredients, excepting vanilla, in top of double boiler. Place over boiling water and beat with rotary or electric mixer until mixture forms peaks. Remove from heat, add flavoring, and beat until frosting has spreading consistency.

VARIATIONS

Burnt Sugar Seven-Minute Frosting.   Add 2 tablespoons Burnt Sugar Sirup (page 91) on removing from heat.

Chocolate Seven-Minute Frosting.   Fold in 3 ounces unsweetened chocolate, melted and cooled, before spreading.

Marshmallow Seven-Minute Frosting. Add 1 cup quartered marshmallows when you remove frosting from heat. Beat by hand until spreadable.

Sea Foam or Brown Sugar Frosting. Use packed measure of brown sugar instead of white. Omit corn sirup or cream of tartar.

WHIPPED CREAM FROSTING or FILLING   *Three* LAYERS

Gelatin is added to make the cream stand up longer.

2 teaspoons plain gelatin
2 cups heavy cream, chilled
½ cup sugar
½ teaspoon vanilla

Soften gelatin in 2 tablespoons cream for 5 minutes. Dissolve over hot water. Cool slightly. Whip cream until stiff. Add sugar gradually, then add gelatin, and beat until mixture stands in peaks. Flavor with vanilla. Frost cake immediately. Chill.

ORANGE CUSTARD FILLING   *Three* LAYERS

Very orangey, a delight for sponge or any plain light cake.

1 cup sugar
2½ tablespoons cornstarch
1 cup orange juice
2 tablespoons lemon juice
2 eggs, beaten slightly
Grated rind of 2 oranges

Mix sugar, cornstarch, and fruit juices. Cook in the top of a double boiler until very thick, stirring constantly. Cover and cook 10 minutes longer, stirring occasionally. Add eggs with orange rind to filling, mixing quickly. Cook 2 minutes longer. Cool.

PINEAPPLE FILLING   *Three* LAYERS

Golden and fruity, it adds glamour to any cake.

½ cup sugar
2 tablespoons flour
2 tablespoons cornstarch
1 cup sirup from can of pineapple

1 tablespoon butter
2 tablespoons lemon juice
1 egg yolk, beaten
1 cup crushed pineapple, well
drained

Combine sugar, flour, and cornstarch and blend well. Add pineapple sirup. Cook and stir until it thickens and loses starchy taste. Add butter, lemon juice, and blend. Remove from heat and fold in egg yolk. Cool. Fold in crushed pineapple.

CRYSTALLIZED ROSE PETALS

A wedding cake, or a cake for a bridal shower or a new baby, may be as beautiful and feminine as a rose itself, with this trimming.

Select highly scented, beautifully colored fresh roses. (This is what hurts, because you are going to tear them apart. But they must be fresh!) Wash them well and drain on paper towels. Scrape off the white pulpy base of the petals, which is bitter. Beat an egg white until slightly foamy, dip a small pastry brush or your fingers into it and brush both sides of each petal thoroughly. Be sure no surplus egg white remains on petals. Sift granulated sugar on both sides and place petals on a tray. Store in the refrigerator until dry. Then assemble to look like roses again, on the cake.

Mint leaves can be prepared in the same way to make leaves for your rose buds.

And What Pies!

WE TEND TO THINK of pies as purely American, but we didn't invent them; we merely made the most of them. A good pie is no better than its crust, and while we have all kinds of pie crust mixes to fall back upon, every good cook should know how to make a tender, flaky, crisp crust that will set its filling off to perfection.

The popular pies among men are the fruit pies, especially apple. We ladies love cream pie, lemon pie (as do the men!), chiffons, and the fluffier concoctions. If there's whipped cream on our pie we groan and take on and talk about our diet—but we lap up every little wisp of it!

All the pies that have pleased my family over the years are here, together with pies that have pleased *Chicago Tribune* readers for a quarter of a century. Many of them have appeared at bake sales, church suppers, picnics. You could make a reputation on any of them—and I hope you will!

You needn't make your own pie crust, but it is more fun, and you'll be proud of pastry you've made yourself. It will taste ever so much better than anything out of a package! Lard is the perfect shortening for pastry; it's the shortest shortening, and it has good flavor. But the fluffed-up shortenings are good, too, and more generally available. If you do use lard, measure just a bit skimpily, a teaspoonful less for a double crust, a tablespoonful less in each cup for the following big recipe which makes four 2-crusters. Otherwise your pie crust may be so tender it crumbles.

There are a half dozen other good recipes and mixing methods, but I am going to tell you about only one—mine.

FLAKY PASTRY

You may keep a pastry mix on hand, or freeze rolled-out crusts with waxed paper between them, so here are recipes for one 2-cruster, and four 2-crust pies. They will make double that many single 9-inch crusts.

ONE PIE	FOUR PIES
2 cups flour	9 cups flour
1 teaspoon salt	4 teaspoons salt
⅔ cup shortening	3 cups shortening
¼ cup water	1 cup water

Spoon flour into cup to measure, and level off. Mix flour and salt in mixing bowl, add shortening and cut it in with a pastry blender, or with your fingertips, until mixture resembles coarse meal. Add water, tossing with a fork to dampen evenly. Don't add water all at once or you'll have wet dough in spots. You may need an extra sprinkle of water. Press dough into a ball.

Divide the dough in half, in the smaller recipe; in 8 parts, in the larger. Roll each part into a circle between two sheets of waxed paper, making it large enough to fit your pie pan.

124

Fit a bottom crust loosely in the pan. If the pie is a single-cruster to be filled after baking, prick it all over with the tines of the fork, and be sure you've built up the rim and fluted it well. Bake single crusts about 12 minutes at 425° F. and cool before filling.

Gash top pastry round for a 2-crust pie to allow steam to escape. Press edges of bottom and top crusts together well and crimp them. Most 2-crust pies are baked at 425° F. for about 40 minutes.

IF YOU WANT A PASTRY MIX

Blend flour, salt, and shortening to crumbs, but do not add water. Divide into four plastic bags. Keep in a covered canister. For each 2-crust pie, use 1 bag and ¼ cup water. Toss and press together right in the bag, if you wish.

GRAHAM CRACKER CRUST

One SHELL (9 or 10-INCH)

Cream pies, chiffon pies, and many others are enhanced by such a crust.

1½ cups crushed graham crackers (about 18)
⅓ cup melted butter
2 tablespoons powdered sugar (granulated is OK)

Combine ingredients in a 9- or 10-inch pie plate and press firmly over bottom and sides. Chill. Bake 8 minutes at 350° F. for a firmer crust.

BRAZIL NUT, ALMOND, or PECAN CRUST

One SHELL

Light, fluffy pies were meant for this kind of foundation.

1½ cups finely ground nuts
3 tablespoons sugar

Mix in pie pan and press firmly over bottom and sides. Bake or not, 8 minutes at 400° F.

CREAM PUFFS
Ten to Twelve SERVINGS

Not at all hard to make, and oh, so glamorous!

½ cup butter or margarine
1 cup boiling water
¼ teaspoon salt

1 cup sifted flour
4 eggs
Cream Puff Filling (see below)

Add butter to boiling water in a saucepan over direct heat. Add sifted flour and salt all at once and stir vigorously until the mixture leaves the sides of the pan in a compact mass. Remove from heat. Add eggs, one at a time, beating vigorously after each. Continue beating vigorously until the batter is smooth and free of lumps. Batter should be stiff enough to hold shape when dropped from a spoon or pastry tube. Drop by tablespoonfuls onto greased baking sheet, 2 inches apart. Pop into a 375° F. oven and bake about 50 minutes. Remove at once from oven and cut one or two slits in the side of each puff. Return to oven for 10 minutes. Cool on a rack. Fill with Cream Puff Filling, using pastry tube.

CREAM PUFF FILLING

½ cup sugar
¼ cup flour
¼ teaspoon salt

1½ cups milk
2 egg yolks
1 teaspoon vanilla

Combine sugar, flour, and salt in the top of a double boiler. Add milk. Cook and stir until thickened and smooth. Add slightly beaten egg yolks, beating them in vigorously. Cook two or three minutes longer. Cool and add vanilla.

CHOCOLATE CREAM FILLING FOR CREAM PUFFS

½ cup sugar
¼ cup flour
2 tablespoons cornstarch
⅛ teaspoon salt
1 egg, slightly beaten
½ cup cold milk

2 cups warm milk
1 tablespoon butter
2 ounces unsweetened chocolate, melted
½ teaspoon vanilla
½ teaspoon almond extract

126

Mix sugar, flour, cornstarch, and salt. Combine egg and cold milk and add to dry ingredients, stirring until smooth. Add warm milk slowly. Cook until thick and smooth, stirring constantly. After it thickens, continue cooking 5 minutes longer. Remove from heat, add butter and melted chocolate, blending thoroughly. Cool, stirring occasionally, then add flavorings.

Fruit-Filled Cream Puffs. Fill puffs with crushed, sweetened straw-berries and whipped cream. Cut off tops for this.

Eclairs. Eclairs may be made from the same dough as Cream Puffs. Shape them into oblongs, 5 inches by 1 inch. Bake in the same way. Frost the filled eclairs with Chocolate Icing (page 117).

Tea or Appetizer Puffs. Make Cream Puff batter according to recipe, but shape the dough into tiny puffs, an inch in diameter, or into small eclairs half the size of the larger ones. Reduce the baking to 30 minutes. Return to oven 5 minutes. Wonderful as appetizers with a lobster or crab meat filling.

APPLE PIE LIKE GRANDMA MADE Six SERVINGS

Dutchess, Wealthy, Jonathan, Greening, McIntosh are names of some of the best pie apples. Fruit should be firm and tart to make good pie. Juicy summer apples usually make the best pies of all.

6 cups pared, sliced apples	1 teaspoon cinnamon (or more)
1 cup white or brown sugar	2 tablespoons butter
2 tablespoons flour	Pastry for 2 crusts (page 124)

Line a deep 9-inch pie pan with pastry, and fill with mixture of apples, sugar, flour, and cinnamon. Dot the apples with butter and adjust the gashed top crust, pressing edges of pastry firmly together. If you roll the upper crust wide enough to allow you to tuck it under the edges of the lower crust at the rim, you can crimp your pie crust into a tightly sealed edge. Sprinkle the top of the pie with a little cinnamon and sugar and bake it at 425° F. for about 45 minutes, or until apples are tender.

APPLE SLICES   *Twelve* SERVINGS

*This was one of our $100-award winners; it has been very
popular.*

FILLING
  3 pounds tart cooking apples,
       pared, cored, cut in
       eighths
  1 cup water
1¼ cups sugar
  1 teaspoon cinnamon
¼ teaspoon salt
  2 tablespoons cornstarch
¼ cup cold water

CRUST
  2 cups flour
½ teaspoon baking powder
½ teaspoon salt
¾ cup lard
  1 teaspoon lemon juice
  2 egg yolks beaten
½ cup water

Bring water, sugar, cinnamon, and salt to boiling point. Add apples
and cook slowly for 10 minutes. Blend cornstarch and ¼ cup cold
water and add to hot mixture. Cook 5 minutes longer, stirring gently.
    Cut lard into sifted flour, baking powder, and salt as for pie crust.
Mix lemon juice, egg yolks, and water, and sprinkle over flour mixture;
blend lightly. Divide into two parts. Roll first piece to fit bottom and
sides of a shallow pan (about 9x13 inches). Fill with apple mixture.
Roll remaining dough to fit top and seal edges. Cut a design in the
crust for steam vents. Bake at 450° F. for 20 minutes, then reduce
heat to 350° F. and bake 30 minutes longer.
    Ice with a thin Confectioners' Sugar Icing (page 117) or sprinkle
with confectioners' sugar. Cut into serving portions.

DUTCH APPLE PIE   *Six* SERVINGS

This is my favorite apple pie, as it was Dad Church's.

  1 quart peeled, sliced, tart apples
¾ cup sugar
½ teaspoon cinnamon
¼ teaspoon nutmeg
  Single pastry shell (page 124)

Lemon Meringue Pie, page 142

Topping
> ¾ cup flour
> ½ teaspoon cinnamon
> ½ cup brown sugar
> ½ cup butter

Mix apples, sugar, and spices. Blend flour, cinnamon for topping, brown sugar, and butter, mixing with finger tips to coarse crumbs. Place apples in pastry shell, and sprinkle with crumb mixture. Bake in preheated 425° F. oven for 45 minutes.

For a super-deluxe pie, coat the apple slices with 3 tablespoons melted butter before adding sugar and spices. I sometimes double the recipe and bake it in a 9x12-inch pan for a crowd, rather than in two pie pans.

APRICOT WHIPPED CREAM PIE *Eight* SERVINGS

What a great big luscious crustful!

> 2 cups dried apricots (1 pound)
> 4 cups water
> ¼ cup quick tapioca
> 1½ cups sugar
> ¼ teaspoon salt
> 1 teaspoon vanilla
> 1 cup whipping cream
> ½ cup toasted coconut
> Baked 10-inch pastry shell (page 124)

Wash apricots, drain, add water, and cook for 20 minutes. Add tapioca and cook for 10 minutes longer, stirring constantly. Add sugar and salt and cook 10 minutes longer, stirring. Remove from heat, add vanilla, and chill. Whip cream. Whip apricot mixture into cream gradually. Pour into baked pastry crust and top with coconut. Chill for several hours before serving. This I love!

129

Glazed Cherry-Cream Pie, page 133

BLUEBERRY or HUCKLEBERRY PIE

We love this pie at our house; it makes our teeth purple!

1 quart fresh blueberries or huckleberries
1 cup sugar
.3 tablespoons flour
   Juice of ½ lemon
2 tablespoons butter
   Pastry for double crust (page 124)

Wash and drain berries. Mix sugar and flour and combine with berries. Turn mixture into pastry-lined pan and sprinkle with lemon. Add a sprinkle of mace, too, if you like. Dot with butter and add gashed top crust. Seal edges of pie. Bake in a 425° F. oven for 40 minutes. Made with the big cultivated Michigan blueberries, a pie like this is heaven itself!

BLACK BOTTOM PIE

Bud Burnham (Norbert, Jr. at weddings and on Sundays) has always thought Mary could make a fortune selling her Black Bottom pies. But who wants to make work out of such a fun pie? It is equally pleasing in a graham cracker or nut crust.

1 tablespoon plain gelatin
2 tablespoons cold water
2 cups milk, scalded
½ cup sugar
1½ tablespoons cornstarch
4 egg yolks, slightly beaten
1½ ounces chocolate, melted

1 teaspoon vanilla
4 egg whites, beaten stiff
¼ teaspoon cream of tartar
⅓ cup sugar
2 tablespoons rum or 2 teaspoons rum extract
Baked pie shell (page 124)

Soften gelatin in cold water. Add blended sugar and cornstarch to scalded milk and cook until thickened. Add small amount of the mixture to the egg yolks, stir, and return to milk mixture. Blend well. To

1 cup of the custard add chocolate and vanilla. Cool and pour into the crust.

To remainder of hot custard, add gelatin and stir until dissolved. Cool. Add cream of tartar and sugar to egg whites gradually, folding in thoroughly. When custard mixture is cool, fold in this meringue and the rum. Pour custard over chocolate filling. If you want to be extravagant, then top the rum filling with slightly sweetened whipped cream and on top of that scatter grated sweet chocolate. Then chill the whole pie for several hours before serving.

BUTTERSCOTCH PIE   *Six* SERVINGS

An old favorite, with some variations.

1 cup firmly packed brown sugar	3 tablespoons butter or margarine
¼ teaspoon salt	1 teaspoon vanilla
5 tablespoons flour	Baked 9-inch pie shell or
1 tablespoon cornstarch	Graham Cracker Crust
2 cups scalded milk	(page 125)
3 egg yolks	Meringue (see below)

Mix brown sugar, salt, flour, and cornstarch, add scalded milk gradually, and cook in the top of a double boiler until thickened and smooth, stirring constantly. Continue cooking 15 minutes longer, stirring occasionally. Beat egg yolks until light and stir a little of the hot mixture into them. Return to double boiler and stir 2 or 3 minutes longer over boiling water. Add butter and vanilla and cool. Pour into pie shell and spread with meringue made by beating 3 egg whites until stiff with a few grains of salt, and folding in 6 tablespoons white sugar. Brown meringue about 15 minutes at 350° F. Or omit meringue and spread pie just before serving with whipped cream, slightly sweetened and flavored with vanilla.

Banana Butterscotch Pie. Slice a layer of bananas over the bottom of the pie shell before adding the butterscotch.

Coffeescotch Pie. Add 2 teaspoons instant coffee to the filling.

Pecan Butterscotch Pie. Fold ½ cup of chopped pecans into the mixture before filling the pie shell.

FRESH CHERRY PIE   *Six* SERVINGS

There was never a better pie!

4 cups pitted sour cherries
¼ teaspoon almond extract
⅓ cup flour or 2½ tablespoons
   cornstarch
1½ cups sugar

⅛ teaspoon salt
1 tablespoon butter
Pastry for double crust
   (page 124)

Add almond extract to fruit, then stir in dry ingredients which have been mixed. Turn into pastry-lined 9-inch pie pan. Dot with bits of butter. Cover with gashed upper crust or lattice strips. Press edges firmly to pie rim. Bake pie in hot oven, 425° F., for 40 minutes.

CHERRY PIE (FROZEN CHERRIES) *Six* SERVINGS

Here is Charlie Church's favorite pie. If there is any left from dinner, he will eat it for breakfast.

2 cans (20 ounces each) frozen cherries
   Juice from thawed cherries, about 1¼ cups
3 tablespoons cornstarch
1 cup sugar
1 tablespoon butter
¼ teaspoon salt
¼ teaspoon almond extract
   Few drops red food coloring (optional)
   Pastry for double crust (page 124)

Defrost cherries until juice will drain away leaving fruit firm and slightly icy. Mix cornstarch with a small amount of cherry juice to make a thin paste. Slowly add remaining juice and cook while stirring until thickened and clear. Remove from heat; add sugar, butter, salt, extract, and coloring. Let cool. Fold sauce into cherries just before turning into pastry-lined 9-inch pie pan. Arrange lattice strips of pastry over filling. Bring lower crust up over edges of lattice and flute. Bake pie at 425° F. for 40 minutes.

GLAZED CHERRY-CREAM PIE   *Ten* SERVINGS

With a dessert such as this your reputation as a hostess-cook is made!

Butter-egg pastry (see below)

CREAM FILLING

½ cup sugar	3 cups milk, scalded
¼ cup flour	4 egg yolks, slightly beaten
¼ cup cornstarch	2 teaspoons vanilla
½ teaspoon salt	1 cup heavy cream, whipped

CHERRY GLAZE

1 can (20 ozs.) frozen tart cherries, thawed	¼ teaspoon salt
¼ cup cornstarch	1 cup cherry juice
¾ cup sugar	¼ teaspoon almond flavoring

To MAKE THE PASTRY: Sift together 1½ cups flour, ¼ teaspoon salt, ¼ cup sugar. Cut in 1 stick butter (½ cup) until mixture is in coarse crumbs. Beat 2 egg yolks with 2 tablespoons cream and sprinkle over flour mixture. Mix with knife or pastry blender and press into a ball on waxed paper. Roll between sheets of waxed paper, fit into deep 10-inch pie pan, prick all over with tines of fork, and bake 15 minutes at 425° F. Cool before filling with Cream Filling, topping with Cherry Glaze.

To MAKE CREAM FILLING: Mix sugar, flour, cornstarch, and salt in top of double boiler. Add milk and cook, stirring constantly, until thick. Cook 10 minutes more, stirring occasionally. Add a small amount of the mixture to the egg yolks. Return to pan and cook 3 minutes longer. Cool, add vanilla, and chill. Cream is folded into filling when the pie is assembled.

To MAKE THE GLAZE: Drain thawed cherries very well. Mix cornstarch, sugar, salt in a heavy pan, add cherry juice and cook and stir until thick and clear. Cool. Add flavoring and cherries. Spoon over filling when it has been placed in the shell.

133

SWEET CHERRY PIE *Six* SERVINGS

A delightful pie, this one—you'll love it!

2 pounds large sweet cherries (about 1 quart) pitted
1 cup sugar
2 tablespoons cornstarch
Juice ½ lemon
Baked pie shell (page 124)

Add blended sugar, cornstarch, and lemon juice to cherries. Let stand until very juicy, then cook over moderate heat until cherries are thick-ened, stirring carefully so that you do not mash cherries. Cover pan and cook gently several more minutes, so that all of the raw starch flavor disappears. Cool filling and place in prepared crust. Top with whipped cream cheese, whipped cream, or ice cream to serve. Or serve plain.

CRANBERRY CHIFFON PIE *Six* SERVINGS

A long-ago invention of mine, presented with pride.

1 cup cooked cranberries and
    juice, strained
⅔ cup sugar
4 eggs, separated
1 tablespoon plain gelatin
¼ cup cold water
½ teaspoon salt
1 tablespoon lemon juice
½ cup cream, whipped
9-inch baked pastry shell
    (page 124)

Cook cranberries in half as much water, by measure, until skins pop. Strain through a sieve and measure 1 cup. Place sauce, ⅓ cup sugar, and egg yolks in top of double boiler. Heat, stirring constantly, until custardy, about 8 minutes. Add to gelatin which has been softened in the water. Add salt and lemon juice. Beat egg whites until stiff with remaining ⅓ cup sugar. Fold into cranberry mixture. Fill baked pie shell and chill until firm. Top with whipped cream just before serving.

CURRANT AND RASPBERRY DEEP-DISH PIE

Six SERVINGS

This is a luscious pie, if you want to know!

2 cups currants, stemmed and washed
2 cups raspberries, washed
⅔ cup sugar
2 tablespoons flour
Pastry for single crust (page 124)

Place fruit and mixture of sugar and flour in an 8-inch casserole and fit the crust over the top, securing it around the edges by pressing firmly. Bake the pie at 400° F. for 30 to 40 minutes. Serve at the table from the baking dish. You can sprinkle the top of the baked pie with confectioners' sugar before serving, if you like.

CHOCOLATE CHIFFON PIE

Eight SERVINGS

Be sure to use the Brazil Nut Crust—it makes this pie!

1½ tablespoons unflavored
    gelatin
¼ cup cold water
3 eggs, separated
½ cup sugar
¼ teaspoon salt
1½ cups milk, scalded

2 ounces chocolate, melted
1 teaspoon flavoring (vanilla, almond or rum)
10-inch Brazil Nut Crust (page 125)
1 cup cream, whipped

Soften gelatin in cold water. Place egg yolks in top of double boiler; add salt and sugar and beat until thick and light. Gradually stir in milk, beating constantly, then add melted chocolate. Cook over hot water, stirring constantly, until custard coats a spoon. Remove from heat and stir in softened gelatin. Add flavoring. Cool. Beat egg whites until stiff, and fold into cooled chocolate mixture; then fold in whipped cream. Pile into pie crust. Chill. Garnish with whipped cream and shaved Brazil nuts before serving.

You can substitute ½ cup rum for ½ cup of the milk. When rum is used, make custard of milk, egg yolks, sugar, and salt, then fold rum into filling with the vanilla.

Mocha Chiffon Pie. Add 1 tablespoon instant coffee to the filling.

OLD-FASHIONED CREAM PIE   *Five* SERVINGS

This pie has a delicate body that holds up well, and real cream flavor.

1½ cups sugar
⅓ cup flour
½ teaspoon salt
2½ cups coffee cream
2 teaspoons vanilla
1 tablespoon melted butter
   Pastry for single 8-inch crust (page 124)

Mix sugar, flour, and salt in a heavy saucepan. Scald cream and stir into the sugar mixture. Cook over moderate heat, stirring constantly, until mixture comes to a boil. Stir in vanilla and butter, and cool to lukewarm. Pour into 8-inch pie shell, and bake for 10 minutes at 450° F., then at 325° F. for 30 minutes longer. Cool thoroughly before cutting.

Use the best pure vanilla for this pie, which is *verree* good!

CREAM PIE   *Six* SERVINGS

This basic recipe has many wonderful variations.

⅓ cup cornstarch
⅔ cup sugar
¼ teaspoon salt
3 cups milk, scalded
3 egg yolks, slightly beaten

2 tablespoons butter
1½ teaspoons vanilla
9-inch baked pie shell
   (page 124)
1 cup cream, whipped

Blend cornstarch, sugar, and salt in top of double boiler. Gradually add milk, stirring constantly. Cook and stir over boiling water until thick, about 10 minutes. Slowly add a small amount of hot mixture to egg yolks, then return to double boiler. Cook 5 minutes. Add butter and vanilla and cool. Fill cooled pie shell and top with whipped cream.

Almond Cream Pie. Add ½ cup toasted shredded almonds to filling.

Banana Cream Pie. Slice two or 3 bananas into shell before adding filling.

Chocolate Chip Cream Pie. Add 1½ ounces unsweetened chocolate, shaved, to the cooled filling.

Coconut Cream Pie. Add 1 cup moist coconut to filling.

Date Cream Pie. Cook 1 cup chopped dates with the filling.

CHOCOLATE CREAM PIE   *Six* SERVINGS

Doesn't everybody love chocolate pie?

      3 squares unsweetened chocolate
   2½ cups milk
      1 cup sugar
      3 tablespoons flour
      2 tablespoons cornstarch
   ½ teaspoon salt
      3 egg yolks
      2 tablespoons butter or margarine
      1 teaspoon vanilla
         Baked 9 inch pie shell or crumb crust (pages 124–5)

Add chocolate to milk and heat in the top of a double boiler. Beat with a rotary beater to blend. Mix sugar, flour, cornstarch, and salt and add gradually to milk and chocolate. Cook, stirring constantly, until thick-ened. Continue to cook 15 minutes longer, stirring occasionally. Beat egg yolks, add to a little of the hot mixture, then return to double boiler and stir over hot water 3 minutes longer. Remove from heat and add butter and vanilla. Cool and turn into pie shell. For meringue topping, whip 3 egg whites with a few grains of salt until stiff and fold in gradually 6 tablespoons sugar. Pile on pie and brown in 350° F. oven.

Two other flavorings are good in chocolate pie. A few drops oil of peppermint (this is strong, so must be used discretely) in addition to the vanilla, or a tablespoon of rum, with or without vanilla, may be used. Or fold in ½ cup crushed peppermint candy.

CUSTARD PIE   *Five* or *Six* SERVINGS

Here are the two methods of baking the same custard filling.
The second is tricky but assures a crisp crust.

    4 whole eggs, or 3 eggs and 2 yolks, slightly beaten
    ½ cup sugar
    ¼ teaspoon salt
    1 teaspoon vanilla
    2½ cups scalded milk
       Nutmeg
       Unbaked 9-inch deep pie shell, chilled (page 124)

Mix eggs, sugar, salt, and vanilla and add gradually to the scalded milk.
Pour into chilled crust, adding the last portion of filling when you have
the pie on the oven rack, to avoid spilling any of the custard mixture.
Bake at 400° F. (oven must be pre-heated to that temperature, of course)
25 to 30 minutes. Test by inserting a silver knife near the center of the
filling. If it comes out clean, remove pie from oven to a rack, immediately, to cool. Sprinkle with nutmeg. Chill.

THE "SLIPPED" METHOD FOR CUSTARD PIE: Use the same recipe, but
bake the pie shell at 425° F. about 15 minutes or until lightly browned,
and cool. Turn the custard mixture into a buttered pie plate of exactly
the same size as the one you used for the crust. Put the pan of custard
filling in a larger pan, set on an oven rack, and pour hot water into the
larger pan to come up about three-fourths of the way on the custard
container. Bake at 350° F. (pre-heated, naturally) for 35 to 40 minutes,
or until a silver knife inserted will come out clean. Cool the filling to
lukewarm, then loosen it carefully all around the edges, shake gently to
loosen at the bottom, and hold the filling over the shell, edge to edge.
Then gently slide the custard out of its pan into the crisp, baked shell,
let it settle there a minute, sprinkle on the nutmeg, and serve at once.
Crisp shell, tender custard!

SOME CUSTARD PIE VARIATIONS

Coconut Custard. If you bake pie and shell together, sprinkle ½ to 1
cup finely cut moist shredded coconut over crust before adding filling.
For the "slipped" method, sprinkle coconut over the custard before
baking.

Maple-Nut Custard. Top pie just before serving with ½ cup chopped toasted almonds or pecans, and drizzle with maple sirup or maple blended sirup.

Nut Custard. Sprinkle bottom of either unbaked or baked shell with ½ cup chopped toasted almonds or pecans. Toast the nuts in 2 tablespoons butter, in a moderate oven, or on top of the range.

Custard pie made by either method should be eaten the day it is made, and shouldn't be cut until serving time.

EGGNOG PIE   *Six* SERVINGS

Rummier pies there are, but I prefer the delicacy of flavor in a pie such as this, which is more egg than nog.

1 tablespoon unflavored gelatin
¼ cup cold water
4 eggs, separated
½ cup sugar
¼ teaspoon salt
½ cup milk
½ cup more sugar for meringue
1 teaspoon vanilla

1 tablespoon rum, whiskey or brandy
Baked 9-inch pie shell or Graham Cracker crust (pages 124–5)
Whipped cream, nutmeg for topping

Soften gelatin in cold water. Beat egg yolks until thick and add sugar, salt, and milk. Heat over hot water, stirring constantly. Add gelatin and stir until dissolved. Cool this custard. Whip egg whites until soft peaks form, then beat in gradually the other ½ cup sugar. Beat until meringue holds a peak. Fold egg whites and flavorings into custard and pour into pie shell. Chill and serve topped with whipped cream. Sprinkle with nutmeg.

DATE SOUR CREAM PIE   *Six* SERVINGS

Two kinds of cream make it doubly delicious.

½ cup sugar
¼ cup cornstarch
1 teaspoon salt
2 cups dairy sour cream
2 eggs, well beaten
2 cups chopped dates

½ cup chopped pecans or wal-
    nuts
1 tablespoon lemon juice
9-inch baked pie shell
    (page 124)
1 cup cream, whipped

Mix sugar, cornstarch, and salt in top of double boiler. Add cream and mix well. Cook, stirring constantly, until thick and smooth. Add small amount of hot mixture to eggs and mix well. Return to double boiler and cook 3 minutes longer. Remove from heat. Add dates, nuts, and lemon juice. Cool. Fill shell. Serve topped with whipped cream.

GOOSEBERRY CREAM PIE   *Five* SERVINGS

Proving that gooseberries are for more than jam.

1 quart gooseberries
1 cup sugar (honey may be
    substituted for half the
    amount)
4 tablespoons flour
2 eggs, separated
⅛ teaspoon salt

¼ teaspoon vanilla
1 tablespoon butter
4 tablespoons sugar for
    meringue
1 baked 8-inch pie shell
    (page 124)

Cook gooseberries (use no water) until soft. Press through sieve and measure 1½ cups of the pulp. Blend sugar and flour and add to goose-berry pulp, in top part of double boiler. Cook and stir over low heat until thickened. Beat egg yolks and add a small amount of the hot mixture to them, beating well. Return all to double boiler and cook over hot water 2 minutes longer, stirring constantly. Remove from heat, add salt, vanilla, and butter; cool slightly. Turn into baked pie shell and top with meringue made by beating sugar into the stiffly beaten egg whites. Brown 15 minutes in a 350° F. oven.

140

CONCORD GRAPE PIE   *Five* SERVINGS

It's decidedly worth the work! What a luscious pie!

 4 cups Concord grapes
 1 cup sugar
 ⅛ teaspoon salt
 3 tablespoons flour or 2½ tablespoons minute tapioca
 1 tablespoon lemon juice
 1 tablespoon butter or margarine
   Pastry for 9-inch double crust (page 124)

Skin grapes, saving skins, and put pulp in saucepan without water. Bring to boil. While hot, put through strainer to remove seeds. Combine strained pulp with skins. Mix sugar, salt, and flour together. Put about ¼ of this mixture on bottom of pastry-lined shell and mix remainder with grapes; add lemon juice. Turn into crust and dot with butter. Cover with top crust and bake in a hot oven, 450° F., for 10 minutes, then reduce heat to moderate, 350° F., and bake 25 to 30 minutes longer. Add a tablespoon of grated orange rind as a variation, if you wish. Your tongue was never more blissfully purple-stained.

GREEN TOMATO PIE   *Six* SERVINGS

If you like tomato preserves, you'll like this pie.

 4 cups sliced green tomatoes
1⅓ cups white or brown sugar
 ¼ teaspoon salt
 3 tablespoons flour
 2 tablespoons cornstarch
 ⅓ cup lemon juice

Grated rind of 1 lemon
3 tablespoons butter or
   margarine
Pastry for 9-inch pie
   (page 124)

Combine sugar, salt, flour, and cornstarch. Dust some of the mixture over bottom of pastry-lined pan. Arrange sliced tomatoes in pan and cover with remaining mixture. Sprinkle lemon juice and rind over top and dot with butter. Adjust top crust or pastry strips. Bake pie at 450° F. for 10 minutes. Reduce heat to 350° F. and bake 25 minutes longer.

LEMON MERINGUE PIE   *Eight* SERVINGS

Note of slight economy: Use 3 egg yolks, and you'll still have a luscious-pluscious pie!

1½ cups sugar
¼ cup cornstarch
¼ cup flour
2 cups boiling water
4 eggs, separated
Grated rind of 2 lemons

Few grains salt
½ cup lemon juice
2 tablespoons butter
½ cup sugar for meringue
Baked 9-inch pie shell
(page 124)

Mix sugar, cornstarch, and flour. Add boiling water gradually, stirring constantly, and cook over direct heat until thickened. Beat egg yolks slightly and stir a little of the hot mixture into them. Then add the yolks, lemon rind, salt, lemon juice, and butter to the thickened filling, stirring constantly, and cook over low heat until filling is clear yellow and thick. Cool slightly, pour into baked shell, and cover with meringue made by beating the egg whites until stiff and gradually beating in the ½ cup sugar. Brown meringue for 15 minutes in a moderate oven, 350° F.

Lime Meringue Pie. Use this recipe, substituting lime juice for lemon juice and lime rind for lemon rind. Add a few drops of green food coloring. This is a glorious pie!

ROSIE'S LEMON PIE   *Six* SERVINGS

The size of this pie may be more to your liking. It's an eggy pie made with more water than milk, nice and lemony. This was the pie Rosemary Fox always had as a child; so of course there is no other lemon pie for her. Rosemary is an ex-Mary Meade assistant but still one of us. "Tart lemon pie" is how this dessert was known years ago.

½ cup flour
1¼ cups sugar
¼ teaspoon salt
1 cup cold water
⅓ cup milk
3 egg yolks beaten
    with 1 white
1 tablespoon butter

Grated rind of 1 lemon
¼ cup lemon juice, or juice of
    2 lemons
8-inch baked pie crust
    (page 124)
2 egg whites
4 tablespoons confectioners'
    sugar

Mix flour, sugar, salt, and water and milk in top of double boiler. Cook over hot water, stirring occasionally, until thickened and smooth. Beat egg yolks and the one white lightly, stir a small amount of the hot mixture into them, then return to the rest of the hot mixture in the double boiler. Cook and stir vigorously until very thick. Add butter, lemon rind, and lemon juice, blend well and cool to lukewarm. Pour into baked shell.

Beat the 2 egg whites until soft peaks form. Gradually add the sugar, beating mixture to stiff peaks. Spread meringue over cooled filling to the edges of the crust. Bake at 350° F. for 12 to 15 minutes, or until meringue is golden. Cool completely before slicing.

LIME CHIFFON PIE   *Six* SERVINGS

Just super-deluxe, that's all!

1 tablespoon plain gelatin
¼ cup cold water
1 cup sugar
½ cup lime juice
½ teaspoon salt
4 egg yolks, beaten

1 teaspoon grated lime rind
Few drops green coloring
4 egg whites, beaten
1 cup heavy cream, whipped
Baked 9-inch pie shell
    (page 124)

Soften gelatin in cold water. Combine half the sugar with salt and egg yolks, and cook in top of double boiler until of custard consistency. Stir in gelatin and grated rind and add a few drops of green coloring. Chill until slightly thickened. Fold second ½ cup sugar gradually into stiffly beaten egg whites. When custard begins to thicken, beat with wire whisk and fold in egg whites. Turn into baked 9-inch pie shell and chill until firm. Top with whipped cream when ready to serve.

143

MAPLE NUT PIE

Six SERVINGS

This pie has a wonderful Vermont flavor!

1 tablespoon plain gelatin	2 egg whites, beaten stiff
¼ cup cold water	1 cup cream, whipped
2 egg yolks, slightly beaten	1 cup finely chopped nuts
¾ cup maple sirup	1 9-inch baked pie shell
¼ teaspoon salt	(page 124)

Soften gelatin in cold water. Mix egg yolks, maple sirup, and salt together and cook over boiling water until slightly thickened. Add gelatin and stir until dissolved. Chill until partially thickened. Fold in egg whites, ½ cup of the whipped cream and ½ cup of nuts, and pour into pie shell. Chill until firm. Garnish with remaining whipped cream and nuts.

MINCE PIE

Six SERVINGS

See page 346 for preparation of mincemeat.

3 or 4 cups mincemeat or 2 cups mincemeat plus 1 to 2 cups chopped apple, cranberry sauce, diced peaches, or other fruit
Pastry for double crust (page 124)

Place filling in unbaked shell, cover with gashed top crust, and bake at 425° F. about 30 minutes.

BAKED PEACH PIE

Six SERVINGS

It's lightly spiced—and nice!

4 cups sliced fresh peaches	¼ teaspoon cinnamon
1 cup sugar (white or brown)	1 tablespoon flour
¼ teaspoon salt	1 tablespoon melted butter
⅛ teaspoon nutmeg or mace	Pastry for double crust
	(page 124)

Fill bottom of pastry-lined 9-inch pan with sliced peaches. Cover with mixture of sugar, salt, spices, and flour and add butter. Adjust gashed top crust. Seal edges of pastry. Bake pie in hot oven, 450° F., for 10 minutes; reduce heat to moderate, 350° F., and bake about 30 minutes longer, or until fruit is tender and crust nicely browned. If peaches are fully ripe, add a tablespoon of lemon juice. And bend your ear—you might sprinkle the peaches with 2 or 3 tablespoons of peach or apricot brandy!

FRESH PLUM PIE   Six SERVINGS

The little tart plums need as much sugar as cherries, for pie. But those big sweet Italian prune plums must have their acid built up with lemon juice. So there really is no right amount of sugar for a plum pie. It depends upon the plums, but all plums make good pie, and some make beautiful pie.

      4–5 cups halved, pitted plums
   1–1½ cups sugar
      2 tablespoons flour
      2 tablespoons butter
        Pastry for 2-crust pie (page 124)

Fill pastry-lined 9-inch pie pan with prepared plums. Mix sugar and flour and sprinkle over fruit. Dot with butter. Adjust top crust, fluting edges of pastry, and trim. Bake at 425° F. for 40 minutes.

For Italian prune plums, use 1 cup sugar, 3 tablespoons flour, and sprinkle the plums with the juice of half a lemon, about 1½ tablespoons. Also add ½ teaspoon cinnamon and ¼ teaspoon nutmeg, if you wish.

PECAN PIE
Six SERVINGS

Not after a heavy meal, please!

⅓ cup butter or margarine
¾ cup firmly packed brown sugar
3 eggs, slightly beaten
1 cup dark or light corn sirup
1 cup whole pecan halves
1 teaspoon vanilla
¼ teaspoon salt
Pastry for one crust (page 124)

Cream butter or margarine and sugar. Add beaten eggs. Stir in corn sirup, pecans, vanilla, and salt just until blended. Do not overbeat. Fill pastry-lined 9-inch pan and bake in hot oven, 450° F., for 10 minutes, then reduce heat to moderate, 350° F., and bake 30 to 35 minutes longer. An inserted knife comes out clean when pie is done. Garnish with additional pecan halves. Cool and serve with whipped cream, or without.

FRESH PINEAPPLE PIE
Six SERVINGS

It will be the best you've ever eaten, I'm sure!

2 cups finely diced
    fresh pineapple
½ cup flour
1 cup sugar
¼ teaspoon salt
1 cup scalded milk
⅔ cup pineapple juice or
    juice and water

3 eggs, separated
1 tablespoon butter
Baked 9-inch pie shell
    (page 124)
6 tablespoons sugar for
    meringue

Cook pineapple in a covered heavy saucepan over low heat until tender, about 20 minutes. Drain, saving liquid.

Mix flour, sugar, and salt in a double-boiler top. Stir in scalded milk and juice. Cook and stir over hot water or low heat until mixture is thick. Cook 10 minutes longer, stirring occasionally. Beat egg yolks and pour a little of the hot mixture over them, stirring vigorously. Return to the pan and cook and stir for 2 minutes longer. Remove from heat and add drained pineapple and butter. Cool, fill baked pie shell, and top with meringue made by beating the egg whites until stiff and folding in 6 tablespoons sugar. Bake at 350° F. until meringue is lightly browned. Cool before cutting.

PUMPKIN or SQUASH PIE   *Six* SERVINGS

This is my family's favorite autumn pie.

1½ cups frozen, fresh cooked, or canned pumpkin or mashed squash

¾ cup brown or white sugar, or honey

¼ teaspoon salt

½ teaspoon ginger

1 teaspoon nutmeg

1 teaspoon cinnamon

3 eggs, slightly beaten

1½ cups milk, scalded

½ cup cream

Pastry for 1 9-inch pie shell (page 124)

Blend pumpkin, sugar, salt, and spices. Add eggs, scalded milk, and cream, beating until smooth. Pour mixture into 9-inch unbaked pie shell. Bake in a hot oven, 450° F., for 10 minutes. Then reduce heat to 350° F. and bake for 30 to 35 minutes, or until filling is set. Serve cold, plus or minus whipped cream.

Use evaporated milk instead of milk and cream for a very rich pie. Whipped cream with chopped candied ginger or chopped toasted almonds in it makes a luxurious garnish.

You can substitute squash for pumpkin in any pumpkin pie—most people can't tell the difference! Mashed sweet potatoes or rutabaga will do, too!

RAISIN CIDER PIE   *Six* SERVINGS

What a big, fat beauty!

2 cups raisins
1½ cups apple cider
1½ cups water
¾ cup sugar
1 cup chopped tart apple, peeled
¾ teaspoon salt
1 tablespoon lemon juice

½ teaspoon grated lemon rind
2 tablespoons butter or margarine
1 teaspoon cinnamon
¼ cup cornstarch
Pastry for 2-crust 9-inch pie (page 124)

Combine raisins, cider, 1 cup water, sugar, apple, seasonings, and butter in a saucepan and bring to the boiling point. Mix cornstarch with remaining water and stir into hot mixture. Cook, stirring constantly, until mixture is thick. Pour into pastry-lined deep pie pan; top with lattice crust. Bake in hot oven, 400° F., for 10 minutes; lower temperature to 350° F. and bake about 35 minutes longer. Cool thoroughly before cutting.

RASPBERRY ANGEL PIE   *Six* SERVINGS

Gorgeous, glorious!

2 teaspoons plain gelatin
2 tablespoons cold water
½ cup sugar
⅛ teaspoon salt
⅓ cup water
2 egg whites, beaten stiff
1 tablespoon lemon juice
1 cup cream, whipped

1 9-inch baked pie shell (page 124)
1 package frozen raspberries, thawed
⅓ cup sugar
4 teaspoons cornstarch
½ cup cream, whipped (optional)

Soften gelatin in cold water. Stir sugar, salt, and water together in a pan until sugar is dissolved. Cook to soft-ball stage, 236° F. Pour sirup in fine stream over egg whites, beating constantly; add lemon juice and

148

continue beating until thick. Dissolve gelatin over boiling water. Combine with first mixture, beating one minute longer. Cool. Fold in whipped cream. Pour into pie shell and place in refrigerator for several hours. Press raspberries through a sieve or cheese cloth to remove seeds. Add sugar mixed with cornstarch. Cook, stirring constantly, until thick. Cool. Spread in center of pie. Garnish with whipped cream and a few raspberries. Refrigerate until serving time.

GLAZED STRAWBERRY or RASPBERRY PIE

Six SERVINGS

This is one of my favorites—a beauty!

1 quart ripe strawberries or raspberries
¾ cup sugar
1 cup water
2½ tablespoons cornstarch
¼ cup sugar
⅛ teaspoon salt
Few drops red coloring
Baked 9-inch pastry shell (page 124)

Wash and stem berries and reserve 1 cup of the less perfect ones for the glaze. Cook this cup of berries with the ¾ cup sugar and the water for 5 minutes. Put through a sieve. Add cornstarch with the ¼ cup sugar and the salt. Cook until thick, add coloring, and cool.

Fill baked pie shell with rest of berries, whole or halved. Pour glaze over pie and chill before serving. The pie is both beautiful and delicious and doesn't need further glamorizing, but of course you may add whipped cream.

Deluxe touch: Spread softened cream cheese (3 ounces, blended with 1 tablespoon cream) over shell before adding berries.

FRESH RHUBARB PIE
Six SERVINGS

Rhubarb is as symbolic of Spring as a robin.

> Pastry for double crust (page 124)
> 6 cups diced rhubarb
> ¼ cup flour
> 1½ cups sugar
> Dash of salt
> 1 egg
> 2 tablespoons butter

Line 9-inch pie plate with pastry. Mix flour, sugar, and salt, and add egg. Stir into rhubarb and fill crust. Dot with butter and add top crust, gashed, or cover with lattice strips. Bake in hot over, 425° F., for 40 to 45 minutes.

I love a deep pie, and this one is generous.

SHOO-FLY PIE
Six SERVINGS

A tiny scoop of ice cream is the perfect topping.

1¼ cups sifted flour
½ cup sugar
¼ teaspoon salt
½ teaspoon nutmeg
1 teaspoon cinnamon
½ cup butter or margarine

1 cup molasses
1 cup cold water
½ teaspoon soda
Pastry shell for 9-inch pie
(page 124)

Sift together the first five ingredients. Cut butter or margarine into flour mixture to resemble coarse crumbs. Mix molasses, water, and soda; pour into unbaked pastry shell. Sprinkle crumbs over liquid. Bake 15 minutes at 450° F.; reduce heat to 350° F., and bake 40 minutes. Serve warm.

DESSERTS and SWEETS

NOT ALL DESSERTS classify neatly into the categories of cakes, cookies, and pies. There are puddings and cobblers, frozen desserts and confections. Yes, candies are dessert, though they are not always served at the end of a meal. This is a section I could easily expand to many times its size. But perhaps instead I will save the other recipes for a book about desserts.

Cobblers, Custards & Others

DESSERTS ARE PASSE. Nobody serves dessert any more," said a woman of my acquaintance, not long ago. Just because she and all of her friends are dieting, she thinks EVERYBODY goes without dessert! You and I know better!

We don't always have cake or pie. Sometimes we like a Baked Custard or a Floating Island, or a Lemon Snow. Now there's a dessert for dieters! Once in a while we enjoy an old-fashioned Bread Pudding or Rice Pudding, and every June we simply wallow in Strawberry Shortcake! The dessert skippers must be very envious when they see us downing a shortcake dripping with bright berries. We are sorry for *them!*

APPLE CRISP

Six SERVINGS

A so-easy, always popular, never-fail dessert.

6 cups sliced cooking apples (about 6 medium)
¾ cup flour
¾ cup brown sugar
½ teaspoon cinnamon (optional)
½ cup butter or margarine

Place sliced apples in buttered baking dish. Mix flour, sugar, cinnamon, and butter until crumbly. Sprinkle over fruit and bake at 350° F. for 30 to 45 minutes or until apples are tender. Serve with whipped cream or ice cream. If apples are past their prime or fully ripe, sprinkle with 1 tablespoon lemon juice before adding topping.

Apple Cheese Crisp. Add 1 cup grated Cheddar or a 3-oz. package of cream cheese to crumbs made with ⅓ cup butter.

Maple Apple Crisp. Use maple sugar instead of brown. So delicious!

Peach Crisp. Just substitute peaches for apples.

OLD-FASHIONED
APPLE DUMPLINGS

Six DUMPLINGS

Droolingly wonderful with that rich, sweet sauce. An exceptional dessert.

6 tart apples, pared, cored
1 recipe Pie Pastry (page 124)
　　or Baking Powder Biscuits (page 34)
1½ cups white sugar
½ cup brown sugar

2 tablespoons flour
½ teaspoon salt
　　Dash of nutmeg
2 cups boiling water
½ cup butter or margarine

Roll pastry thin and cut into 6 six-inch squares. Place an apple in the center of each square and sprinkle with a little sugar and nutmeg or cinnamon. Dampen edges of dough and bring opposite corners together over apples. Seal well. Place dumplings in a deep baking dish. Make sirup by blending sugars, flour, salt, and nutmeg, and adding boiling water and butter. Bring to boil, and pour over dumplings. Bake covered at 425° for ½ hour. Uncover and bake until apples are tender and dumplings are browned, basting occasionally with sauce.

Old-Fashioned Peach Dumplings.   Make them the same way.

Cheese Apple Dumplings.   Roll ½ cup grated sharp Cheddar cheese into pastry or biscuit dough.

OLD-FASHIONED BREAD PUDDING

Eight SERVINGS

Put in raisin bread and stale doughnuts when you have them.

1 quart dry bread cubes (½ inch)
½ cup washed seedless raisins
2 cups scalded milk
2 beaten eggs
½ cup brown or white sugar
½ teaspoon salt
1 teaspoon cinnamon
½ teaspoon nutmeg
1 teaspoon vanilla
   Lemon Sauce (see below)

Combine bread cubes and raisins in greased 1½-quart casserole. Add milk to eggs, sugar, salt, cinnamon, nutmeg, and vanilla. Beat with rotary beater. Pour over bread and raisins. Bake at 350° F. for 1 hour. Serve warm with Lemon Sauce.

   Small amounts of fruit you may have sitting in the refrigerator could be added—cranberry sauce or cherries or peaches.

LEMON SAUCE: Mix ½ cup sugar, 1 tablespoon cornstarch, a sprinkle of salt. Add 1 cup hot water and cook and stir until thickened. Add 1 teaspoon grated lemon rind, 3 tablespoons lemon juice, 1 tablespoon butter.

LEMON BREAD PUDDING   *Six* SERVINGS

One of the very best.

2½ cups ½-inch bread cubes
2 cups milk
2 eggs, slightly beaten
¾ cup sugar
⅛ teaspoon salt
⅛ teaspoon nutmeg

Grated rind 1 lemon
3 tablespoons lemon juice
⅓ cup butter or margarine,
      melted
¼ cup currants or raisins

Soak bread in milk ½ hour. Combine remaining ingredients and mix with bread. Bake in a buttered casserole set in a shallow pan of water, at 350° F. for 50 minutes, or until a knife comes out clean when inserted in center.

Queen's Pudding. Make pudding with 3 egg yolks. As soon as baked, spread with jelly or marmalade and top with meringue made by beating 2 of the whites until stiff and beating in ¼ cup sugar gradually. Brown at 350° F. for 15 minutes.

BLUEBERRY SLUMP   *Six* SERVINGS

One of the best berry desserts that ever stained your teeth!

1 quart blueberries
1 tablespoon flour
1 cup sugar
   Juice of ½ lemon
1 cup flour

2 teaspoons baking powder
½ teaspoon salt
3 tablespoons sugar
3 tablespoons butter
½ cup milk

Mix flour and sugar with washed berries, place in greased baking dish (an 8-inch square glass casserole is fine), and sprinkle with lemon juice. Sift flour, baking powder, salt, and sugar together for batter. Cut in the butter, then add milk and stir vigorously to blend. Spoon over berries. Bake at 425° F. about 20 minutes. Serve pudding warm with cream.

BAKED CUSTARD   *Six* SERVINGS

Individual custards are most attractive, but a casserole will do.

- 1 quart scalded milk
- 4 eggs, beaten slightly
- ¼ cup sugar
- ¼ teaspoon salt
- 1 teaspoon vanilla
- Dash of nutmeg

Stir milk gradually into eggs. Add sugar and seasonings and mix just until sugar is dissolved. Turn into custard cups or a 1½-quart casserole and place cups or casserole in a pan of hot water and bake at 350° F. about 35 minutes or until firm in the center. The water should come up on the sides of the custard dishes at least an inch. Chill, then unmold cups; serve casseroled custard from the dish, at table. Serve plain or with crushed sweetened strawberries, peaches, or other fruit.

SOME VARIATIONS OF BAKED CUSTARD

Brown Sugar Custard.   Place 2 tablespoons brown sugar in each custard cup before pouring in custard mixture. When you turn these out, you have a sauce.

Caramel Custard.   Stir ¾ cup sugar in a heavy skillet over low heat until it forms a golden-brown sirup. Pour a small amount of the sirup into each custard cup and twirl to coat the sides evenly. Then add custard and bake. This is a delicious sauce for baked custards.

Chocolate Custard.   Melt 1½ ounces unsweetened chocolate with milk when you scald it.

Honey Custard.   Use honey in place of sugar.

Rum Custard.   Substitute ¼ cup light rum for ¼ cup of the milk, but don't scald it with the milk. Add it with sugar.

SOFT CUSTARD   *Four* SERVINGS

Possibly more popular as a sauce than as a dessert by itself.

2 eggs or 4 yolks
2 cups milk
1/8 teaspoon salt

1/4 cup sugar
1 teaspoon vanilla

Beat eggs slightly as milk is scalding in the top of a double boiler. Add sugar and salt to eggs. Add hot milk, stirring constantly, and return to the double boiler. Cook and stir over hot, not boiling, water until a clean spoon dipped into the custard will come out with a thin coating. Cool quickly. Add vanilla. Chill. Serve by itself for dessert or as a sauce for puddings, fresh fruit, or cake.

SOME VARIATIONS OF SOFT CUSTARD

Caramel Custard. Needs two extra tablespoons of sugar. Melt the sugar to a light golden brown in a heavy pan, pour into the scalding milk, stir until dissolved, and proceed as with plain soft custard.

Chocolate Custard. Calls for a square of unsweetened chocolate and 2 extra tablespoons of sugar. Melt chocolate in the milk and make according to the foregoing recipe.

Coffee Custard. Make this by adding 1 1/2 teaspoons instant coffee.

Orange Custard. May be made by substituting a cup of orange juice for a cup of milk.

ORANGE   *Six to Eight* SERVINGS
FLOATING ISLANDS

Meringue-topped soft custard—pretty, delicious.

3 egg yolks, slightly beaten
1 teaspoon grated orange rind
1/8 teaspoon salt
1/4 cup sugar
2 cups scalded milk

1/2 teaspoon vanilla
1 cup orange sections
2 egg whites, beaten stiff
1/4 cup confectioners' sugar

Combine egg yolks, grated orange rind, salt, sugar; gradually add hot milk, and stir constantly over hot water until mixture coats a spoon; about 5 minutes. Add vanilla and cool quickly. Arrange orange sections in dessert dishes and cover with custard. Fold sugar into egg whites and drop by spoonfuls into boiling water. Cover and simmer 5 minutes, then lift out with slotted spoon and place on top of custard.

CHERRY COTTAGE PUDDING   Six SERVINGS

A de luxe version of an old family favorite. Omit the cherries and serve the cake with Lemon Sauce (page 155) and you'll have simple Cottage Pudding.

¼ cup butter or margarine
¾ cup sugar
1 egg
½ teaspoon lemon extract
1¾ cups sifted flour
2½ teaspoons baking powder
½ teaspoon salt
⅔ cup milk
1 cup pitted large fresh sweet cherries, well drained
Cherry Sauce (see below)

Cream shortening and sugar until light. Add egg; beat until smooth and fluffy. Stir in flavoring. Add sifted flour, baking powder, and salt alternately with milk, beating until smooth after each addition. Fold in cherries. Bake in greased pan at 350° F. for 35 to 45 minutes. Cut into squares and serve warm with Cherry Sauce.

CHERRY SAUCE. Pit and cut in half 1 cup fresh sweet cherries, add ¼ cup water and ¼ cup sugar and cook over low heat 5 minutes. Blend 1 tablespoon cornstarch with 1 cup orange juice and add to cherries. Cook until thick and clear. Add ¼ teaspoon almond extract. Serve warm.

DATE TORTE

Six SERVINGS

Quick and simple, but very good.

1 cup finely chopped dates
½ cup walnuts, chopped
½ cup sugar
3 eggs, well beaten
2 tablespoons flour
1 teaspoon baking powder

Mix ingredients and pour into a greased pan, about 7x11 inches. Bake at 350° F. for 30 minutes. Serve plain or topped with whipped cream or ice cream.

AUNT HARRIET'S THANKSGIVING DATE PUDDING

Sixteen SERVINGS

A dessert that can be made several days before you serve it.

1 pound dates, cut fine
1 cup boiling water
1 teaspoon soda
1 cup sugar
1½ cups sifted flour
1 teaspoon baking powder
1 teaspoon butter

1 egg
1 cup chopped walnuts or
   pecans
½ cup sugar
⅔ cup boiling water
Whipped cream

Pour the cup boiling water over half the dates and add soda. Let this mixture stand while mixing second group of ingredients. Sift flour, sugar, and baking powder. Mix in the date sauce and add beaten egg, butter, and ½ cup nuts. Blend and spread mixture in greased jelly-roll pan. Bake at 350° F. for 30 minutes. Spread over the top a date-nut sauce made by combining the rest of the dates and ½ cup nuts with the ½ cup sugar and last amount of boiling water. This sauce should be mixed while cake is baking. The topping will remain moist and keep the cake moist. Serve slices with sweetened whipped cream.

160

Caramel Apples, page 175

INDIAN PUDDING   *Six to Eight* SERVINGS

An old New England favorite.

3 cups milk
⅓ cup yellow cornmeal
½ cup dark molasses
¼ cup sugar
1 teaspoon salt

½ teaspoon cinnamon
¼ teaspoon nutmeg
2 tablespoons butter
½ cup raisins, optional
1 cup cold milk

Heat 3 cups milk in top of double boiler. Add cornmeal, molasses, sugar, salt, spices, and butter. Cook over hot water, stirring occasionally, 20 minutes, or until mixture thickens. Add raisins, if used, and stir. Pour into a 1½-quart casserole and add remaining cold milk without stirring. Bake at 300° F. for 2½ hours. Serve warm with cream or vanilla ice cream.

LEMON SNOW   *Six* SERVINGS

Light, frothy, and most refreshing.

1 tablespoon (envelope) plain
    gelatin
¼ cup cold water
1 cup hot water
½ cup sugar

⅛ teaspoon salt
¼ cup lemon juice
1 teaspoon grated lemon rind
2 or 3 egg whites

Soften gelatin in cold water, dissolve in hot water and add sugar, salt, and lemon juice and rind. Chill until mixture begins to thicken, then beat egg whites stiff. Beat gelatin until fluffy and fold into egg whites. Chill until firm and serve in dessert glasses with Soft Custard (page 158).

Lemon Fluff. Use egg yolks as well as whites. Beat them slightly, add water, sugar, and salt, and cook until thick over hot water. Add gelatin and proceed as for Snow.

Lime Snow. Same, but with lime juice and rind. Add a few drops of green coloring.

161

Barbecued Spareribs, page 262

PINEAPPLE SNOW

Six SERVINGS

A favorite dessert of my childhood.

1 flat can crushed pineapple (1 cup)
1 tablespoon (envelope) plain gelatin

½ cup sugar
¼ teaspoon salt
2 tablespoons lemon juice
2 egg whites

Drain pineapple well and add water to sirup to make 1¼ cups. Soften gelatin in ½ cup of the cold liquid; add to gelatin with sugar and salt and stir until dissolved. Stir in pineapple and lemon juice. Chill until mixture is slightly thicker than consistency of unbeaten egg whites. Beat egg whites stiff; add gelatin mixture. Place the bowl in ice water. Beat until it begins to hold shape. Turn into 1 large mold or 6 or 8 smaller ones and chill until firm. Unmold and serve with Soft Custard Sauce (page 158).

ORANGE PUFFS

Ten SERVINGS

Use a large kettle for these. They cook a long time and absorb a heavenly orange flavor.

1½ cups sifted flour
2½ teaspoons baking powder
½ teaspoon salt
½ cup sugar
1 egg, beaten

½ cup milk
½ cup melted butter or margarine
1 teaspoon orange extract

SIRUP: 1 cup sugar, 1 cup water, 3 tablespoons butter or margarine, grated rind of 1 orange, 1½ cups orange juice, ½ teaspoon salt.

Sift together flour, baking powder, salt, and sugar. Combine egg, milk, melted butter, and flavoring. Add to dry ingredients and blend. Drop by spoonfuls into boiling sirup, cover tightly, and simmer for 1 hour. Serve hot with sirup in which they were cooked as sauce. To make sirup, just combine all ingredients in heavy, large kettle. Heat to boiling, then add dumplings. Puffs will expand during cooking.

PLUM CRUNCH   *Six* SERVINGS

This sweet, crunchy dessert is wonderful served warm.

3 cups pitted small blue plums, cut in quarters
3 tablespoons brown sugar
5 tablespoons sugar
¼ teaspoon nutmeg

TOPPING: 1 egg, well beaten, 1 cup flour, 1 cup sugar, 1 teaspoon baking powder, ¼ teaspoon salt, ½ cup butter, melted.

Place plums in 7x11-inch pan. Mix brown sugar, granulated sugar, and nutmeg and sprinkle over fruit. Beat egg in a bowl and add sifted dry ingredients. Mix with pastry blender or fingers until crumbly. Sprinkle over plum mixture. Pour butter over all. Bake at 375° F. 45 minutes.

OLD-FASHIONED RICE PUDDING *Four* SERVINGS

The long, slow cooking is responsible for the characteristic texture of this eggless pudding.

⅓ cup raw rice
1 quart milk
½ cup granulated sugar
½ teaspoon salt
½ teaspoon cinnamon
½ teaspoon nutmeg
½ cup raisins
1 tablespoon butter

Rinse rice in hot water. Mix with remaining ingredients except raisins and butter. Bake in greased casserole uncovered at 275° F. for 3 hours. After the first hour add the raisins and butter, mixing well. Serve warm or cold.

Chocolate Rice Pudding.   Add ¼ cup cocoa or 1 ounce melted chocolate.

STRAWBERRY SHORTCAKE   *Six* SERVINGS

For many of us, there's but one kind of strawberry short-cake: the rich biscuits that grandma and mama made, split, buttered and buried under bright crushed berries, and drenched with cream. Cake topped with strawberries is not Strawberry Shortcake—it is only cake topped with straw-berries. Biscuits with a skimpy berry topping aren't short-cake, either. There must be at least a quart of berries for four servings. Skimp on the biscuits, if you wish, but not on the fruit. And crush the berries, since it is strawberry juice soak-ing into buttery biscuits that makes shortcake so good. Keep a few whole berries for garnish, if you want to, but squash the rest of them with a fork, a potato masher, or even your lily-white hands! Do this shortly before serving the short-cake, and add the sugar you like at that time.

Raspberries, peaches and other fruits may be turned into shortcake in this same manner.

> 1 batch Baking Powder Biscuits (page 34) with 2 table-spoons sugar added, and double the shortening (use butter)
> Soft butter
> 1½–2 quarts strawberries, sweetened and crushed
> Cream or whipped cream

Divide your prepared shortcake dough in half and roll each half to fit a 9-inch round pie pan or layer cake pan. Place one round in the pan, spread with soft butter, and place the second round on top. Bake at 400° F. about 20 minutes. Have the berries ready. Place the shortcake on a serving platter, break the two layers apart and fill with berries. Put the remaining berries on top. Serve warm with cream or whipped cream. Individual 2-story shortcakes may also be baked.

MOTHER CHURCH'S ENGLISH CHRISTMAS PUDDING

Six POUNDS

Mother C. boils this in a napkin, but steaming may be easier.
We think it the finest of plum puddings.

1 quart raisins
1 pint currants
1 cup cut citron
1 quart chopped apples
1 quart beef suet, chopped
1 quart soft bread crumbs
8 eggs, separated
2 cups sugar
2 teaspoons grated nutmeg
2 teaspoons salt
1 quart flour
3 cups milk, cider or fruit juice

Combine fruits and add a cup of the flour, or enough to flour them thoroughly. Beat egg yolks until light and gradually beat in sugar. Add nutmeg and salt, then part of the flour. Stir to mix. Add fruit, suet, and crumbs alternately with rest of liquid. Add remaining flour. Beat egg whites stiff and fold in last. Fill greased molds ⅔ full and steam 4 to 5 hours or longer.

We always serve two sauces with this pudding, Vanilla Sauce and Hard Sauce, because Brother-in-law Bill Kapple grew up eating two sauces on pudding, and at family dinners insists on these two. Either is sufficient for most people.

VANILLA SAUCE: Mix ½ cup sugar, a few grains salt, 1 tablespoon cornstarch. Add 1 cup water and cook over moderate heat until thickened and clear. Add 2 tablespoons butter, 1 teaspoon vanilla and a fleck of nutmeg. Serve warm.

HARD SAUCE: Cream ⅓ cup butter and work in 1 cup powdered sugar, ½ teaspoon vanilla and if you like, a dash of nutmeg. Chill. Sauce may be flavored with lemon juice and grated rind.

HEAVENLY HASH
Four SERVINGS

*When you cook rice to accompany the meat, cook plenty
and save some for this.*

1 cup cooked rice
1 cup canned or sweetened fresh fruit, diced or sliced
1 cup heavy cream, whipped and sweetened

Combine and pile into sherbet glasses. Baby marshmallows or chopped
nuts may be added.

MINCEMEAT-STUFFED APPLES WITH LEMON SAUCE
Four SERVINGS

Delicious! Wonderful sauce.

4 baking apples, Rome Beauties or other
½ cup mincemeat

LEMON SAUCE
½ cup butter
½ cup sugar
1 egg, beaten
3 tablespoons water
3 tablespoons lemon juice
1 tablespoon grated lemon peel

Wash and core apples and fill each with 2 tablespoons mincemeat. The
other ingredients are the sauce.

Cream butter and sugar, add egg, then water, lemon juice, and peel.
Pour over apples and bake at 350° F. for about 40 minutes or until
done. Serve with the sauce.

166

Frozen Desserts

THERE ARE PLENTY of ice creams and sherbets to be found in any drug store or supermarket, but they aren't like the ones you can make at home in an ice cream freezer or a refrigerator tray. Those frozen desserts you make yourself are the kind that are talked about and remembered—Avocado and Mint Sherbets, Grape Ice Cream, and the custardy-smooth ice cream you make in an electric freezer. They are a joy to make, and we like all those compliments afterwards!

LICK-THE-DASHER ICE CREAM

Three to Four QUARTS

It's kind of silly to make ice cream in a freezer when you can get any kind you want at the supermart. But this is one of the fun things at the farm. Everybody loves homemade ice cream and the children wait for a chance at the dasher. There's no turning of the crank; a motor does that. We just cook up the custard, chill it, pour it into the freezer can and set the whole thing up with the proper ice and salt, and a heavy duty cord that snakes across the lawn from the kitchen to the willow tree. It is under the willow that our ice cream is made.

2 cups sugar
¼ cup cornstarch
¼ teaspoon salt
4 cups milk
4 eggs, beaten
2 tablespoons vanilla
4 cups light cream

Mix sugar, cornstarch, and salt in the top of a double boiler. Blend in milk gradually and cook over hot water, stirring occasionally until mixture is thickened, about 12 to 15 minutes. Blend a small amount of the hot mixture into the eggs, then stir the eggs into the rest of the mixture. Cook 4 or 5 minutes more, stirring constantly. Chill custard. (Important, for smooth ice cream). Add vanilla and chilled cream. Fill gallon freezer container not more than ⅔ full. Freeze in hand-cranked or electric freezer with a mixture of 1 part ice-cream salt to 6 parts crushed ice. When mixture is frozen, the electric motor grinds to a halt; the hand crank can no longer be turned. Remove the dasher and repack the freezer with ice and salt—1 part salt to 8 parts ice. Cover with a rug or blanket and let cream ripen in the freezer for about 2 hours. Or pack into containers and transfer to a home freezer for hardening. That is less romantic by far!

SOME LUSCIOUS VARIATIONS

Butter Pecan. Use brown sugar instead of white, and add 1 cup chopped pecans, toasted or sautéed in butter.

168

Chocolate. Add 4 ounces unsweetened chocolate, melted, and ½ cup more sugar to the basic mix.

Lemon. Omit the vanilla and add a can of lemonade concentrate. Cousin Jeannie Baxter and I invented a special lemon ice cream with a cupful of fresh lemon juice and the grated rind of a couple of lemons. We think it is divine, but you need to add one more cup of sugar.

Peach or Strawberry. Add to the mix 2 cups puréed, slightly sweetened fruit.

Dozens of other variations are possible. I often add an extra egg. Sometimes we can't get ice-cream salt (rock salt), and have to substitute flake salt, intended for canning. It doesn't work quite as well. We often use ice cubes instead of crushed ice, and they work fine.

GRAPE ICE CREAM — *Six* SERVINGS

Oh, this one's luscious!

- 1 pound Concord grapes
- ½ cup sugar
- 2 tablespoons light corn sirup
- 2½ tablespoons lemon juice
- ¼ teaspoon salt
- 2 egg yolks, slightly beaten
- 1 cup cream, whipped

Slip skins from grapes and place pulp in a heavy saucepan. Cook, stirring constantly, for 5 minutes. Add skins and cook 5 minutes longer. Force through a food mill or sieve. Add sugar, corn sirup, lemon juice, and salt to grape purée and bring to boiling point. Add small amount to egg yolks and mix. Return to pan and cook for 3 minutes, stirring constantly. Chill over ice cubes. Fold in cream. Turn into refrigerator tray and chill with control set at coldest point until set. Beat in a bowl until smooth. Return to tray and freeze until just firm.

GINGER ICE CREAM   *Six to Eight* SERVINGS

"Remember this for an unusual, wonderful dessert" say my
notes on this recipe.

½ cup chopped preserved ginger
⅓ cup water
½ cup sugar
3 egg yolks, slightly beaten
½ tablespoon (½ envelope) plain gelatin
1 tablespoon cold water
1 pint heavy cream, whipped

Combine the ginger with the water, sugar, and egg yolks and cook
over hot water, stirring constantly, until mixture coats a spoon. Remove
from heat and add gelatin which has been softened in cold water. Stir to
dissolve. Cool and fold into whipped cream. Freeze without stirring.

GRAPEFRUIT SHERBET   *Six* SERVINGS

*This is superb! It's a perfect meat course accompaniment—
but might be appetizer or dessert.*

1 tablespoon plain gelatin
¼ cup cold water
¾ cup sugar
½ cup hot water
2½ cups grapefruit juice
2 egg whites, beaten stiff

Soften gelatin in cold water. Boil sugar and hot water 2 minutes. Add
gelatin and stir to dissolve. Cool. Add grapefruit juice. Freeze to a
mush. Turn into chilled bowl and beat quickly until smooth. Fold in
egg whites, return to tray and finish freezing. Stir several times.

Grapefruit Mint Sherbet. Add a few drops of peppermint extract
and enough food coloring to tint pale green. Most refreshing!

AVOCADO SHERBET

Six SERVINGS

Just the right tang! You can't buy anything like this!

½ cup sugar
½ cup water
½ cup sieved avocado
3 tablespoons lemon juice

½ cup pineapple juice
1 egg white, beaten stiff
2 tablespoons sugar

Boil sugar and water a minute; cool. Add avocado and fruit juices. Freeze until mushy. Beat the 2 tablespoons sugar into egg white. Turn fruit mixture into chilled bowl. Fold in egg white. Freeze until firm, stirring once. Excellent as meat or fish course accompaniment.

LEMON SHERBET

One QUART

A simple, economical recipe for a really lemony sherbet.

2 cups sugar
2 cups water

2 egg whites, beaten stiff
1 cup lemon juice

Boil the sugar and 1 cup water 5 minutes. Beat this sirup, a little at a time, into the beaten egg whites; then add lemon juice and second cup of water, beating in well. Turn into pan and freeze until mushy; beat in chilled bowl quickly but thoroughly. Return to pan and freeze firm.

PINEAPPLE WHIPPED-CREAM SHERBET

Six SERVINGS

This is a favorite at our house. It's Aunt Edna's recipe.

Juice of 2 oranges and 1 lemon
1 cup canned crushed pineapple
1 cup sugar
1 cup cream, whipped

Fold ingredients together and freeze at coldest temperature, stirring once.

MINT SHERBET   *Six* SERVINGS

Garnish each scoop with a few fresh mint leaves.

  1 cup sugar
  2 cups water
  ½ cup (packed) fresh mint
  1 tablespoon plain gelatin
  ½ cup cold water
  1 cup bottled or fresh lemon juice
    Few drops green coloring
  2 egg whites, beaten stiff

Boil sugar and water 5 minutes. Add bruised mint, cover, and steep
for 1 hour. Strain out mint. Soften gelatin in cold water, dissolve over
hot water, and add with lemon juice and coloring to tint pale green.
Freeze mushy, beat in a chilled bowl until fluffy, and fold in egg whites.
Freeze firm.

CHERRY MOUSSE   *Six to Eight* SERVINGS

Pink and creamy—at holiday time toss in ½ cup pistachios.

  1 No. 2 can pitted sour cherries or 2½ cups fresh cherries
  ⅔ cup sugar
  4 drops red coloring
  ⅛ teaspoon salt
  2 teaspoons plain gelatin
  2 tablespoons cherry juice
  ¼ teaspoon almond extract
  1⅔ cups heavy cream, whipped

Drain cherries, reserving liquid for other use. Grind or chop cherries
and add sugar and coloring. Boil 1 minute. Remove from heat, add
salt. Soften gelatin in 2 tablespoons of the drained juice, and dissolve
in hot cherry mixture. Chill. Add almond extract; fold into whipped
cream. Freeze.

Sweet-Tooth Delights

MY FAVORITE FUDGES and those of my friends, relatives, and also of readers of the food columns in the *Chicago Tribune* are collected here. They are fun to make, and delicious to eat. You need a candy thermometer to make them perfectly, but the old soft-ball, hard-ball tests in water are a fair guide in cooking. Drop a tiny portion of sirup from a teaspoon into cold water to make such a test.

CANDY-MAKING TESTS

SOFT BALL: 234° to 240° F. Sirup forms a soft ball in cold water; can be picked up, but flattens. Use for fudges, penuche, and fondant.

FIRM BALL: 242° to 248° F. Forms firm ball in cold water and holds shape unless pressed. Use for caramels.

HARD BALL: 250° to 265° F. Forms hard ball in cold water but is plastic and chewy on removal. Use for divinity, taffy, and caramel corn.

SOFT CRACK: 270° to 290° F. Separates into heavy threads in cold water and will make crackling sound when rapped against side of cup. Use for butterscotch, taffy.

HARD CRACK: 295° to 310° F. Separates into threads which are hard and brittle. (Care must be taken to avoid scorching, caramelizing and melting at this temperature.) Use for brittles and glacés.

ALMOND or PEANUT BRITTLE

Here's my favorite brittle; I've made it for years and years!

2 cups sugar
1 cup light corn sirup
½ cup water
2 cups blanched almonds or raw peanuts (or use salted
    Spanish peanuts)
2 teaspoons soda
1 teaspoon vanilla
1 teaspoon butter

Cook sugar, sirup, and water to 280° F. (medium crack stage). Do not stir except to mix. Add nuts and let them cook in the sirup about 3 minutes, or until they have turned golden brown. Add soda and remove at once from heat. Mixture will foam. Add butter and vanilla and pour into buttered pans as soon as foaming has subsided. Use a jelly-roll pan, cooky sheet, or two 9x9-inch pans. Break up candy when cold.

PECAN AND PEANUT-BUTTER ROLL *Two* ROLLS

Keep the rolls wrapped in foil and slice the candy as you want it. Children love this stuff.

2 cups sugar
1 cup light brown sugar
½ cup light corn sirup
1 teaspoon vinegar

1 cup milk
½ cup peanut butter
Confectioners' sugar
1 cup chopped salted pecans

Combine sugars, sirup, vinegar, and milk. Cook to soft-ball stage (236°–238° F.). Cool to room temperature, then beat until creamy. Add peanut butter and blend. Knead on board dusted with confectioners' sugar until firm, shape into 2 rolls 10 inches long, 2 inches in diameter, and cover with chopped pecans, pressing them in gently. Slice when firm.

CARAMEL APPLES   *Eight* APPLES

Here's the best recipe I've found for a caramel coating that permits you to keep all your gold inlays.

½ cup brown sugar
½ cup white sugar
½ cup dark corn sirup
1 can sweetened condensed milk
1 teaspoon vanilla
1 teaspoon butter
8 medium Jonathan or Winesap apples, on skewers

Combine sugars, sirup, and milk in a heavy saucepan. Cook to 230°–234° F., stirring constantly. Remove from heat and add butter and vanilla. Dip skewered apples, one at a time, twirling to coat smoothly. Immerse immediately in ice water and place on heavy waxed paper to set. Reheat sirup over hot water, if necessary, while you're dipping.

SURPRISE CARAMEL KISSES   *Two* DOZEN

They're chewy, molasses flavored, deliciously different.

1 cup sugar
¾ cup molasses
⅛ teaspoon salt
⅓ cup butter
½ cup light cream or evaporated milk
1 teaspoon vanilla
2 dozen salted almonds

Mix all ingredients except last 2 in a saucepan and cook slowly to 252° F. (firm ball stage). Remove from heat; add vanilla. Pour sirup onto buttered platter or cooky sheet. Cool. When cool enough to handle, cut into 1¼-inch squares. Place a whole almond in the center of each and roll caramel into a ball completely covering the nut. Wrap candy in waxed paper.

175

KNEADED CHOCOLATE FUDGE   *Two* POUNDS

A wonderfully smooth, creamy candy.

> 1 pound (2½ cups) light brown sugar
> 1 pound (2 cups) granulated sugar
> 3 ounces unsweetened chocolate, finely cut
> 2½ tablespoons light corn sirup
> ⅓ cup cream
> ¾ cup water
> ⅛ teaspoon salt
> 1 teaspoon vanilla
>   Chopped nuts (optional)

Bring to boil in covered pan all ingredients except vanilla and nuts;
uncover and boil to soft-ball stage (235° F.). Wipe away crystals from
pouring side of pan and pour into shallow pan. Let cool undisturbed.
When cool, stir with heavy spoon until creamy. Add vanilla and nuts
and stir until mixture forms a cheesy mass. Knead in the hands or
on a board until soft and plastic. Pat into a buttered or waxed-paper-
lined pan and press to uniform thickness. Cover with waxed paper
and let stand until firm. The fudge should be ready to eat in 10 minutes.

DIVINITY FUDGE   *One* POUND

Heavenly divinity, we always called it at home.

 2 cups sugar
 ½ cup light corn sirup
 ½ cup hot water
 ⅛ teaspoon salt

 2 egg whites
 1 teaspoon vanilla
 1 cup broken nuts

Cook sugar, sirup, and water in a heavy saucepan to 265° F. (hard-
ball stage). Do not stir after boiling starts. Wipe away sugar crystals
from the sides of the pan and pour sirup in a thin stream over stiffly
beaten egg whites (beaten as sirup is nearing end of cooking), beating
constantly with electric mixer or rotary beater. When mixture be-

comes thick and begins to lose gloss, add vanilla and nuts and drop from a spoon onto waxed paper, or pour into greased pan, about an inch thick.

Holiday Divinity. Add only ½ cup nuts, plus ½ to 1 cup candied red and green cherries. Flavor with rum or brandy extract instead of vanilla, if you wish.

WONDERFUL FUDGE   *Five* POUNDS

You'll need your preserving kettle to make this big batch of fudge, but it is ever so easy, despite all those different kinds of chocolate, and why not make a big batch?

Portions can be packaged to store in the freezer if you don't need so much candy at one time.

½ cup (1 stick) butter
1 tall can (14½ ozs.) evaporated milk
2 pounds sugar (4½ cups)
½ pound marshmallows
2 ounces unsweetened chocolate
1 12-ounce package (or two 6-oz. packages) semi-sweet
      chocolate pieces
3 bars (4 ozs. each) sweet chocolate
1 tablespoon vanilla
2 cups chopped pecans, walnuts, or other nuts

Stir together in a large heavy pot or dutch oven, over moderate heat, the butter, canned milk, and sugar. Bring to a boil. Cover.

Boil 5 minutes and turn off heat. Add marshmallows and stir until melted. Add the chocolate, one kind at a time, stirring as it melts. Add vanilla and nuts. Blend. Pour into buttered pan and smooth out evenly. This quantity is exactly right for a jelly-roll pan, 10x15 inches. Let stand until firm, then cut into 1-inch squares.

Whole half-pecans may be pressed into the tops of the pieces. And I have found it isn't really necessary to use three different kinds of chocolate. Use what you have, but make sure you use the same weight, a total of 26 ounces.

PENUCHE
Sixty-four PIECES

Delicious brown sugar fudge!

3 cups packed brown sugar or 2 cups brown, 1 cup white
    sugar
1 cup milk, cream or evaporated milk
1 tablespoon butter, if you use milk
2 teaspoons vanilla
  Few grains salt
  Walnuts or pecans

Cook mixture of sugar, milk to 238° F. (soft-ball stage). Remove from heat, add butter, vanilla, salt. Cool to lukewarm. Beat until mixture begins to hold shape. Pour into buttered 8-inch pan, cut into squares, and press a nut half into the top of each piece.

If you'd rather, add a cup of coconut with the butter and vanilla; then skip the nuts.

AUNTIE'S PRALINES
Two DOZEN

Aunt Genorie Lovrien's pecan pralines are the best I've ever eaten, and the junior members of our household squeal with glee when a pre-Christmas box of them arrives.

1 cup brown sugar
2 cups white sugar
1 cup evaporated milk or cream
3 tablespoons corn sirup
¼ teaspoon salt

2 tablespoons butter
1 teaspoon maple flavoring
1 teaspoon vanilla
1 cup broken pecans
½ cup pecan halves

Cook sugars, cream, sirup, and salt to soft-ball stage (236° F.). Remove from heat. Add butter and flavorings. Stir until sirup begins to thicken. Add broken pecans and drop from a spoon into cakes, on waxed paper placed on a cooky sheet. Press pecan halves into the surface, working quickly, as the cakes harden fast. When hardened, remove from waxed paper with a spatula and wrap individually.

To make Sherry Pralines, replace ¼ cup of the evaporated milk or cream with sherry.

LEMON PATTIES   Three DOZEN

This creamy, lemony candy is extremely easy to make, and
so good for after dinner!

2¾ cups confectioners' sugar
  2 tablespoons evaporated milk or cream
  3 tablespoons melted butter or margarine
  1 tablespoon lemon juice
4–6 drops yellow color

Mix ingredients and knead with hands to distribute coloring evenly.
Shape into roll and wrap in waxed paper. Chill and slice. Of course,
you can make other colors and flavors, too. An assortment of flavors
in pastel colors would be lovely on a tea table.

PHYL'S IMPOSSIBLY DIVINE TOFFEE

My sister-in-law, Phyllis Lovrien, makes the crunchiest,
butteriest, most sublime toffee I've ever eaten. She makes
it by the bucketful, literally, at Christmas time. Once she
sent me a good-sized planter filled with the rich and fattening
candy. What diabolical temptation!
   The electric blender is great for chopping the nuts as fine
as you wish.

1 cup butter (½ lb.)   1 tablespoon corn sirup
1 cup granulated sugar   1 cup chopped almonds
3 tablespoons water   Semi-sweet chocolate

Cook the butter, sugar, water, and corn sirup to the crack stage (290° F.).
Add half the almonds and cook 3 minutes more. Pour into a well-
buttered 9x9-inch pan and let get cold. Invert the pan and candy will
fall out. Spread it with melted semi-sweet chocolate pieces or bar
chocolate and sprinkle with rest of nuts. Break apart.
   A toffee recipe from my files suggests laying 3 small bars of sweet
chocolate on the surface of the toffee while it is hot, then spreading it
as it melts. You could do it that way. Also, pecans or other nuts might
be used.

179

CHOCOLATE·MINT SALT WATER TAFFY

One hundred fifty PIECES

Just the thing for an old-fashioned taffy pull. Such fun!

4 ounces unsweetened chocolate
1 tablespoon butter
2 cups sugar
1 cup light corn sirup
1 cup water

1½ teaspoons salt
½ teaspoon peppermint extract
  or a few drops oil
  of peppermint

Melt chocolate and butter in top of double boiler. Mix rest of ingredients, except extract, in a large kettle and cook over high heat, stirring constantly, until sugar is dissolved. Lower heat and continue cooking without stirring to 262° F. (hard-ball stage). Remove from heat, add chocolate and butter, stirring only enough to blend. Pour into a shallow greased pan. Put flavoring in center of the mass and work carefully into the mixture. When cool enough to handle, remove from pan, divide into pieces, and pull until somewhat lightened in color. When cold divide into bite-sized pieces.

Salt Water Taffy in Mixed Flavors. Omit the chocolate, cook the sirup to 262° F. and pour the hot sirup into several greased pans. Add various flavorings—mint to one batch, vanilla to another, rum extract to a third—and add food coloring, too, if you wish. Mix and pull.

CHRISTMAS HARD CANDIES   *Sixty-four* PIECES

Make separate batches for separate colors and flavors.

  2 cups sugar
½ cup hot water
½ cup light corn sirup
½ teaspoon anise, peppermint, wintergreen, or lemon extract
  Red, green or yellow food coloring

Mix sugar, water, and sirup and cook without stirring to hard crack stage (310° F.). Add flavoring and coloring during last minute on the burner, remove from heat, pour into greased 8-inch square pan and mark in squares.

MOLASSES TAFFY One hundred fifty PIECES

This stuff is really good!

2/3 cup molasses
1/3 cup light corn sirup
1 1/2 cups firmly packed
    brown sugar
1 1/2 tablespoons vinegar

1/2 cup water
1/4 teaspoon salt
1/8 teaspoon soda
1/4 cup butter or margarine

Cook sirups, sugar, vinegar, water, and salt in a large, heavy saucepan, stirring until sugar dissolves, then stirring only occasionally until mixture reaches 265° F. (hard-ball stage). Remove from heat and stir in soda and butter; turn into large, greased, shallow pan and let cool until you can handle it. Butter your finger tips, cut off pieces of candy and pull and twist until candy changes color to bronze. Twist in shape or cut into 1-inch pieces with scissors dipped in cold water. Wrap in Saran.

POPCORN BALLS One DOZEN

These are the kind you want for a children's party, or for Hallowe'en "tricks or treats."

1/3 cup molasses
1/3 cup light or dark corn sirup
1/3 cup water
1 cup sugar
1/2 teaspoon salt

2 tablespoons butter
    or margarine
2 quarts popped corn
2 cups salted peanuts

Combine molasses, sirup, and water in a saucepan; add sugar and salt. Stir and heat until sugar dissolves, then cook rapidly to 265° F. (hard-ball stage). Add butter. Pour sirup slowly over corn and nuts, stirring to coat all kernels. While mixture is still warm, shape into balls with the hands.

    For a children's party or to tie on a Christmas tree, wrap the balls in colored plastic wrap, tie with bright ribbons in contrasting color, and add name tags, if you wish.

181

ORANGE-SUGARED WALNUTS   *One* QUART

Crunchy and delicious, they have just enough orange flavor.

2½ cups walnut halves
1 cup sugar
⅓ cup light corn sirup
¼ cup water
3 tablespoons orange concentrate
1 teaspoon grated orange rind

Cook sugar, sirup, water, and orange concentrate (frozen or canned) to 240° F. (soft-ball stage), remove from heat, and add orange rind and nuts. Stir until sirup begins to appear cloudy. Turn out on waxed paper and break apart with two forks.

TOASTED PUMPKIN SEEDS

Pumpkin seeds, and squash seeds also, make a delectable snack. Remember this when your youngsters are carving a Jack-o'-Lantern. Wash the seeds, free them from the membrane at the same time, and dry them on paper towels. Then spread them in a shallow pan, dribbling salad oil over them and sprinkling lightly with salt. Place them in a 300° F. oven to brown lightly and become crisp. It takes about 40 minutes.

Sunflower seeds are good this way, too, but they have an outer husk that is inedible and must be cracked off as you munch them. The tiny morsel within is sweet and delicious, but you may not think it worth the effort. Sunflowers grow 2 feet in diameter out our way, and one sunflower has a powerful lot of seeds. It seems a shame not to do *something* with them, especially when they are supposed to be so nutritious.

The MAIN COURSE

MEAL PLANNING does not begin in chronological order, with the appetizer choice. You start by choosing the meat or the fish or poultry or cheese dish which is to be the main part of your meal. Then you work around that, filling in with vegetables and salad. Afterwards, you think about the appetizer and the dessert. Here is the heart of the menu, and in this section of the book I hope you will find good ideas for every day in the year.

Chicken &
Other Poultry

GOOD OLD CHICKEN comes to mind whenever you can't think of anything else to serve, and what a blessing this versatile meat is! It's inexpensive and everybody likes it—have you ever heard of anyone who doesn't? These virtues are sufficient, but chicken has more to offer. It is low calorie, high protein (when you're careful about butter), and may be prepared in a thousand different ways to taste like a thousand different kinds of meat.

Turkey is almost as versatile, and is a better choice sometimes when you have a crowd to feed. Duck and goose and game birds are rarer treats, not as popular perhaps, but versatile, too. I wish I had a few hundred more pages to include all of the chicken, turkey, duck and pheasant recipes I'd like you to know about! But then this book would be too awkward to use, wouldn't it?

BAKED CHICKEN BREASTS   *Eight* SERVINGS

Here's a dish you go away and forget for two hours—
then you come back and find dinner is ready. With a
salad, it's a great luncheon dish for the club.

    4 large chicken breasts, split
    ½ cup butter
       Salt, pepper
    1 cup raw rice
    1 can undiluted cream of mushroom soup
    1 can undiluted cream of chicken soup
    1 can undiluted cream of celery soup

Dip the chicken pieces in melted butter or brush with butter, and
season with salt and pepper. Mix rice and soups and spread in a
shallow buttered casserole. Top with chicken breasts and bake at 300° F.
for 2 hours.

BAKED CHICKEN SOUFFLE   *Nine* SERVINGS

This was one of our Chicago Tribune *$5 "favorite" recipes,*
contributed by a Michigan reader, which has been extremely
popular. At one PTA luncheon where it was served, every
guest demanded a copy of the recipe!

    4 cups diced cooked chicken
    9 slices white bread, crusts re-
        moved
    ½ pound fresh mushrooms,
        sliced
    ¼ cup butter
    1 can (8 ozs.) water chestnuts,
        drained, sliced
    ½ cup mayonnaise
    9 slices process sharp cheese

    4 eggs, well beaten
    2 cups milk
    1 teaspoon salt
    1 can undiluted mushroom soup
    1 can undiluted celery soup
    1 jar (2 ozs.) pimiento, cut
        fairly fine
    2 cups buttered coarse bread
        crumbs

Turkey may be used, of course, in place of chicken. Line a large, flat
buttered baking or roasting pan with the bread. Top with chicken. Cook

mushrooms in butter for 5 minutes. Spoon over chicken. Add water chestnuts. Dot with mayonnaise. Top with cheese. Combine eggs, milk, and salt and pour over chicken. Mix soups and pimiento and spoon over mixture. Cover with foil; refrigerate overnight if you wish. Then bake at 350° F. for 1½ hours, uncover, top with crumbs, and brown 15 minutes more.

BREAST OF CHICKEN WITH VIRGINIA HAM

Six SERVINGS

Epicurean!

    6 breasts young chicken, boned
    6 slices cooked Virginia ham

SAUCE

    3 tablespoons butter or margarine
    3 tablespoons flour
    1 cup chicken stock
  ½ cup cream
    2 egg yolks, slightly beaten
      Salt, paprika
    2 tablespoons sherry

Place chicken breasts in kettle and barely cover with water. Add salt, a few slices of onion, bay leaf, a few peppercorns, and a few slices of lemon. Cover and cook gently until just tender. Drain and reserve stock. When ready to serve, reheat with melted butter or margarine in a covered pan, but do not allow breasts to brown. Serve on slices of hot ham and cover with hot sauce.

TO PREPARE SAUCE: Melt butter or margarine, blend in flour, and add chicken stock and cream gradually while stirring over low heat. Stir a little of the hot sauce into the beaten egg yolks, and stir this mixture into remaining sauce. Season to taste with salt and paprika and add sherry.

BARBECUED FRYER · · · · · · · · · · · · *Four* SERVINGS

One of the best of all barbecued chicken recipes—looks and eats good!

1 frying chicken, cut up
1 medium onion, chopped
½ green pepper, chopped
½ clove garlic, mashed
      with 1 teaspoon salt
⅓ cup butter
⅓ cup vinegar

⅓ cup water
½ cup catsup
2 teaspoons
      Worcestershire sauce
½ teaspoon pepper
½ teaspoon paprika
2 tablespoons brown sugar

Combine ingredients except chicken and simmer gently for 40 minutes. Dredge chicken in seasoned flour; brown in ⅓ cup fat in a heavy skillet. Lower heat and cook 15 minutes. Pour hot sauce over chicken, cover tightly, and cook slowly for about 30 minutes or until chicken is tender.

BUFFET CHICKEN FOR A CROWD · · · · · *Twelve to Fifteen* SERVINGS

You can put it together the day before.

1 stewing chicken (4–5 lbs.)
      in pieces
1 clove garlic, sliced
1 teaspoon salt
1 cup diced celery
1 green pepper, chopped
1 onion, chopped
2 tablespoons olive oil
3½ cups (No. 2½ can)
      tomatoes
½ teaspoon curry powder

1 8-ounce package noodles
½ cup chopped blanched
      almonds
1 cup sautéed sliced fresh
      mushrooms
1 cup sliced ripe olives
2 cups whole kernel corn,
      drained
Salt, pepper
1 cup grated cheese

Simmer chicken with 3 cups water, 1½ teaspoons salt, and ¼ teaspoon pepper until tender. Remove meat from bones and dice. Save broth. Mash garlic with the 1 teaspoon salt. Fry garlic, celery, green pepper, and onion in olive oil until softened but not browned. Add tomatoes and curry and simmer uncovered about 30 minutes. Meanwhile, cook noodles in broth. Combine tomato mixture, noodles, almonds, mushrooms, olives, corn, and chicken. Season well. Place in casserole about 9x13x2 inches. Sprinkle with cheese. Bake in 325° F. oven about 1 hour.

CHICKEN SPIRAL LOAF   *Six* SERVINGS

Here's an easy and pleasing dish with leftover chicken.

CHICKEN FILLING
> 1 cup diced cooked chicken
> 1 cup chopped celery
> ¼ cup chopped green pepper (optional)
> 1 tablespoon chopped onion
> 3 sliced hard cooked eggs
> ½ teaspoon salt

PASTRY
> 1½ cups flour
> ½ cup corn meal
> 1 teaspoon baking powder
> 1 teaspoon salt
> ½ cup shortening
> ½ cup milk

Combine all ingredients for chicken filling, mixing well. To make pastry, sift dry ingredients, cut in shortening until mixture resembles coarse crumbs; add milk, tossing lightly until mixture will just hold together. Knead gently a few seconds on a lightly floured board. Roll dough to form a 10x12-inch rectangle. Transfer dough to baking sheet. Spoon chicken filling onto dough, spreading evenly. Roll, beginning on the long side, as for jelly roll. Place end of fold underneath. Seal ends by pressing the dough together over the filling. Bake in a hot oven, 425° F., for 20 to 25 minutes. Slice and serve with Cheese Sauce.

TO MAKE CHEESE SAUCE: Melt 1 cup shredded or grated sharp cheese in 1½ cups Medium White Sauce (page 282), well seasoned. Good with mushroom soup sauce or chicken gravy, too.

CHICKEN A LA KING
Six SERVINGS

Popular everywhere with everybody.

2½ cups diced cooked chicken
1 cup sliced mushrooms
2 tablespoons chopped
    green pepper
3 tablespoons chicken fat
    or butter

3 tablespoons flour
2 tablespoons chopped pimiento
1 teaspoon onion juice
2 cups milk and chicken broth
    Salt, pepper
1 beaten egg yolk

Cut chicken meat across the grain, using kitchen scissors. Brown mushrooms and green pepper lightly in chicken fat or butter; add flour and blend. Add milk and chicken broth, cook and stir until thickened, add salt and pepper to taste. Add chicken, pimiento, and onion juice. Stir a little of the mixture into the beaten egg yolk, turn it back into the creamed chicken, and heat gently for only a few minutes. Serve hot on toast triangles, or in patty shells or noodle nests. Split salted almonds make a nice garnish.

CHICKEN AND
BROCCOLI CASSEROLE
Six to Eight SERVINGS

This is our version of a famous entrée, Chicken Divan.

4 meaty breasts of chicken,
    simmered tender
2 packages frozen broccoli or
    1 bunch fresh
½ cup slivered toasted almonds
¼ cup butter
2 tablespoons flour

2 cups cream or cream
    and chicken stock
2 egg yolks
Salt
Juice of ½ lemon
Dash of cayenne pepper
Grated cheese

Slice cooked chicken breasts as thin as possible. Cook frozen broccoli 5 minutes, or trimmed fresh broccoli about 10 minutes, in boiling, salted water, and place in bottom of greased casserole. Sprinkle with the almonds and overlap the sliced chicken on top. Make a sauce by blending butter and flour, adding cream gradually. Stir to smoothness. Beat egg yolks and add lemon juice. Stir into cream sauce. Season with salt and cayenne. Pour over chicken and broccoli in the casserole and sprinkle with grated cheese. Brown in 375° F. oven for 20 minutes.

Of course, chicken and turkey can be used interchangeably in any similar dish.

ORANGE-FRIED CHICKEN   *Four or Five* SERVINGS

Deliciously orange, and a little bit peppery, too!

1 young chicken, 2–2½ pounds, in pieces	½ teaspoon salt
	½ teaspoon dry mustard
4 teaspoons grated orange rind (2 oranges)	⅛ teaspoon pepper
	¼ teaspoon Tabasco sauce
⅔ cup orange juice	Flour mixture for coating

Place chicken, one layer deep, in a shallow dish. Combine half the orange rind (2 teaspoons) with juice, salt, mustard, pepper, and Tabasco. Pour mixture over chicken and let stand from 1 to 3 hours. Drain, reserving the marinade mixture for the gravy.

Combine remaining orange rind with ¾ cup flour, 2 teaspoons paprika, 1½ teaspoons salt, and ⅛ teaspoon pepper in a paper bag, or in a can with a tight cover. Shake chicken pieces, a few at a time, in this container, until they are well coated with flour mixture. Save any extra flour after coating the chicken, for gravy seasoning and thickening.

Brown chicken in ½ inch hot fat in a heavy skillet; turn occasionally to brown evenly. When chicken is lightly browned, 15 to 20 minutes, add 1 tablespoon water and cover skillet tightly. Cook slowly until thickest pieces are fork tender, 20 to 30 minutes, turning occasionally for even browning. Uncover and continue cooking slowly to recrisp coating, about 5 minutes. Remove chicken to warm platter and prepare the gravy.

GRAVY: Pour all but 2 tablespoons drippings from skillet. Add water to the marinade mixture to make 1½ cups in all. Add 2 tablespoons reserved flour mixture and a little salt and pepper, and heat until mixture bubbles. Add marinade mixture all at once and cook, stirring constantly until thickened. Season further, if necessary.

COUNTRY FRIED CHICKEN   *Four* SERVINGS

Always serve it with milk gravy.

1 frying chicken (2½ to 3½ lbs.)
   Fat for frying
½ cup flour, or ⅓ cup cornmeal plus 2 tablespoons flour
½ teaspoon salt
   Pepper or paprika

Use a frying pan large enough so chicken will cook without crowding. In it heat enough fat to come to a depth of ¼ to ½ inch. Roll the well-dried pieces of chicken in flour or cornmeal mixture combined with salt and pepper or paprika. Brown on all sides over moderate heat, about 20 minutes. Use a fork and spoon to turn the pieces so they will not be pierced. Cover and cook over low heat until chicken is tender, 20 to 40 minutes, depending on size of pieces.

OVEN-FRIED CHICKEN   *Eight* SERVINGS

This is my favorite way of cooking chicken for a crowd. You may use all the parts of chicken or just half-breasts or drum-sticks. Several large panfuls may be baked in one big oven.

2 frying chickens, cut up
1 cup flour
2 teaspoons salt
½ teaspoon pepper
1½ cups butter or margarine

Shake chicken pieces in a bag with mixture of flour, salt, and pepper. Melt butter in a shallow pan in a 375° F. oven. Remove pan from oven, place chicken in pan and turn over, so that both sides are buttered. Bake 30 minutes, then turn pieces and bake 30 minutes more. Chicken should be brown and crisp. Gravy may be made from drippings.

   Barbecue sauce may be added when you turn the pieces, if you wish. It is important that the chicken be in just one layer, and not crowded.

GRILLED CHICKEN ORIENTAL   *Eight* SERVINGS

Mary Meade staff assistant Helen Dickinson loves entertaining with this chicken dish which most youngsters as well as adults enjoy.

Chickens may be quartered or cut into pieces instead of split; you'd then have twice as many portions. That's a good idea if you have much other food.

     4 broiler-fryer chickens, split
     1 cup barbecue sauce (bottled, or the one on page 202)
 ½ cup vinegar
 ½ cup orange marmalade
 ¼ cup soy sauce

Rub grill or hinged broiler with oil to prevent sticking. Place chicken halves, bone side down, on grill. Brush with mixture of remaining ingredients. Cook about 8 to 10 inches from well-burned-down coals, about 45 minutes to an hour. Brush frequently with sauce. Turn chicken for last 10 minutes of cooking, to brown the skin side.

PLANTATION   *Four* SERVINGS
CHICKEN SHORTCAKE

As easy to fix for many as a few.

     4 squares hot, thin corn bread
     4 slices baked ham, size of corn bread
     4 slices light meat of chicken
     4 slices dark meat of chicken
 1¼ cups hot chicken gravy or mushroom sauce
     4 broiled mushroom caps
       Grated Parmesan cheese

If corn bread isn't thin, split two squares and butter them. On each square place a slice of ham, topped with light and dark chicken meat. Top with hot sauce, garnish with mushroom caps, sprinkle with cheese, and slip under the broiler until bubbly. Turkey is wonderful this way, too, of course.

193

CHICKEN STEW WITH DUMPLINGS

Six SERVINGS

The old-fashioned fat hen has all but disappeared from our markets, having been replaced by the broiler-fryer, the young chicken that is supposed to be the all-purpose chick. I regret this, for there is nothing like a hen for a chicken stew or for chicken and noodles. The excess chicken fat is marvelous for cooking, and the hen yields broth for soup and gravy with unmatched flavor.

If you were brought up on a farm or in a very small town, maybe you have had a rare delicacy, unborn chicken eggs cooked in broth. No? Well, you missed something!

If you can't find a hen for stew, use a broiler-fryer, or two of them. They cook in much less time than the flavorsome hen.

1 stewing hen, cut up
2 teaspoons salt
5 peppercorns
1 onion
1 carrot
1 bay leaf
2 or 3 stalks celery, with leaves
   Dumplings (see next page)

Place chicken in a heavy pot with enough water to cover the pieces well. Add salt, peppercorns, onion, carrot, bay leaf, and celery. Heat to boiling, lower heat to simmering, cover and cook 2 to 3 hours (much shorter time if you use a broiler-fryer) or until meat is tender enough to fall from bones. Cool chicken in stock, then remove bones if you like, and strain stock. Chill it so that you can remove the fat from the surface. Thicken the stock for gravy by measuring a tablespoon of flour for each cup of broth, blending it smooth with some of the broth, then cooking with all of it until thickened. If you wish to add other vegetables, cook separately 3 quartered potatoes, 2 sliced carrots, and 1 cup peas and then add to chicken. Drop the dumplings on the boiling stew, cover tight and don't peek for 15 minutes.

DUMPLINGS: Mix 1½ cups flour, ½ teaspoon salt, 2 teaspoons baking powder. Add 1 tablespoon chicken fat or oil to ⅔ cup milk and stir into dry mixture to make a soft dough. A tablespoon of minced parsley may be added for parsley dumplings. Drop batter from a tablespoon onto the stew.

HOMEMADE NOODLES AND CHICKEN

My friend Virginia Hutton makes everything from scratch, including noodles. "They're so much better!" says Virginia. I don't know why she was surprised to discover that her ten-year-old Jim had written this essay at school:

THE MOST DELICIOUS SMELL WHEN I AM HUNGRY
As soon as I walk in the door, I smelled something that made me as hungry as could be. The smell is so heavenly I could almost flip my lid. Even when I have a stuffed nose I can smell it. My mother cooks it a special way. It is chicken and noodles.

If you'd like to try your hand at homemade noodles, they're really quite easy to make.

> 4 eggs
> 1 teaspoon salt
> 2⅔ cups flour (about)

Beat the eggs, add the salt and enough flour to make a very stiff dough. Knead on a floured board for 3 or 4 minutes, then roll out very thin in a sheet. Cover with a towel and let stand 20 minutes. Then roll up as you'd roll jelly roll, cut into narrow strips, unroll them, and lay out to dry. Noodles may be made a week ahead and stored in a container.

Cook the noodles tender in chicken broth. You can use the recipe for Chicken Stew, substituting noodles for the dumplings, and omitting the thickening for the gravy.

CHICKEN TETRAZZINI   *Eight* SERVINGS

Multiply by two for a party. An excellent dish!

1 4-pound stewing chicken	3 tablespoons butter for sauce
1 teaspoon salt	3 tablespoons flour
½ pound fresh mushrooms, sliced	2 cups chicken broth
	1 cup heavy cream
3 tablespoons butter	2 tablespoons sherry
½ pound spaghetti	Parmesan cheese

Cover chicken with hot water, add salt, and simmer until tender. Cool in broth, then shred chicken, putting skin and bones back in broth. Cook broth down to a little more than 2 cups, so that when strained, you'll have 2 cups for the sauce. Sauté mushrooms in butter for two or three minutes, and cook spaghetti in boiling, salted water.

Make sauce by blending butter and flour, adding broth and stirring over low heat until smooth and thickened. Add cream and sherry. Divide sauce. Add chicken to one part and spaghetti and mushrooms to other. Put spaghetti in baking dish, making a well in the center for the chicken mixture. Cover casserole with grated Parmesan cheese. Bake at 375° F. until lightly browned and hot. Serve at once.

COMPANY CHICKEN LOAF   *Twelve to Fifteen* SERVINGS

Very nice for a luncheon or buffet supper.

4 cups diced cooked chicken (5-lb. stewing chicken)
1 cup cooked rice
¼ cup diced pimientos
1 tablespoon grated onion
2 cups soft bread crumbs, firmly packed
1 cup milk
2 cups rich chicken broth
4 eggs, beaten
1 teaspoon salt
¼ teaspoon pepper

Combine ingredients. Taste and add more seasoning if desired. Bake in a 2-quart baking dish at 325° F. until firm, about 1 hour, or until knife inserted in center will come out clean. Cut in squares or thick oblong pieces.

This is nice served with chicken giblet gravy with 1 can mushroom soup added.

HAWAIIAN COCONUT CURRY

Six to Eight SERVINGS

(My favorite curry for parties—just exotic enough!)

2 cups grated fresh coconut
(or packaged coconut)
3 cups milk
2 cloves garlic, chopped
1 tablespoon chopped fresh
ginger root (or ½ teaspoon
powdered ginger)
2 medium onions, chopped
2 apples, cored and diced

2 tablespoons curry powder
½ cup softened butter or
margarine
½ cup flour
½ teaspoon salt
½ cup top milk or cream
3 cups diced cooked chicken,
shrimp, or lobster meat

Combine coconut and milk and bring to simmering. Add garlic, ginger, onions, and apples. Blend curry powder and 2 tablespoons of the butter. Add to the coconut mixture and cook slowly for 3 hours, stirring occasionally. Remove from the heat and let stand in a cool place several hours or overnight. Squeeze through several thicknesses of cheese cloth. Blend flour with the remaining butter and add to the strained mixture. Cook, stirring constantly, until thickened. Add salt and top milk; add chicken or fish and continue to cook over low heat (in a chafing dish is fine) for 30 minutes. If chicken is used, 1 cup finely diced pineapple may be added.

Serve with rice and the following accompaniments: Crisp chopped bacon, chutney, preserved kumquats, sweet pickles, grated coconut, sliced lemon, chopped cashews or peanuts, grated hard-cooked eggs. Curry is attractively served from a heated hollowed pineapple shell with rice molded in individual servings and garnished with chopped parsley. (Note: Grate the coconut in your blender to save those knuckles!)

SCALLOPED CHICKEN SUPREME   *Six* SERVINGS

Almonds add a pleasing crunch.

1½ cups cooked rice
2 cups chicken broth
3 tablespoons butter
  or chicken fat
6 tablespoons flour
1½ cups milk
1½ teaspoons salt
¼ teaspoon pepper

2 cups diced cooked chicken
1 pimiento, cut fine
1 cup cooked mushrooms,
  sliced
½ cup blanched almonds,
  slivered
Buttered bread crumbs
Paprika

Add ½ cup chicken broth to rice and mix. Melt butter, stir in flour, and blend. Add chicken broth with milk, stirring constantly, and cook until mixture thickens. Add salt and pepper. Butter a large casserole and place a layer of rice on bottom, then a layer of chicken; cover with gravy. Sprinkle with pimiento, mushrooms, and almonds. Repeat until all ingredients are used. Sprinkle top with buttered bread crumbs and paprika. Bake in a moderate oven, 350° F., for 30 minutes.

CHICKEN LIVERS EN BROCHETTE *Six* SERVINGS

A Japanese hibachi will cook them perfectly.

6 slices bacon, cut in quarters
12 large mushroom caps
6 small onions, cut into 3 slices each
1 pound chicken livers, washed, drained, and cut in halves

On each of six metal skewers, impale a mushroom cap, a quarter slice of bacon, a chicken liver half, and a slice of onion. Add another piece of bacon, chicken liver, and onion slice. Repeat procedure again, adding another piece of bacon, liver, onion slice. End with a piece of bacon and a mushroom cap. Arrange skewers on broiling pan, brush with melted butter or bacon drippings; broil 10 minutes on each side. Serve immediately. For crisp bacon, partly cook it before skewering.

STUFFED DRUMSTICKS
Four SERVINGS

Unusual and attractive for a luncheon.

8 meaty drumsticks, simmered tender, bones removed
½ pound chicken livers, sautéed in butter
½ cup fine dry bread crumbs
1 small can button mushrooms, chopped fine
  Salt, pepper
  Stock or wine to moisten
1 slightly beaten egg
¼ cup milk
  Fine dry crumbs for coating

It will be easy to slip the "sticks" out of the drumsticks, once cooked. Use a sharp, pointed knife to loosen meat from bone ends. Mince the cooked livers and combine with crumbs, mushrooms, and seasonings, adding mushroom liquid, stock or wine (any dry wine) to moisten slightly. Stuff the boned drumsticks with this mixture. Dip into mixture of egg and milk, then into the crumbs, and sauté in butter until well browned. Serve two to a customer. Minced celery and a little onion may be added to this filling.

CHICKEN or TURKEY SALAD
Twelve SERVINGS

There's not a hint of the customary celery in this good salad, but you could add it, if you like. A perfect party dish!

4 cups diced chicken or turkey
  (½-inch cubes)
1 cup sliced ripe olives
½ cup sliced stuffed olives
½ cup chopped green pepper
⅓ cup minced parsley
1 cup mayonnaise

1 teaspoon salt
½ teaspoon pepper
½ teaspoon mace
¾ teaspoon tarragon,
  crushed fine
1½ cups heavy cream,
  whipped

Combine ingredients, folding in whipped cream last. Chill in a lettuce-lined bowl before serving.

199

BUFFET CHICKEN SALAD   *Ten* SERVINGS

*Here's how to make chicken salad look (and taste) abso-
lutely beautiful!*

1 quart diced cooked chicken, or chicken and
    cooked veal or ham
2 cups seedless grapes, or halved, seeded light grapes
1 cup sliced toasted almonds or pecans
    Mayonnaise
    Salt
    Cantaloupe rings
    Watercress

Combine chicken, grapes, and almonds with mayonnaise to moisten,
and salt as needed. Serve in melon rings on watercress, or mold by
pressing into a bowl, then turning it out on a platter, and garnishing
with melon balls or slices and clusters of grapes. Decorate with watercress.

CRANBERRY-TURKEY   *Eight to Ten* SERVINGS
SALAD LOAF

*A lovely holiday season salad; reverse the layers if you
wish to emphasize the cranberry red.*

TURKEY LAYER
  1 tablespoon (envelope)
     plain gelatin
2¼ cups turkey or chicken
     bouillon or broth
½ teaspoon salt
  1 teaspoon onion juice
  2 cups diced turkey
½ cup chopped celery
  2 tablespoons chopped
     green pepper

CRANBERRY LAYER
  2 cups cranberries
1¼ cups water
¾ cup sugar
  1 tablespoon (envelope)
     plain gelatin
  1 tablespoon lemon juice
½ teaspoon salt
½ cup chopped celery
½ cup chopped apple
¼ cup chopped nuts

For turkey layer, soften gelatin in ¼ cup cold broth. Heat remaining broth and add salt, onion juice, and softened gelatin. Remove from heat, stir until dissolved, then cool. When mixture begins to thicken, add turkey, celery, and green pepper. Turn into a loaf pan and chill until firm.

For cranberry layer, cook cranberries in 1 cup water until skins pop, about 7 minutes. Strain through fine sieve, add sugar, and simmer 5 minutes. Soften gelatin in remaining ¼ cup water and dissolve in hot cranberry juice. Add lemon juice and salt, then cool. When mixture begins to thicken, fold in celery, apple, and nuts. Pour on top of firm turkey layer and chill. When ready to serve, unmold on crisp greens and accompany with mayonnaise.

HOT CHICKEN SANDWICHES   *Forty* SERVINGS

Doris Schacht of my staff reports that a successful luncheon for the women of her church featured Hot Chicken Sandwiches with a minimum of work. A lime gelatin and cottage cheese salad and a relish tray of carrot sticks, celery curls, and olives were served with the sandwiches.

  1 bunch green onions
½ pound butter or margarine
  7 cans condensed cream of mushroom soup
3½ cups milk
  7 cups diced cooked chicken (2 stewing chickens
        should do it)
  2 large sandwich loaves white bread (40 slices)
  1 2-pound package process cheese, sliced
10 medium tomatoes, cut into 4 slices each
  2 (3 ozs.) packages grated Italian-type cheese

Chop onions, including tops, and sauté in butter or margarine. Add soup or milk; heat until creamy. Add chicken and stir lightly. Toast bread and lay slices in shallow baking pan. Top each with a slice of cheese, then a large spoonful of chicken mixture, covering toast completely. Top each portion with a slice of tomato and sprinkle with grated cheese. Bake at 350° F. for 15 minutes.

BARBECUED TURKEY ON A SPIT

A 10-to-14-pound turkey is the right size to cook on your rotisserie, if you're not a man. A bigger bird is extremely awkward to handle, and if it starts going *klunk-klunk*, it takes a man of muscle to fix it properly on the spit again. It's very important to get the turkey balanced on the spit before you start cooking.

Start your charcoal fire a good half hour before you begin cooking. The coals must look gray, not black or red. You need only a layer of them. If you need to add more charcoal, do it a few pieces at a time.

Your turkey should be completely thawed, if you use a frozen bird. Salt and pepper the inside well. The bird usually is not stuffed. If you do stuff the turkey, sew up the openings or you are likely to find the filling dropping into your fire.

Truss the bird by tying feet firmly to tail and wrapping cord around the body to hold the neck skin and wings in place. Center on your spit and be sure the prongs of the spit are anchored firmly in the bird. Rub the turkey with salad oil.

Start the motor and expect a done turkey in something like 4 hours. It will take about 15 to 20 minutes per pound, as a rule. After 2 hours, baste the bird with a barbecue sauce, if you like, swabbing it on at intervals with a dish mop.

The bird is done when the flesh pinches soft.

BARBECUE SAUCE   *Three* CUPS

This sauce is good on chicken, beef, and other meats, as well as turkey.

1 large onion, chopped
½ cup butter or margarine
1 cup chili sauce
½ cup water
¼ cup wine vinegar
2 tablespoons brown sugar

1 tablespoon Worcestershire
   sauce
1 teaspoon dry mustard
1 teaspoon salt
1 teaspoon paprika
   Dash of cayenne
¼ teaspoon black pepper

Sauté onion in butter several minutes, then add other ingredients and simmer 30 minutes. If sauce seems too thick, dilute it with water.

If you have an electric blender, put all the ingredients into it, whirl them smooth, and then cook gently for about 10 minutes.

SMOKED TURKEY

If you haven't a barbecue grill with a cover, it is possible to create a dome with heavy foil on a wire frame. You need something to keep the smoke around the big bird as it cooks.

   1 turkey (12–15 lbs.)
   4 cups chopped celery with leaves
1½ cups chopped onions
1½ cups chopped parsley
     Sprigs of fresh thyme, dill, and rosemary,
       if you have them
 ½ cup oil for basting sauce
   1 cup white table wine
     Salt, pepper, salad herbs
     Hickory chips

Build your charcoal fire at one side or end of the grill, and when it is burning evenly, place a foil drip pan beside the fire and under the grill where the turkey will rest. Make your foil pan a little larger all around than the turkey, using a double thickness of heavy foil, turning up foil on all sides and mitering the corners.

Salt and pepper the turkey inside and fill it with mixture of celery, onions, and herbs. Mix salad oil and wine with salt, pepper, and salad herbs for basting. Skewer openings of turkey and truss it. Brush with basting sauce. Place on grill and put a piece of foil against the side of the turkey which is toward the fire, to protect it from too much heat. Cover grill and adjust damper for slow-burning fire. Allow about 5 hours for the turkey to smoke and cook, adding damp hickory chips to the fire at the beginning, middle, and toward the end of cooking and adding new charcoal when needed. Baste the bird now and then with your sauce.

HOW TO ROAST A TURKEY

Here's something that *has* improved since Grandma's day: the turkey, and how to roast it. Modern turkeys are compact, meaty, tender-fleshed, and it has been a long time since any cook had to do a pin-feathering job. I can remember plucking pinfeathers out of a turkey for a whole evening, before Thanksgiving, using tweezers, paring knife and finally twisted paper torches to get the hairs.

The following time chart, accepted by poultry packers as the best general guide to cookery, needs to be used with common sense. Turkeys vary, and one may cook a little quicker or a little slower than this schedule. To test for doneness, move the drumstick up and down (it should move freely), and pinch the flesh of thigh and drumstick (it should feel soft). Use mitted fingers for that test!

Roast turkey uncovered except for a loose tent of foil over the breast when the turkey is half or two-thirds done. Set the oven at 325° F.

Roast a 6– 8 pound turkey	2–2½ hours
" " 8–12 pound "	2½–3 hours
" " 12–16 pound "	3–3¾ hours
" " 16–20 pound "	3¾–4½ hours
" " 20–24 pound "	4½–5½ hours

If you have a meat thermometer, insert it in the thickest part of the inside thigh muscle, being careful not to touch bone. Roast the turkey to 185° F. Baste now and then with butter or barbecue sauce if you wish. Let the bird stand a few minutes before carving to re-absorb its juices and firm up for the knife.

SAGE AND CELERY STUFFING

Fourteen to Eighteen Pound TURKEY

Here's the old-fashioned flavor but the texture is fluffy, not heavy as was the old-time stuffing.

4 quarts lightly toasted bread cubes
2 medium onions, chopped
1 quart chopped celery and tops
1 tablespoon salt

½ teaspoon pepper
1 teaspoon dried sage
1 teaspoon poultry seasoning
1 cup (½ pound) butter, melted
Broth or stock to moisten

Sauté the onion and celery lightly in a little of the butter, if you wish. Combine all ingredients lightly. Cooked, ground, or chopped giblets may be added to the stuffing.

SAUSAGE AND CORNBREAD STUFFING

Fourteen to Eighteen Pound TURKEY

This is my Thanksgiving day special; it is savory and good.

2 quarts lightly toasted bread cubes
2 quarts broken up cornbread (bake a double batch)
1 pound bulk pork sausage
1 teaspoon poultry seasoning

½ teaspoon salt
½ cup chopped onion
1 cup chopped celery
2 tablespoons minced parsley
Stock or milk to moisten

Combine breads in a large bowl. Cook sausage, breaking it up well. Add sausage and drippings to bread, tossing lightly. Add seasonings and other ingredients. The sausage fat is the only fat you use in this stuffing.

CASSEROLED TURKEY WITH MUSHROOMS

Six SERVINGS

Here's creamed turkey de luxe.

½ pound fresh sliced
    mushrooms
¼ cup butter
¼ cup flour
½ teaspoon salt
⅛ teaspoon pepper
1 teaspoon minced onion

1 cup clear turkey
    or chicken broth
    or bouillon
1 cup cream
2 cups diced cooked turkey
¼ cup chopped green pepper
¼ cup sliced ripe olives

Sauté sliced mushrooms in butter five minutes. Sprinkle flour over mushrooms and add salt, pepper, and minced onion. Stir until blended. Gradually add turkey or chicken broth and cream. Stir constantly until thickened and smooth. Add turkey, green pepper, and ripe olives. Cook only until turkey is heated through. Transfer mixture to a hot casserole or chafing dish. Top with a sprinkle of finely chopped parsley.

CREAMED TURKEY AND HAM GOURMET

Five or Six SERVINGS

See what a little wine can do!

¼ cup butter or margarine
¼ cup flour
1¼ cups milk or milk and cream
½ cup turkey or chicken stock
    or bouillon
¼ cup sauterne
½ teaspoon monosodium
    glutamate

Dash of mace
Salt, pepper
1 cup diced cooked turkey or
    chicken
1 cup diced cooked ham
1 4-ounce can sliced mushrooms,
    drained

Melt butter, stir in flour, and add milk and stock. Cook, stirring, until mixture boils and thickens. Gradually stir in wine. Add remaining ingredients. Serve piping hot in patty shells or in a rice or noodle ring.

TURKEY A LA QUEEN
Twelve SERVINGS

Pineapple may replace some or all of the grapes in this excellent buffet dish.

1½ quarts (6 cups) cooked turkey, cut in large pieces
1½ quarts well-seasoned Cream Sauce (see below)
½ cup sherry
1 pound mushrooms, sliced and sautéd in butter
6 cups red and green grapes, halved and seeded

Stir sherry into sauce (white table wine may be substituted) and add turkey and mushrooms. Heat thoroughly and stir in the grapes last. Serve with rice, if you wish. Or serve with reheated turkey dressing, if this is a leftover combination.

CREAM SAUCE: Melt ¾ cup butter (1½ sticks) and blend in ¾ cup flour and 1½ teaspoons salt. Add gradually 6 cups milk and cream or milk, cream, and chicken broth, or turkey stock. Cook and stir to smooth sauce. Taste for salt, and add some pepper. If you wish, you may sauté the mushrooms in the butter before adding the flour instead of doing them separately.

DUCK GRILLED OUT OF DOORS

Quarter thawed ducklings and remove necks and backbones. Simmer these for soup or stock. With a sharp knife score the skin of the ducks at 1-inch intervals. Rub the quarters with salt, pepper, and paprika; also with garlic or garlic salt, if you wish. Put them in a baking pan and toss in a cupful of chopped celery with tops and ½ cup of chopped onion. Bake at 350° F. for 1½ hours. Then transfer to charcoal grill and cook 3 to 5 inches above well-burned-down coals for about 20 minutes, until tender and brown. Turn pieces, and if you wish, brush with Barbecue Sauce (page 202) at intervals during grilling.

Of course, you may grill the duck from scratch, but you get a lot of spattering and it takes a little longer. I prefer this method. The duck acquires just as much charcoal flavor.

DUCK WITH SAUERKRAUT AND CARAWAY

Four SERVINGS

A European-style treat.

1 duckling (4–5 lbs.) quartered
1 medium onion, chopped
1 apple, peeled, cored, and chopped
1 teaspoon caraway seeds
3 cups sauerkraut
1 tablespoon cornstarch
2 tablespoons cold water
Salt, pepper

Brown duck quarters in heavy skillet or Dutch oven in ¼ cup oil. Drain off all but 2 or 3 tablespoons fat. Sauté onion and apple in the fat a few minutes; add caraway and kraut. Mix lightly and place duck on top, seasoning duck with salt and pepper. Cover and cook gently until duck is tender, about 1½ hours.

Remove duck to serving platter (crisp skin under broiler, if you like). Combine cornstarch and water, add to kraut, and stir constantly until thickened. Serve kraut around the duck.

SPIT-ROASTED DUCK

Four SERVINGS

Two ducklings usually may be spitted together for twice as many portions. Press them tightly, legs touching, breasts outward.

1 duckling (4–6 lbs.)
Salt, pepper
Celery, parsley, and onion, or orange slices for stuffing
Basting Sauce (see next page)

Score the skin of the duck or ducks at 1-inch intervals, using a sharp knife. Fill cavity, after salting and peppering it, with chopped celery, parsley, and onion in any proportion you like, or with small onions stuck with cloves, or with sliced oranges. The filling is not necessary, but seems to add flavor, and enriches the delectable aroma of the roasting duck.

Skewer neck skin to back and insert spit through center of duck, fixing it firmly with prongs and set screws to balance perfectly. Tie cord around legs of bird and around breast to hold wings in place.

Place hot charcoal briquets at back of fire box with a foil drip pan in front of them. Cook duck 2½ to 3 hours on the revolving spit, brushing with basting sauce the last 45 minutes, if you wish. The duck is done when the drumstick feels very soft when pressed between your fingers (use a pad or other finger protector). Cut duckling into four quarters to serve. To divide, split lengthwise through the breastbone, then cut to one side of the backbone. Divide halves just above the thigh. Poultry shears or a sharp heavy knife will do the job neatly.

BASTING SAUCE: Barbecue Sauce (page 202) or a mixture of 1 can (8 ozs.) tomato sauce, 2 tablespoons soy sauce, ¼ cup orange marmalade, and 1 teaspoon mustard.

ROAST WILD DUCK

Wipe out the duck cavity with a cloth saturated in red wine, brandy, or vinegar. Sprinkle salt and freshly ground pepper into it, also a little garlic salt, if you wish. Fill the bird with wild rice cooked in chicken broth or consommé and seasoned with a little onion and melted butter. Or fill with seeded or seedless grapes or orange sections and an onion or two, or with sliced apples and prunes. Any of these will add flavor and fragrance.

Cook duck giblets in water to cover with a slice of lemon, salt, a stalk of celery and a few whole peppercorns. Lay bacon strips over the duck breast.

Roast on a rack in an open roasting pan at 450° F. for 30 minutes. Or roast at 325° F. for an hour. Either way should give you delicious, juicy duck. I think I prefer the higher temperature for the shorter time. Make gravy from the drippings and the giblet stock, adding the chopped liver, and if you wish, a little red wine.

The duck may be brushed with melted currant jelly to glaze it, 10 minutes before it is done.

A wild duck serves two generously, but if the carver makes thin slices, it will stretch to satisfy four appetites if they aren't too ravenous. The breast is about all there is to the bird.

PHEASANT IN CREAM GRAVY

Three or Four SERVINGS

Salt pork or bacon seasons the cream gravy; the bird is delicious this way.

1 pheasant, cut up
  Flour, salt, pepper
6 slices salt pork or thick bacon

3 tablespoons flour
2 cups milk

Flour and season the pheasant. Cook salt pork or bacon and set aside. Brown the pheasant in the drippings, cooking evenly. Cover the skillet and let the bird cook gently until tender, half an hour or more. Transfer to a hot platter and lay the salt pork or bacon over the pieces. Add flour to fat in skillet, blend well, then add milk. Cook and stir to a smooth sauce. Season with salt and pepper, if necessary. If you used salt pork, you may need no more salt. Serve gravy with or around the pheasant.

WINE-BAKED PHEASANTS

Six SERVINGS

Wild rice, or a mixture of brown rice and wild rice (less expensive), makes the perfect accompaniment.

3 pheasants, split in half
  Butter, salt, pepper
6 strips bacon

1 cup red table wine
1 onion
¼ teaspoon thyme or rosemary

Brush pheasants with butter all over and sprinkle inside with salt and pepper. Lay in a shallow pan and brown on each side under the broiler. Then place skin side up in the pan and place a bacon strip on each. Pour wine over birds, place onion in the pan, and sprinkle thyme or rosemary over the pheasants. Bake at 325° F. for an hour or longer, until pheasants are very tender, basting several times with the wine and drippings. Meanwhile cook giblets in water with an onion, a stalk of celery, and salt and pepper, until tender. Use the stock with the drippings to make a sauce or gravy, adding the sliced liver to it. Pheasants may be covered for the first half of baking, if you wish.

PHEASANTS WITH SOUR CREAM SAUCE: Prepare the birds in the same way, but just before serving, stir into the gravy 1 cup sour cream.

Fish & Seafood

ALL MY BROTHER Keith has to do to go fishing is walk down to the beach, climb in his boat, and go *put-put* off to where he thinks the fish may be biting on Lake Minnetonka. He fishes Canadian lakes sometimes, as well as Minnesota's. And I now give him credit for being an excellent fish cook.

He was patient, but stubborn, the day he and Phyl were holding a fish fry for about twenty relatives. Phyl, daughter Phyllis Ann, and sister (this one), all home economists, were offering unnecessary advice and telling the poor man he couldn't possibly fry so many fish in butter. The butter would scorch, because of the salt. He would ruin the fish.

So he cooked fish for twenty *in butter,* and it was absolutely delicious! "That's the way the Indian guide cooked our fish, and that's the way I'm going to cook these," said he. The fillets were dipped in milk, then in "Aunt Jemima" (pancake mix), and fried quickly in lots of butter. As the fillets browned and cooked, he placed them on a warming ledge over the charcoal grill, and filled the skillet with a new batch.

It's easy, if an Indian guide shows you how!

BARBECUED FISH   *Six to Eight* SERVINGS

A recipe from Texas where they barbecue everything!

1 red snapper (3–4 lbs.)
   whitefish, or bass
2 tablespoons chopped onion
1 tablespoon fat
2 tablespoons brown sugar
2 tablespoons vinegar

¼ cup lemon juice
½ teaspoon salt
3 tablespoons Worcestershire
1 cup catsup
½ cup water
   Salt and pepper

Clean fish and place in greased shallow pan. Brown onion in fat; add brown sugar, vinegar, lemon juice, salt, Worcestershire sauce, catsup, and water. Simmer 5 minutes. Sprinkle fish with salt and pepper and pour sauce over it. Bake at 425° F. for 10 minutes; reduce heat to 350° F. and continue baking 35 to 45 minutes longer.

CANADIAN INDIAN   *Three* QUARTS
GUIDE'S CHOWDER

Any fish you catch go into this kind of chowder. Bass and walleye are very good. Some guides might add some cooked bacon.

4 cups diced potatoes
   (about 3 medium)
3 cups diced onions
1 tablespoon salt
¼ teaspoon coarse
   black pepper

1 quart boiling water
5 cups diced raw fish
   (¾-inch cubes)
2 cups milk
2 cups half-and-half or cream
   Chopped parsley

Add potatoes, onions, salt, and pepper to 1 quart boiling water. Cook about 12 minutes or until vegetables are almost tender. Add fish and cook 10 minutes. Add milk and cream. Heat 15 minutes more without allowing chowder to boil. Serve garnished with parsley.

GRANDMOTHER'S FINNAN HADDIE

Six SERVINGS

Milk makes a less expensive dish, but it's better with cream. Wonderful for breakfast as well as supper.

2 pounds finnan haddie
2 bay leaves
¼ teaspoon each, pepper, marjoram, and thyme
2 tablespoons chopped parsley

2 cups light cream
2 teaspoons lemon juice
1 tablespoon grated onion
2 tablespoons butter or margarine

Cover fish with hot water, add seasonings, and simmer until fish will flake. Drain. Place in a casserole and add cream, lemon juice, and grated onion. Dot with butter or margarine and bake at 350° F. for 10 minutes, or until heated through.

FISH MOUSSE

Six to Eight SERVINGS

A pound of frozen fillets will start you on this excellent dish, or use the leftovers of a fish fry.

2 tablespoons sugar
1 teaspoon salt
1 teaspoon dry mustard
½ cup vinegar
2 egg yolks, beaten
1 tablespoon (envelope) plain gelatin

¼ cup cold water
1 tablespoon horseradish
2 cups flaked cooked fish
1 cup chopped celery
1 cup heavy cream, whipped
Stuffed olives
Pimiento

Combine sugar, salt, mustard, and vinegar with egg yolks in top of double boiler. Cook over hot water, stirring constantly, until thickened. Add gelatin which has been softened in cold water. Stir to dissolve. Add horseradish. Cool until slightly thick and fold in fish, celery, and whipped cream. Arrange sliced stuffed olives and strips of pimiento in an oiled fish mold. Pour in mixture and chill until firm. Turn out on greens to serve.

213

FOILED FISH DINNERS   *Six* SERVINGS

These are such fun for a cookout. A vegetable may be added to the package, too. Green beans or peas, perhaps.

6 fish steaks or fillets, any kind
  Salt, pepper
  Lime or lemon juice
2 medium potatoes, cooked 10 minutes and sliced
2 onions, sliced
6 pats butter or margarine

Place fish steaks on squares of heavy foil. Sprinkle with seasonings and lemon or lime juice. Put several slices of potato and onion over fish. Add more salt and pepper. Top with a pat of butter. Seal the packets with a double fold of foil and grill over charcoal for about 20 minutes, or bake in a 400° F. oven for that long.

Fish fillets may be stuffed, rolled, and packaged this way with lemon juice and butter. Even a large fish may be stuffed, wrapped in foil, and grilled. It is especially good if some barbecue sauce is poured over it before wrapping. A 3- or 4-pound fish will take about half an hour, and should be turned once.

FISHERMAN'S PUFF   *Six* SERVINGS

Salmon and mashed potatoes are inexpensively casseroled.

1 pound flaked salmon, cod, or tuna
2 cups mashed potatoes
½ cup warm milk
2 tablespoons minced parsely
1 teaspoon minced onion
1 tablespoon lemon juice
3 eggs, separated
1 teaspoon salt
  Dash of pepper
1 tablespoon butter or margarine, melted

Combine fish, potatoes, milk, parsley, onion, lemon juice, and egg yolks. Then add salt and pepper and fold in the stiff-beaten egg whites. Pile lightly into buttered baking dish and pour the melted butter over the top. Bake at 350° F. for 30 minutes.

214

HADDOCK TOMATO ROLL-UPS   *Four* SERVINGS

A beautiful color combination, a piquantly flavored stuffing.

2 pounds haddock fillets
½ cup chopped onion
¼ cup minced parsley
½ cup shredded raw spinach
2 carrots, grated
Juice of 1 lemon

1 teaspoon salt
⅛ teaspoon pepper
2 tablespoons butter or
    margarine
¼ teaspoon basil
½ cup tomato sauce

Combine vegetables, lemon juice, salt, and pepper, and spread on fillets. Roll and fasten with string or toothpicks. Simmer in a pan with ¾ cup water, 1 tablespoon lemon juice 8 to 10 minutes, covered. Meanwhile combine butter, basil, and tomato sauce, and heat through. Remove fish from water and drain. Place on heated platter and cover with tomato sauce. Garnish with parsley and lemon wedges.

HALIBUT or TUNA STEAK   *Four* SERVINGS
WITH TOMATOES

Any thick fish steaks can be prepared like this. Not for meatless Fridays, but good.

2 slices salt pork
1 onion, sliced
1 pound halibut or tuna steak, about 1 inch thick
    Salt, pepper
1 cup canned tomatoes
¼ cup sliced ripe olives
    Buttered bread crumbs

Cut pork into strips, and place half in a baking pan. Place half the onions on top, then the halibut seasoned with salt and pepper. Add tomatoes, olives, and remaining onion. Top with remaining salt pork strips, and sprinkle with buttered crumbs. Bake at 375° F. for 30 minutes.

BAKED STUFFED LAKE TROUT   *Six* SERVINGS

Mackerel, whitefish, and others of baking size are awfully good this way, too.

1 3-pound lake trout
3 cups dry bread crumbs
¼ cup chopped onion
¼ cup chopped parsley
1 cup chopped celery
2 beaten eggs
1 teaspoon salt
¼ teaspoon paprika
Milk to moisten stuffing

Have fish cleaned, scaled, and head and tail removed. Or remove head and tail just before serving. Wipe with damp cloth; sprinkle lightly inside and out with salt. Combine stuffing ingredients, fill fish, and close cavity, using skewers and string. Place in greased baking dish, brush with butter, and bake at 400° F. 10 minutes per pound. Serve with parsely and lemon cups filled with tartar sauce.

GRILLED BROOK TROUT   *Four* SERVINGS

Note that 4 trout make 4 servings—I won't say 4 fish will feed 4 people! Not out of doors, anyway.

4 cleaned brook trout
Salt, pepper
Lots of melted butter

Hold trout head back with fingers through gill opening and shake salt and pepper into body cavity. Brush fish well with butter and gently place on or between grills, 5 to 7 inches above hot coals. Cook only 3 to 4 minutes to the side.

216

Hot Chicken Sandwiches, page 201

TROUT BARBECUE
Six SERVINGS

Try this recipe with any fish of around a pound in weight.

6 trout, ¾–1 pound each
Salt, pepper
Flour, oil
⅓ cup white table wine
⅓ cup barbecue sauce
Juice of 1 lemon
Oregano

Season fish with salt and pepper. Coat with flour. Fry in oil until half done, about 10 minutes. Place in baking pan. Mix wine with barbecue sauce and lemon juice. Add 2 tablespoons water. Baste fish before placing in 375° F. oven, and baste twice while baking for 30 minutes. Sprinkle with oregano and serve hot.

SALMON LOAF
Six SERVINGS

Lemon juice does a lot for this well-seasoned mixture.

1 pound can salmon, flaked
¼ cup lemon juice
3 tablespoons butter or
   margarine
3 tablespoons flour
½ teaspoon salt
2 cups milk

2 tablespoons minced onion
¼ cup chopped celery
   (with tops)
2 eggs, beaten
1 cup dry bread crumbs
1 cup cooked peas
   Lemon Sauce (see below)

Add lemon juice to salmon. Melt butter, blend in flour and salt, and add milk. Cook to smooth sauce. Add onion, celery, eggs, crumbs, peas, and salmon. Bake in greased 9x5-inch loaf pan or a ring mold, at 350° F. for 45 minutes.

Serve with **cream sauce,** to which you've added 1 cup fresh chopped cucumber and a little lemon juice.

217

TOP – *Fish Fry (Perch), page 211*
BOTTOM – *Shrimps Creole, page 226*

HERRING SALAD

This is the smörgasbord classic of the Swedes; it is good eating for a picnic, barbecue, or buffet supper. It keeps well, so make it 2 or 3 days early.

2 large salt herring
4 medium potatoes, boiled and diced fine
4 medium beets, cooked and diced fine
2 cups finely diced cooked veal or canned luncheon meat
1 dill pickle, cut fine
3 tart apples, pared and diced fine

1 small onion, minced
1 cup cooked carrots, diced fine
⅓ cup vinegar
2 tablespoons sugar
½ cup heavy cream
Sour cream or whipped cream for garnish
Sliced beets, hard cooked egg, greens

Skin and bone herring and soak overnight in cold water. Cut fine. Mix fish with potatoes, beets, meat, pickles, apples, onion, and carrots. All ingredients should be cut very fine. Add salt if needed.

Add sugar to vinegar and mix with salad. Add cream enough to make a smooth mixture which should not be too moist. Pack it firmly into a wet bowl, cover, and chill. Turn out on a platter. It will keep its shape. Garnish with a blob of sour or whipped cream and a few beet slices. Sprinkle with sieved hard-cooked egg. Tuck in a few greens here and there.

PICKLED SMELTS   *Two* QUARTS

Prepared like this, the fish will keep 3 to 4 weeks in the refrigerator. They're a delicious appetizer.

Fresh smelts, cleaned
2 cups vinegar
2 cups water
2 teaspoons salt
20 peppercorns

18 whole allspice
5 bay leaves
4 slices lemon
3 slices onion, separated in rings

Boil all pickling ingredients except the lemon 30 minutes. Add lemon, boil 5 minutes. Remove lemon slices. Place the cleaned fish in the liquid a few at a time and simmer until tender enough to pull out a fin (fin and tail are left on the fish in this recipe). Pack in sterilized glass jars with thinly sliced onions here and there. Distribute the lemon slices through the jars. Pour over the boiling liquid. Do not seal, but cover with the lids. The liquid turns to a jelly.

SMOKED FISH   *Six* SERVINGS

I well remember when son Charles smoked his first fish. He had caught only one small one, and there were at least twenty of us around. But each of the twenty tasted one small bite of the fish, so his work was admired.

Of course, if you have more or fewer fish, you'll have more or fewer servings. But 6 fish make the smoking worth while!

6 cleaned fish, about 1 pound each ,
1 cup salt
1 gallon water
¼ cup salad oil

Remove heads of fish just above gills. Cut along backbone almost to the tail. The fish should lie flat in one piece. Rinse fish. Add salt to water and put the fish in this brine for 30 minutes.

To smoke the fish, use a charcoal fire in a barbecue grill with a hood or cover that closes to make a smoker. Soak 1 pound of hickory chips in 2 quarts water. Let fire burn down to low, even heat. The coals should look gray. Place a third of the wet chips on the charcoal. Rinse fish in fresh water and place, skin side down, on a well-greased grill over the smoking fire. Cover grill and smoke for 1½ hours, adding remaining wet chips every 15 minutes to keep the fire smoking. Increase the temperature by adding more charcoal and opening the draft. Brush fish sparingly with oil. Cover and cook 15 minutes. Brush again with oil and cook 10 minutes more, or until lightly browned.

TUNA-NOODLE CASSEROLE   *Eight* SERVINGS

One, two, three! It's in the oven, and you know it's good!

    ¼ cup butter or margarine
    1 green pepper, chopped
    2 tablespoons finely chopped onion
    1½ cups milk
    ¼ cup chopped pimiento
    ½ pound process cheese, cubed
    3 eggs, well beaten
    ½ teaspoon salt
    ¼ pound noodles, cooked
    2 cans tuna (6½–7 ozs. each), flaked

Place butter, green pepper, onion, milk, pimiento, and cheese in a double boiler. Stir occasionally until cheese is melted. Stir in eggs and salt. Mix with noodles and tuna; pour into a large buttered casserole. Place in a shallow pan of hot water and bake at 350° F. for 35 minutes.

SWEET-SOUR TUNA   *Six* SERVINGS

The recipe was a prize winner and a popular one.

6 slices canned pineapple, cut
    into sixths
2 tablespoons butter
⅔ cup pineapple juice
2 large green peppers, cut into
    1-inch pieces
2 tablespoons cornstarch
2 teaspoons soy sauce

2 tablespoons vinegar
⅓ cup sugar
1 cup chicken bouillon
2 cans tuna, 6½–7 ozs. each
½ teaspoon salt
⅛ teaspoon pepper
Chinese noodles

Sauté pineapple in butter 5 minutes. Add ⅓ cup pineapple juice and green pepper. Cover and simmer 10 minutes. Mix cornstarch with remaining pineapple juice. Add to pineapple with soy sauce, vinegar, sugar, and bouillon. Cook, stirring constantly, until thick. Add tuna and seasonings and heat through. Serve over crisp noodles.

220

WALLEYE SPECIAL

The walleye pike is one of the best game fish and one of the best to eat. You are lucky to catch one of 2 to 4 pounds weight, which is average, but in deep, dark waters among rocks and ledges you may find a 15-pounder. There's a lot of good eating on such a fish!

This method is good for all kinds of fresh-caught fish.

Fillet the walleye into large pieces. Dip into beaten eggs, then into crushed cornflakes or crackers, and fry in ½ inch hot cooking oil until brown and crusty. Cook only until fish flakes easily with a fork. Add salt and pepper and serve hot.

BROILED WHITEFISH AMANDINE
Four to Six SERVINGS

This could be the best fish you ever ate!

  1 whitefish (2–3 lbs.) scaled, boned, split
½ teaspoon each, garlic salt, salt, paprika
    Dash pepper
¼ cup melted butter

SAUCE: ½ cup slivered almonds, ⅓ cup butter, 2 tablespoons lemon juice, 2 tablespoons minced parsley

Line shallow baking pan with foil and brush foil with melted butter. Lay fish, meaty side up, on foil. Sprinkle with seasonings, dribble with butter. Broil 12 to 15 minutes, 2 inches from heat. Meanwhile, sauté almonds 5 minutes in butter, remove from heat, and add lemon juice and parsley. Place fish on hot platter and cover with sauce.

DEVILED CRAB   *Four* SERVINGS

A simple way to prepare a really delicious dish.

2 6-ounce packages frozen crab meat, thawed
2 tablespoons butter or margarine
1 cup medium white sauce
1 teaspoon dry mustard
  Dash cayenne pepper or Tabasco sauce
1 tablespoon minced parsley
1 teaspoon minced onion
1 teaspoon Worcestershire sauce
½ cup grated sharp cheese

Sauté crab meat a few minutes in butter. Add white sauce and seasonings, with more salt if necessary. Fill individual shells or casseroles with the mixture and top with cheese. Bake until lightly browned on top, about 20 minutes, at 375° F.

BACK-YARD CLAMBAKE   *Twelve* SERVINGS

If you live on the seashore, you know about clambakes, and you may think this kind is a poor imitation. But it's lots of fun for a party, and the food is exactly as good as it would be on the seashore! This recipe is from the Bureau of Commercial Fisheries, U.S. Dept. of the Interior.

12 dozen steamer clams
12 baking potatoes
12 ears of corn, in the husks
12 live lobsters, 1 pound each
  Lemon wedges
  Melted butter

Wash clam shells thoroughly. Wash potatoes and cut off ends. Remove corn silk from corn and replace husks.

For steaming, use a large metal container, similar to a 30-gallon galvanized garbage can with a tight-fitting lid. Have made 5 baskets with folding handles, to fit inside the container. The bottoms of the baskets should be made of 1/2-inch galvanized wire mesh. Place three 6-inch-high supports in the bottom of the container.

Put water into the container to a depth of about 5 inches. Place potatoes in a basket and put the baskets on the supports. Finish filling container by placing corn in the next basket, lobsters in the next two, and the clams in the top basket. Cover container and place it over a hot fire. Steam for 1 hour. Remove baskets. Crack lobster claws. Serve with lemon and butter.

OYSTER STEW   *Eight* SERVINGS

I am one who thinks oyster stew tastes more oystery warmed up the second day. I prefer oyster stew on the second day, although it sometimes has a slightly curdly appearance.

   2 pints fresh oysters, medium size, with their liquor
   1/2 cup butter
   2 cups light cream, scalded
   1 1/2 quarts milk, scalded
      Paprika, if you like
   1 teaspoon salt
      Lots of pepper

Pick over oysters for any bits of shell and heat them with the butter until the edges curl, just a minute or two. Add cream and milk, heat to just under the boiling point and add seasonings. Do not allow stew to boil or it will curdle. Serve hot with oyster crackers.

Some professionals use clam broth as part of the liquid in an oyster stew. Others will heat a sliced onion in the milk, then remove it.

SCALLOPED OYSTERS   *Eight* SERVINGS

*Nobody has ever been able to improve upon the old-fash-
ioned, simple scallop with crackers and milk or cream.*

2 pints medium oysters, drained and picked over
2 cups strained oyster liquid and cream or milk
3 cups crumbled crackers
   Salt, black pepper
½ cup melted butter

Butter a shallow casserole and make 2 layers of oysters in it, with
crackers between and on top. Sprinkle each layer of oysters with salt
and pepper. Pour melted butter over the casserole, then add the oyster
liquid and cream, trickling the mixture around the edges of the casserole so that it comes up under the top cracker layer. Bake at 400° F.
for 20 to 25 minutes, until browned.

BAKED SEAFOOD SALAD   *Six to Eight* SERVINGS

Delicious, and simplicity itself!

½ cup chopped green pepper
¼ cup minced onion
1 cup chopped celery
1 cup cooked or canned crab-
   meat
1 cup cooked or canned shrimps
1 cup mayonnaise
½ teaspoon salt

1 teaspoon Worcestershire
   sauce
2 cups cornflakes, crushed, or
   1 cup fine dry crumbs
Paprika
2 tablespoons butter or margarine

Combine green pepper, onion, celery, fish, mayonnaise, salt, and Worcestershire, and mix lightly. Place mixture in individual shells or shallow baking dish. Sprinkle with crushed cornflakes or crumbs and
paprika. Dot with butter. Bake at 350° F. about 30 minutes. Serve
with slices of lemon.

SCALLOPS IN GARLIC BUTTER
Eight to Ten SERVINGS

They remind you a little of Oysters Rockefeller or Shrimps de Jonghe.

1 pound scallops
¼ pound butter, melted
1½ teaspoons each, chopped
    chives, parsley
¼ teaspoon tarragon

¼ teaspoon garlic salt
½ teaspoon onion salt
    Dash of black pepper
    Fine dry bread crumbs

Mix butter and seasonings. If large scallops are used, cut into pieces—if small, leave whole. Arrange 8 to 10 baking shells or ramekins on a baking sheet. Place some of butter mixture in bottom of each shell. Put some of the scallops in each shell, then top with remaining butter mixture. Sprinkle with crumbs. Bake at 350° F. for 10 minutes. Serve hot, to begin a meal, or as an hors d'oeuvre.

BROILED BARBECUED SHRIMPS
Four SERVINGS

Use your table broiler, and prepare these in front of your guests.

2 pounds raw shrimps, shelled,
    veined
⅓ cup minced onion
3 tablespoons olive oil
1 cup catsup
⅓ cup lemon juice
2 tablespoons brown sugar

½ cup hot water
2 teaspoons prepared mustard
2 tablespoons Worcestershire
    sauce
¼ teaspoon salt
1 teaspoon chili sauce

Sauté onion in olive oil for 5 minutes. Add remaining sauce ingredients and simmer 10 minutes. Place shrimps on a heatproof platter and cover with sauce. Broil about 5 inches from heat 5 to 7 minutes. Turn once during broiling.

SHRIMPS AND HALIBUT EPICUREAN

Four SERVINGS

Very, very good!

1 pound cooked shrimps
1 pound sliced halibut
1 clove garlic
6 shallots, chopped (or green onions)
1 fresh tomato, peeled and chopped
1 cup beef bouillon or consommé

½ cup sauterne or other dry white wine
Juice of ½ lemon
1 tablespoon Worcestershire sauce
1 teaspoon salt
Dash of black pepper
Pinch of tarragon
Dash Tabasco

Peel and vein shrimp. Steam halibut until tender, and break into coarse chunks. Mash garlic clove slightly and sauté in 3 tablespoons butter or oil for 2 or 3 minutes. Remove from pan and add shallots. Cook until soft, then add tomato, bouillon, wine, lemon juice, and seasonings. Simmer sauce until it cooks down a bit, then add fish, heat through, and serve on hot, fluffy rice.

SHRIMPS CREOLE

Six SERVINGS

Wine could replace ½ cup tomato juice, for more exotic flavor.

1 medium onion, chopped
1 green pepper, chopped
1 cup sliced fresh mushrooms
¼ cup oil
3 tablespoons flour
1 No. 2 can tomato juice (2½ cups)

2 cups chopped fresh tomatoes
1 teaspoon chili powder
1 teaspoon minced parsley
1½ teaspoons salt
¼ teaspoon pepper
1½ pounds shrimps, cooked
Hot cooked rice

Cook onion, green pepper, and mushrooms gently in oil until soft. Blend in flour, then gradually add tomato juice, chopped tomatoes, and seasonings. Cook until thickened. Add shrimps. Simmer 15 minutes. Serve on freshly cooked hot rice.

226

SHRIMP CURRY   *Eight* SERVINGS

An easy one for a party.

½ cup butter or margarine
1 clove garlic, minced
   very fine
1½ cups chopped onion
1 bay leaf
3 tablespoons curry powder
3 tablespoons flour

1½ teaspoons salt
1½ cups water or 1 cup stock
   and ½ cup dry
   white wine
3 pounds raw shrimp, peeled
   and cleaned,
   butterfly style

Melt butter in large frying pan, add garlic and onion, and sauté until golden. Add bay leaf, curry, flour, and salt, and blend. Stir in liquid. Cook and stir until mixture thickens and comes to a boil. Add shrimp and simmer gently, stirring occasionally to prevent sticking, for 20 minutes. Serve on fluffy rice with curry accompaniments such as raisins, chutney, chopped nuts.

SWEET AND PUNGENT SHRIMPS *Four* SERVINGS

This dish is attractive and kind to your taste buds.

1 pound cooked shrimps,
   shelled and deveined
¼ cup brown sugar
2 tablespoons cornstarch
½ teaspoon salt
¼ cup vinegar
1 tablespoon soy sauce

Juice from No. 2 can
   pineapple chunks
1 green pepper,
   cut in thin strips
2 small onions, sliced and
   separated into rings
Drained pineapple chunks

Mix brown sugar with cornstarch and salt in a heavy saucepan. Stir in vinegar, soy sauce, pineapple juice, and cook to a smooth sauce, stirring constantly. Add green pepper, onions, and pineapple and cook 2 or 3 minutes. Remove from heat and add shrimps. Let stand about 10 minutes. Just before serving, bring to the boiling point. Serve with hot rice, or on chow mein noodles.

CURRIED SHRIMP SALAD WITH MELON

Eight SERVINGS

*An utterly divine combination which makes a beautiful sum-
mer luncheon.*

4 pounds shrimps, cooked, shelled, deveined
1 cup mayonnaise
1½ tablespoons grated onion
2 tablespoons lemon juice
1½ cups chopped celery
1½ teaspoons salt
½ cup dairy sour cream
1½ tablespoons curry powder
2 large honeydew melons, quartered, seeds removed

To the shrimps add the mayonnaise, onion, lemon juice, celery, salt, and
sour cream blended with the curry. Chill. Cut melon balls; chill balls
in mixture of 2 tablespoons lemon juice and ⅓ cup salad oil. Scrape
out remaining melon and chill the boat-shaped shells. To serve, fill the
shells with shrimp salad and garnish with the melon balls.

SEAFOOD EN BROCHETTE

Broil these out of doors for a summer cook-out.

Scallops wrapped in bacon
Peeled raw shrimps
Chunks of bananas or pineapple, or both
Mushroom caps
Butter, brown sugar, salt

String the shellfish, fruit, and mushroom caps on skewers, brush with
butter, sprinkle lightly with salt and a little brown sugar. Or roll the
fruit in brown sugar before skewering it. Grill or broil 10 to 15 minutes, turning once for even cooking. Use long skewers for meal-size
portions, small ones for appetizer size.

Beef,
Veal,
Lamb,
Pork,
& Ham

BEEF IS "MEAT" to most Americans, especially to midwesterners who would forget that there is more to a steer than roasts and steaks, were it not that hamburgers are so popular with the younger generation and ground beef dishes so reasonable. There are many equally good cuts in other kinds of meat—lamb, for example, and many cooks are beginning to discover that.

In this collection of recipes may be found some real gems of indoor and outdoor cookery. I hope readers will try the unfamiliar ones as well as those that just naturally sound good, because there will be some happy surprises.

ROAST PRIME RIBS OF BEEF

This is the great American dinner. An 8-pound standing rib roast should care for 8 hearty appetites and provide leftovers, as meat is trimmed these days.

Stand the roast in a shallow pan so that the ribs make a natural rack. Roast at 325° F. for about 3 hours for rare beef; 3½ hours for medium.

A thermometer in the center of the roast (don't let it rest on fat or bone) will tell you more exactly when the meat is cooked to perfection. A reading of 140° F. equals rare-in-the-middle beef; 160° F. is medium. Some of your guests are bound to be unhappy if you cook the beef well done. I venture to say most will want it pink. Salt and pepper the beef before or during roasting, as you wish.

The meat is easier to carve 20 minutes after it comes from the oven. That's lucky for the hostess who wants to bake rolls.

ROAST BEEF WITH YORKSHIRE PUDDING
Eight SERVINGS

"Auntie" Evans was the plump and jolly nurse at our house whenever there was a new baby, and sometimes between-times. When she was in her nineties she came for a visit and made a last batch of her famous Beef and Yorkshire Pudding. Auntie was Welsh, and her version of this classical dish had more gravy and thus was better than any other I've ever tasted.

1 4-pound pot roast, floured, salted, and peppered
  Drippings
2 onions
  Water

PUDDING: 1 cup flour; ½ teaspoon salt; 2 eggs, beaten; 1 cup milk.

Brown meat well in drippings, add onions to the pan, and pour in a cup of water. Cover and cook gently on top of the range or in a 325° F. oven, adding more water from time to time in order to have a generous amount of gravy.

To Make Pudding: Mix flour and salt. Add milk to eggs and pour into flour. Beat smooth. If meat is cooked on top of the range, pour off drippings and gravy into an 8-inch square pan. Heat in a 400° F. oven, then pour in Yorkshire pudding and bake about 40 minutes. Serve with the beef and more gravy. Pour the pudding batter around an oven-braised hunk of beef in its good brown gravy, and turn the heat up to 400° F. for the baking.

Yorkshire pudding may be baked in fat-skimmed drippings from prime ribs or another oven roast. I sometimes accumulate drippings in the freezer for this purpose, as there isn't enough of this good goo from the average oven roast.

BEEF STROGANOFF   *Four* SERVINGS

One of our most popular recipes, this is a dish to make dinner an occasion.

1½ pounds sirloin steak or fillet of beef
¼ cup flour
2 teaspoons salt
4 tablespoons butter or margarine
1 cup finely chopped onions
½ pound mushrooms, sliced
1 small clove garlic, finely minced
1 cup sour cream

Slice meat in ½-inch strips. Dredge strips in flour seasoned with salt, then set aside. Sauté onions and mushrooms in 2 tablespoons butter for 5 minutes. Remove vegetables; add 2 tablespoons more butter to skillet and add meat strips. Brown evenly on all sides. Return onions and mushrooms. Add garlic and blend in sour cream. Mix thoroughly and heat through on moderate heat. Serve with rice or noodles.

BEEF STEW
WITH RED WINE

Eight to Ten SERVINGS

Madeline Holland, a former member of the Mary Meade staff, is one of our favorite people and a top-notch home economist and food publicist. This is Mad's favorite stew, and I hope it will be yours, too.

3 strips bacon, fried crisp
3 pounds beef chuck, cubed
½ cup flour
1 tablespoon salt
½ teaspoon pepper
2 carrots, ground
1 cup water
1–1½ cups dry red wine

8–10 medium onions, peeled
8–10 medium potatoes, pared
8–10 medium carrots, scraped
1 tablespoon Worcester-
   shire sauce
1 package (10 ozs.) frozen
   peas, thawed

Set aside cooked bacon. Coat meat with flour, salt, and pepper, and brown in bacon fat. Add carrots, 1 cup water, and 1 cup wine. Cover and cook very slowly (on top of the range, in the oven, or in the electric fry pan) for 2½ hours, adding remaining wine at the end of 2 hours. Add vegetables, except peas, and cook 25 minutes. Add Worcestershire sauce and peas and cook 5 minutes longer or until peas are just tender. Thicken drippings with any remaining flour. Garnish with bacon.

BEEF STEW
WITH PARSLEY DUMPLINGS

Four SERVINGS

Make veal stew in the same manner.

1 pound beef for stew
  Flour, salt, pepper
2 tablespoons fat
1 cup water
12 small onions
8 carrots, pared and cut in half lengthwise
  Parsley Dumplings (see next page)

Have meat cut into 2-inch cubes. Dredge in seasoned flour. Heat fat in deep kettle, then brown meat in it well on all sides. Add liquid, cover kettle tightly and simmer 1½ to 2 hours, or until tender. About 30 minutes before the end of cooking time, add vegetables and more liquid if necessary. Cover tightly and continue cooking. About 15 minutes before end of cooking time, drop dumplings gently on top of stew, cover, and finish cooking. Arrange meat, vegetables, and dumplings on hot platter; thicken liquid for gravy, using 1 tablespoon flour for each cup of liquid.

PARSLEY DUMPLINGS: Sift 1 cup flour, 2 teaspoons baking powder, and ½ teaspoon salt together. Cut in 1 tablespoon fat. Break 1 egg into a cup measure, add enough milk to make ½ cup of liquid. Stir liquid and 2 tablespoons chopped parsley into flour, mixing to a soft dough. Dip a tablespoon into stew broth, then scoop up a spoonful of batter and slip it on top of vegetables in kettle. Work quickly and arrange dumplings so that steam circulates around all sides. Do not remove cover while dumplings are cooking.

CHUCK WAGON CHOW   *Six* SERVINGS

This is the kind of food that goes over big with a bunch of Boy Scouts or a camping-out crew of almost any age.

2 pounds round steak, cut into 1-inch cubes	2 tablespoons salad oil
1½ teaspoons salt	2 medium onions, diced
½ teaspoon pepper	1 green pepper, diced
1 tablespoon chili powder	1 can tomato sauce
1 or 2 garlic cloves, minced (optional)	2 cans kidney beans

Sprinkle salt, pepper, and chili powder on beef, also the garlic, if used. Brown meat lightly in oil. Add onions and green pepper and cook until tender and transparent. Add tomato sauce. Cover and simmer until meat is tender, about 1 hour. Add beans and cook 10 minutes more. This combination doubles or triples readily for a crowd. Use a heavy iron skillet or Dutch oven.

CUBED-STEAK ROLLS *Four* SERVINGS

These are attractive little packages; well seasoned, too.

4 cubed steaks (minute steaks)
1 small onion
½ green pepper
2 strips bacon
3 pieces celery
2 carrots

½ teaspoon salt
¼ teaspoon paprika
Flour, drippings
1 clove garlic, minced
1 cup water or stock

Grind onion, green pepper, bacon, celery, and carrots. Add salt and paprika. Spread vegetable mixture on steaks, roll, and tie or fasten with toothpicks. Dredge with flour and brown in hot drippings. Add garlic and stock or water. Cover and simmer until tender, about 1½ hours. Or bake at 325° F. until tender.

AUNT KATIE'S CASSEROLE *Ten* SERVINGS

The boys spent a week with Aunt Katie and came back asking for this dish. So I had to get the recipe which she had gotten from a friend who had gotten it from a friend in California, who had gotten it, I think, from a Pillsbury Bake-Off. It has been changed some, in going from hand to hand, but as Kathleen Kapple serves it, the casserole is perfection for family or company.

2 pounds round steak, cut in 1-inch cubes
¼ cup flour
1 teaspoon salt
¼ teaspoon pepper
½ teaspoon paprika
1 jar whole small onions
2 cans condensed cream of chicken soup with
1 can water
Herb Dumplings (see next page)

Brown the meat in a deep skillet in fat trimmings or drippings, after pounding in the flour, salt, pepper, and paprika with a meat mallet or edge of a saucer. Add the onions, soup, and water. Bake at 350° F. for 40 to 45 minutes. Meanwhile, make the Herb Dumplings.

DUMPLINGS: Sift together 2 cups flour, ½ teaspoon salt, 4 teaspoons baking powder. Stir in ¾ cup milk and ¼ cup oil. Add 1 teaspoon poultry seasoning and 1 tablespoon each of celery seed and poppy seed. Prepare a cup of crushed cornflakes. Drop the dumpling mixture into the crumbs, then place on top of the meat. Bake 15 to 20 minutes longer.

LONDON BROIL Four to Six SERVINGS

Choice quality flank steak is tender enough to broil if you do it quickly, then carve it on the diagonal. There's lots of flavor in this inexpensive cut, which is becoming a popular barbecue meat.

    1 flank steak, top quality, about 2 pounds
      French dressing (the oil-and-vinegar kind)
    1 teaspoon salt
      Lots of black pepper
    2 tablespoons soft butter

Pour about ¼ cup dressing over a well-scored flank steak and let stand several hours in the refrigerator. Drain well and broil about 2 inches under broiler unit (set temperature at BROIL or 550° F. and let the oven pre-heat 10 minutes) for 5 minutes per side. Season with salt and pepper when you turn the meat, and brush with butter. Season second side and brush with butter before serving on a hot platter. See that the carver has a very sharp knife, and ask him to slice on the diagonal for tender texture, making very thin slices.

The steak may be cooked over charcoal. Brush with barbecue sauce, if you wish.

Flank steak may be rolled around bread stuffing, braised tender (1½-2 hours), and served with mushroom sauce (see page 238).

COUNTRY FRIED STEAK   *Four* SERVINGS

*With so many fancied-up round steak preparations, we
mustn't forget this old-fashioned platter full of good eating.*

1½ pounds round steak, cut ½ inch thick
¼ cup flour
1½ teaspoons salt
¼ teaspoon pepper
   Bacon drippings for frying
2 cups milk

Pound flour and seasonings into steak and fry in about 3 tablespoons
very hot drippings until brown on each side. Transfer to a hot platter
and make gravy from drippings and milk. You'll probably need to add
a little more flour to the skillet, 1 or 2 tablespoons, before adding the
milk and stirring a smooth gravy. Taste for seasonings. You may need
a little more salt.

FARMERS' STEAK (SWISS STEAK) *Six* SERVINGS

*Granny always pounded the steak with the edge of a thick
saucer to tenderize it and work in the flour. There are meat
tenderers which break up the connective tissue with a few
hammer strokes—but they really don't work any better than
that saucer!*

2 pounds round steak cut 2 inches thick
½ cup flour
2 teaspoons salt
½ teaspoon pepper
1 or 2 onions, chopped or sliced
   Sliver of garlic, mashed, if you want it
1 cup water, stock, tomato juice, or tomato sauce

Pound mixture of flour, salt, and pepper into steak on both sides, using meat tenderer or the edge of a sturdy saucer or plate. Brown on both sides in hot drippings or oil (about 3 or 4 tablespoons). Add onion, garlic, and liquid. Cover and simmer gently until meat is very tender, adding more liquid from time to time as you need it. About 1½ hours should be sufficient time. Mashed potatoes or boiled noodles are what you want with this dish.

GREEN PEPPER STEAK   *Six to Eight* SERVINGS

This is our version of a dish that is a favorite in restaurants from coast to coast.

3 pounds round steak, cut 1½ to 2 inches thick
⅓ cup flour
2 teaspoons salt
½ teaspoon pepper
¼ cup drippings
2 medium onions, sliced thin
1 green pepper, cut julienne
1 cup beef bouillon
3 green peppers, cut julienne
3 tomatoes, cut into wedges
¼ cup butter
½ teaspoon salt
½ cup Burgundy

Pound flour and seasonings into meat with a mallet. Brown on both sides in drippings. Add onions, 1 green pepper, and bouillon. Cover pan and let ingredients simmer for 1 to 1½ hours or until meat is tender. Sauté the 3 green peppers and the tomatoes in butter for 5 minutes. Sprinkle with salt. Place meat on heated platter. Stir Burgundy into meat drippings and heat. Pour drippings over meat and top with peppers and tomatoes. If you wish, thicken drippings with flour or cornstarch.

STUFFED FLANK STEAK *Four to Five* SERVINGS

Rolled and braised until very tender.

1 flank steak, 1½ pounds, well scored
2½ cups coarse bread crumbs
½ cup chopped celery
2 tablespoons chopped onion
1 tablespoon chopped green pepper
1 teaspoon salt
¼ cup melted butter
1 egg
Salt pork or bacon strips

Blend bread crumbs, celery, onion, and pepper. Add salt and melted butter and enough hot water to moisten slightly; add egg. Spread dressing on flank steak and roll up lengthwise. Tie. Brown on all sides in hot fat; place in heavy kettle or casserole and lay strips of salt pork or bacon over the top. Cover and cook over low heat or in 325° F. oven 1½ hours to 2 hours. Slice and serve with mushroom gravy.

SPANISH STUFFED STEAK *Six* SERVINGS

This is a fine Cuban version of beef rolls, obtained from a hotel cook at Varadero.

2 pounds beef round, sliced thin
Salt, pepper
1 onion, chopped
1 tablespoon lemon juice
6 carrot strips

6 dill pickle strips
6 ham strips
2 cups tomato sauce
½ onion, chopped
½ green pepper, chopped

Cut meat into portions and sprinkle with salt, pepper, onion, and lemon juice. In each piece, wrap a strip each of carrot, pickle, and ham. Tie or skewer the rolls and brown all around in drippings or butter. Use a canned tomato sauce, if you like, adding the onion and green pepper. Pour over the meat and cover. Simmer gently for about 1½ hours, or until meat is very tender. May be baked covered at 350° F.

STEAK AND PEA SOUP   Four SERVINGS

Joanne Will's great-grandma on the Will side came from Alsace, as did her recipe for something the Wills call "steak and pea soup." It is a prosaic name for a very good dish, a combination of meat and potato and pea soup seasoned with the steak drippings.

1 sirloin steak for 4, 1-inch thick
4 medium red potatoes, peeled and diced
4 to 6 cups water

1 package frozen peas
¼ cup butter
Salt, pepper

Pan-fry steak in a large skillet or electric fry pan to the degree of doneness you like. Meanwhile, cover potatoes with salted water, heat to boiling and cook 5 minutes. Add frozen peas and cook 5 minutes more. Remove steak to a hot well-and-tree platter, and keep it warm. Add butter to the steak drippings, with a little water. Scrape to get all the meat particles and brown a little. Add this pan gravy to the potato and pea soup. Season to taste with salt and pepper. Green onions could be added to the soup. Steak and soup are served at the same time.

PLANKED STEAK DINNER   Four SERVINGS

Practice on your family, then serve guests this way!

Sirloin steak, 1½–2 inches
    thick
Salt, pepper, salad oil
Mashed potatoes

8 large mushroom caps, buttered
1 egg white, beaten slightly
1 teaspoon paprika
1 package frozen peas, cooked

Broil the steak rare, season with salt and pepper, and place on wooden plank brushed with salad oil. Use a pastry bag or two spoons to make a border of potatoes around the plank, close to the edge. Arrange mushroom caps on plank. Brush potato border with egg white and sprinkle with paprika. Bake at 450° F. about 12 minutes, or until potatoes are browned. Remove plank from oven, fill in gaps around meat with hot peas, and serve at once.

VARIATION: Include halves of tomato with buttered crumbs on the plank when it goes into the oven.

BARBECUED STEAK   *Six* SERVINGS

Nice for a busy day—fix it early, refrigerate, then shove it into the oven later.

2 pounds round steak, cut 1½ inches thick
1½ teaspoons salt
¼ teaspoon pepper
2 tablespoons drippings
⅓ cup minced onion
½ cup minced celery

2 tablespoons brown sugar
2 teaspoons prepared mustard
2 tablespoons Worcestershire sauce
2 teaspoons lemon juice
1 can tomato soup, undiluted

Rub salt and pepper into steak and pound with meat tenderer. Brown in hot drippings in heavy frying pan. Place in a casserole. Combine remaining ingredients and pour over meat. Cover casserole and bake at 350° F. for 1½ to 2 hours or until tender.

BARBECUED BEEF   *Eight* to *Twelve* SERVINGS

This is the kind of meat I like to prepare in twice these amounts in order to freeze some of it.

1 4-pound sirloin tip roast or 4 pounds boned rump roast
Salt
Pepper

SAUCE

1 medium onion, chopped
3 tablespoons drippings or oil
1 tablespoon sugar

1 teaspoon dry mustard
1 teaspoon salt
¼ teaspoon pepper
1 teaspoon paprika
½ cup catsup
½ cup water
¼ cup vinegar
1 tablespoon Worcestershire sauce
Few drops Tabasco sauce

SIRLOIN TIP ROAST: Place in shallow pan, fat side up, season with salt and pepper. Roast at 325° F. for 30 to 45 minutes per pound, depending upon degree of doneness desired. After half of roasting time has elapsed, pour barbecue sauce over meat, continue roasting, basting meat two to three times during final cooking period.

BONED RUMP ROAST: Rub roast with salt and pepper. Heat 1 tablespoon fat or drippings in kettle and brown meat on all sides. Pour barbecue sauce over meat, cover kettle, and cook in 325° F. oven about 4½ hours or until meat is tender. Remove cover last half hour of cooking and spoon sauce over meat. Serve beef, sliced thin, in toasted rolls.

TO PREPARE SAUCE: Cook onion in oil until golden brown. Add combined remaining ingredients and simmer for 15 minutes.

POT ROAST WITH ONIONS   *Eight* SERVINGS

So good with boiled noodles!

>   1 4-pound chuck or rump pot roast (if boned and rolled, it will
>   go farther)
> ½ cup flour
>   1 tablespoon salt; pepper
>   3 tablespoons fat
>   3 large onions, sliced
>   1 green pepper, diced (optional)
>   1 clove garlic, minced
>   2 cups water, stock, tomato juice or wine

Flour and season the meat and brown well on all sides in hot fat. Add onions, green pepper, and garlic and ½ cup of the liquid. Cover and cook gently 3 to 4 hours, or until meat is very tender, adding remainder of liquid in ½ cup portions, from time to time. Transfer to hot platter and thicken liquid for gravy.

WITH VEGETABLES: Add 1 hour before serving 6 medium pared potatoes, 6 scraped carrots, 12 small peeled onions.

BEEF BRISKET WITH HORSERADISH SAUCE

Six SERVINGS

A zesty horseradish sauce complements the flavor of fresh beef brisket.

3 or 4 pounds fresh boneless
    beef brisket
Salt and pepper

HORSERADISH SAUCE
1 tablespoon butter
1 tablespoon flour

1 cup milk
½ cup horseradish
1 tablespoon lemon juice
¼ teaspoon salt
    Dash pepper
1 tablespoon pimiento

Wipe meat with damp cloth. Place in kettle; cover with water. Season with salt and pepper; simmer for 3 to 4 hours, or until meat is tender. Cool in stock. Slice thin and reheat in stock.

TO PREPARE HORSERADISH SAUCE: Melt butter and mix to smooth paste with flour. Add milk slowly, stirring constantly, until mixture boils. Drain horseradish and add with remaining ingredients to sauce. Serve sauce hot over drained meat.

BEEF IN HERB WINE SAUCE   *Four to Six* SERVINGS

A $100 favorite recipe is this one, and it's great for guests.

3 or 4 medium onions, sliced
2 tablespoons bacon drippings
2 pounds lean beef (sirloin tip
    preferred) cut into 1½-
    inch cubes
1½ tablespoons flour
1 cup beef bouillon
1½ cups dry red wine
¼ teaspoon marjoram

¼ teaspoon thyme
¼ teaspoon oregano
1 teaspoon salt
½ teaspoon pepper
½ pound fresh mushrooms,
    sliced lengthwise,
    sautéed in
¼ cup butter

Sauté onions in bacon drippings until yellow, remove from pan, add meat cubes, sprinkle lightly with flour, and brown meat. When meat is well browned, add ¾ cup beef bouillon, 1 cup red wine, and the herbs and seasonings. Cover pan tightly and simmer over low heat (or in 300° F. oven) about 2 hours, adding remaining bouillon and wine in several bastings. Add onions and mushrooms and cook 20 to 30 minutes longer, or until meat is tender.

TENDERLOIN TIPS WITH MUSHROOMS

Eight SERVINGS

If you plan a buffet supper, this dish is a good one to choose. It can be made ahead, but leave the sour cream for the warm-up.

  1 pound mushrooms, sliced
  1 small onion, minced
  ½ cup butter
  3 pounds tenderloin tips, cut into thin diagonal strips
  ½ cup flour
  ¼ teaspoon pepper
  1 clove garlic mashed with 2½ teaspoons salt
  1 cup dry red wine
  1 green pepper, cut into thin strips
  1 jar (2 ozs.) pimiento, chopped
  2 cups sour cream
  Minced parsley

Cook mushrooms and onion in butter 5 minutes. Remove from pan. Dredge meat in flour seasoned with pepper and garlic salt. Brown meat in remaining butter. Turn into casserole; add mushrooms and onion. Pour wine into skillet and scrape brown meat particles from pan; add to casserole and mix. Cover and bake at 375° F. for 30 minutes. Stir in green pepper, half of the pimiento, and the sour cream. Bake uncovered 5 minutes longer or until heated through. Sprinkle with parsley and the remaining pimiento, and serve.

SAUERBRATEN

Eight SERVINGS

That delicious raisin gingersnap gravy is famous.

4 pounds beef (chuck, rump, round)	2 cups vinegar or vinegar and wine
2 teaspoons salt	2 cups water
1/4 teaspoon pepper	Fat for browning
1 onion, sliced	1/4 cup sugar
3 bay leaves	1/4 cup raisins
1 teaspoon peppercorns	4–6 gingersnaps, crushed

Rub meat well with salt and pepper. Place in a large dish with onion, bay leaves, and peppercorns. Heat vinegar and water and pour over meat to cover. Cover dish and let stand in refrigerator 12 to 36 hours, turning occasionally. Drain, wipe dry. Brown meat in fat in a heavy skillet. Add onion and a small amount of spiced vinegar. Cover and simmer slowly until tender, about 3 to 4 hours. Melt sugar in a skillet, add the strained liquid very gradually, then add raisins and gingersnaps and cook until thickened and smooth. Add a tablespoon or two of thick sour cream to the gravy for extra flavor. Highly seasoned potato dumplings are the usual accompaniment.

CHEESEBURGERS DE LUXE

Six SERVINGS

These are hamburgers for adults; they're company specials.

1 1/2 pounds ground round steak or chuck	6 strips bacon, cooked and crumbled
1 1/2 teaspoons salt	6 slices Cheddar cheese, cut with doughnut cutter
1/4 teaspoon pepper	6 hamburger buns, split and toasted
6 thick tomato slices	

Season meat with salt and pepper and form into 6 large patties. Broil until brown on both sides. Place a slice of tomato on each patty, sprinkle with crumbled bacon, and top with cheese slice. Return patties to broiler and heat until cheese is melted. Serve on toasted buns. If you wish, serve the cheeseburgers open face; top each with a mushroom which has been sautéed in butter.

SUPER BURGERS   *Four* SERVINGS

These burgers are big, big, BIG! Make smaller ones, if you'd rather, and serve 6 or more.

1 egg
1 small green pepper,
   quartered
½ small onion
½ cup chopped celery
1 can tomato soup, undiluted
1 teaspoon salt

¼ teaspoon pepper
1½ pounds ground beef
12 crackers, crushed
½ small onion, chopped
   (for sauce)
2 tablespoons butter

Place egg, green pepper, ½ onion, celery, ⅓ cup soup, salt, and pepper in blender container. Blend until vegetables are finely chopped. (If you do not have a blender, grind vegetables in a food chopper.) Mix with beef and crackers and form into 4 patties. Place them on rack of pre-heated broiler. Cook burgers on both sides to the degree of doneness you wish.

Cook remaining onion in butter for 5 minutes. Add the rest of the soup; simmer for 5 minutes. Serve sauce over burgers.

THE BROMLEYS' MEAT LOAF   *Eight* SERVINGS

"I was raised on this loaf, which is slightly red because of the salt pork in it," says Margaret Bromley Piont, Mary Meade's right arm in the office. "It's delicious cold."

2 pounds ground beef
¼ pound ground salt pork
¾ cup fine cracker crumbs
1 cup milk, scalded

1 egg, slightly beaten
1 teaspoon crushed sage leaves
¼ teaspoon each: celery salt,
   onion salt, salt, pepper

Have the meat man grind meats together. Reserve ¼ cup crumbs. Add remainder to milk. Add egg, milk mixture, and seasonings to meats. Mix well but lightly. Pack into a 9½x5½-inch loaf pan and top with the saved crumbs. Bake 1½ hours at 350° F.

MEAT LOAF, PLAIN OR PLANKED

Eight SERVINGS

Beef and pork are an excellent combination for a good loaf.

2 pounds ground beef
1 pound ground pork
2 cups soft bread crumbs
1 medium onion, minced
2 eggs

1 tablespoon salt
¼ teaspoon pepper
1 can (1 lb., 12 ozs.) tomatoes
1 green pepper, chopped

Mix meat, bread crumbs, onion, eggs, and seasonings. Shape into a loaf in a shallow pan. Combine tomatoes and green pepper and pour over loaf. Bake uncovered at 350° F. for 1 hour 15 minutes. Serve plain, or place loaf on a plank and pipe (using pastry bag) fluffy mashed potatoes around loaf. Brown potatoes and loaf at 500° F. for about 10 to 15 minutes.

MEAT BALLS IN SAUCE

Six SERVINGS

Serve these savory beef-and-pork balls on spaghetti or rice, then sit back and listen to those squeals of joy!

1 pound ground beef
½ pound ground pork
½ cup rolled oats or bread
     crumbs
1 small onion, minced
1½ teaspoons each: salt and
     prepared mustard
¼ teaspoon pepper
1 cup milk
¼ cup drippings

SAUCE
½ pound mushrooms, sliced
2 tablespoons butter
1 clove garlic, mashed with
     1 teaspoon salt
1 can (1 lb., 12 ozs.)
     tomatoes, forced through
     a food mill
¼ teaspoon pepper
1 cup sour cream

Combine meat, oats, onion, seasonings, and milk. Mix well and let stand for 10 minutes. Drop from a tablespoon into hot drippings and brown on all sides. Cook mushrooms in butter for 5 minutes. Combine with remaining ingredients except sour cream. Pour mixture over meat balls and simmer for 30 minutes. Stir in cream, heat through, but do not boil. Serve sauced meat balls over spaghetti.

SOME BEEFY CAMPING-OUT SPECIALTIES

Pat O'Donnell is an old hand in hospital and school kitchens and doesn't mind getting up at 4:30 a.m. when she's cooking for 35 or 40 kids at a church camp. She can spout easy recipes for beefy dishes faster than I can write them down. Her recipes don't all have names, but you'll have no difficulty with them, even in this capsule form. For a lot of people, you just double or triple the amounts.

1. Brown a pound of ground beef lightly in a skillet, add salt and pepper, a can of corn and another of spaghetti.

2. Brown 3 pounds of ground beef lightly, not too much, add a chopped onion, salt and pepper, a can of chili con carne, and 3 cans of kidney beans.

3. Brown a pound of ground beef and then just add a can of condensed vegetable soup or chicken gumbo or cream of chicken soup to season the meat and give it a Sloppy Joe texture. Serve the mixture in buns.

To finish off such a meal, if you've been blueberry picking, Pat says you can make a fine cobbler over an open fire. You just put the berries in a skillet with sugar and butter, then drop on top biscuits made with a mix, cover, and cook until "puffy and nice."

Marg McCarthy has a contribution to this kind of cooking. Her ten youngsters like this goulash: Cook 1 pound of small macaroni shells. Brown 2 pounds of hamburger and add two 1-pound jars of spaghetti sauce. Mix with the shells and serve hot.

CORNED BEEF WITH MUSTARD SAUCE

Ten to Twelve SERVINGS

Here's a genuine 14-karat gold-plated husband pleaser.

6–8 pounds corned beef brisket
2 cloves garlic
4 bay leaves
   Whole cloves
⅓ cup brown sugar, packed

1 tablespoon prepared mustard
⅓ cup catsup
3 tablespoons vinegar
3 tablespoons water

Roll and tie the corned beef, cover with water, and simmer with the garlic and bay leaves 5–6 hours, or until very tender.

Cool in the liquid. Drain (save that juice for other cooking, especially vegetables), stud the fat side with cloves, and cover with mustard sauce made by blending remaining ingredients. Bake uncovered in slow oven at 275° F., about an hour, basting occasionally with the sauce.

Rather have corned beef and cabbage? Then omit cloves and mustard sauce, and add a cabbage cut in wedges to the corned beef when cooked tender. Cook another 15 minutes, or until the cabbage is tender. Other vegetables such as turnips, onions, carrots and potatoes could be added earlier, for the last half hour of cooking. Slice corned beef very thin, across the grain.

WONDERFUL CORNED BEEF HASH: Grind some of the corned beef and all of the vegetables, on the second day, and bake or fry until browned.

ANCHOVY LEG OF VEAL

Twelve SERVINGS

Here's a pot roast of unusual distinction.

1 6-pound leg of veal
6 boned anchovies, sliced
1 clove garlic, sliced
   Salt, pepper
6 whole cloves
1 medium-size onion, sliced

1 bay leaf
¾ cup water
½ cup butter
   or margarine
¼ cup fine bread crumbs
½ cup heavy cream

248

Spit-Roasted Lamb, page 254

Trim and wipe leg of veal, make small incisions over surface, and fill with strips of anchovies and garlic. Sprinkle with salt and pepper, and stick with cloves. Place in roasting pan and put onion, bay leaf, water, and 1/4 cup butter around meat. Roast, covered, at 325° F. about 3 1/2 hours. Baste occasionally with liquid in pan. Turn meat over, dust with crumbs, dot with remaining 1/4 cup butter. Roast, uncovered, about 20 minutes longer, or until crumbs are browned, pouring cream over meat 10 minutes before removing from oven. Remove to hot platter. Strain liquid in pan, thicken if necessary, and serve with meat.

VEAL CURRY FOR THE BUFFET   *Ten* SERVINGS

This is a delicious curry, hot but not too hot.

2 1/2 pounds veal, cubed
1/4 cup drippings
3 medium onions, chopped fine
6 stalks celery, chopped fine
2 apples, minced
1/4 cup curry powder (use less if you prefer a mild curry)
2 cups well-seasoned meat stock or bouillon
1/4 cup molasses or brown sugar
1/2 teaspoon ginger
1/4 teaspoon black pepper
1 tablespoon Worcestershire sauce
1/2 teaspoon Tabasco sauce (or less)

Brown cubed meat in drippings. Add onions, celery, and apples; cover, and cook until meat is tender. Add curry powder to meat stock, simmer 5 minutes. Add molasses and remaining seasonings to meat mixture. Simmer gently 20 minutes. Serve with a big bowl of rice, and smaller dishes containing raisins, shredded fresh coconut, chopped, hard-cooked egg, chopped peanuts, and chutney.

Roast Turkey, page 204

VEAL AND NOODLE CASSEROLE Six SERVINGS

Lots of good flavor!

1½ pounds lean veal, cubed
1 small onion, diced
2 tablespoons butter
1½ teaspoons salt
¼ teaspoon pepper
½ cup water
1 package (8 ozs.) noodles, cooked

¼ pound mushrooms, sliced and sautéed
1 cup thinly sliced celery
⅔ cup sour cream
1 tablespoon flour
Buttered soft bread crumbs

Brown veal and onion in butter. Add salt, pepper, and water; cover and cook until meat is tender. Mix meat and drippings in pan with remaining ingredients except crumbs. Pour into a large casserole and cover with crumbs. Bake in a moderate oven (350° F.) for 40 minutes.

LIVER, COUNTRY STYLE   Six SERVINGS

It's baked in cream sauce with bacon.

6 slices bacon, cut in pieces
2 tablespoons flour
1 teaspoon salt
⅛ teaspoon pepper
2 cups milk
1 pound sliced beef or veal liver
¼ cup buttered bread crumbs

Fry bacon in heavy skillet until crisp. Remove bacon; add flour, salt, and pepper to drippings, stirring until smooth. Stir in the milk and cook until thick and smooth, stirring constantly. Roll liver slices in flour and brown in hot fat in another skillet. Place alternate layers of liver slices, bacon, and gravy in a buttered casserole. Top with buttered crumbs and bake at 350° F., about 45 minutes or until tender.

LIVER AND PINEAPPLE EN BROCHETTE

Chicken livers are delicious this way, too!

¾ pound veal liver
6 slices bacon
18 pineapple chunks

Cut liver and bacon into inch squares and alternate with pineapple on skewers, ending with bacon. Brush liver with butter or French dressing. Arrange skewers in slanting position on broiler pan so that bacon will baste liver as it cooks. Cook 10 to 12 minutes, turning several times to brown all around. Serve on skewers, or push off onto toast.

WIENER AND SAUERKRAUT SCALLOP

Niece Phyllis Ann likes this kind of country cooking, and I do, too!

1 pound wieners
1 can cream of mushroom soup
1 teaspoon caraway seed
1 can (1 lb.) sauerkraut
4 cups diced cooked potatoes
¼ teaspoon paprika
2 tablespoons butter, melted
½ cup soft bread crumbs or cornflake crumbs

Cut 5 wieners in bite-size pieces. Combine soup, caraway, and kraut. Add potatoes and wieners. Place in a 7x11x2-inch casserole. Combine paprika, melted butter, and bread crumbs and sprinkle over the top of the casserole. Bake at 350° F. about 25 minutes. Arrange remaining wieners on top of casserole and bake 10 minutes more.

ROAST LEG OF LAMB   *Twelve* SERVINGS

*Garlic and herbs are favorite seasonings for roast lamb. This
wonderful meat deserves to be more popular than it is. It
is succulent and flavorsome.*

    1 leg of lamb, about 6 pounds
      Salt, pepper
      Dried thyme (optional)
      Garlic (optional)

Rub leg of lamb with salt, pepper, and thyme; also with cut clove of
garlic, or garlic salt, if you wish. Or cut tiny slits in the meat and
insert slivers of garlic. Roast in the open pan, on a rack, at 325° F.
about 3 hours, or to 175° F. by your meat thermometer. Let stand
20 to 30 minutes in a warm place for easier carving.

SOME VARIATIONS

Lamb with Rosemary.   Rub dried rosemary or dried mint into meat
before roasting.

Glazed Lamb.   When lamb is ⅔ done brush with mixture of ½ cup
melted currant jelly, 2 teaspoons oregano, juice of 1 lemon, ½ clove
garlic, mashed (if garlic isn't used in meat earlier). Baste occasionally.
Skim off fat, and make gravy from drippings.

Sprigged Lamb.   Cut 25 or 30 slits in the meat and insert sprigs of
fresh parsley, mint, or watercress.

CURRIED LEFTOVER LAMB   *Four* SERVINGS

*This is one of my pet leftover dishes. Use the recipe with
veal, too.*

    2 cups sliced leftover lamb
    2 tablespoons butter
    1 tablespoon minced onion
    1 teaspoon curry powder (or more)
    2 tablespoons flour

252

2 apples, cut in small dice
1½ cups meat stock or bouillon

Brown lamb lightly in butter with onion. Add curry and flour and stir well. Add apples and stock. Cook and stir until sauce thickens and meat is thoroughly hot. Add salt and pepper, if necessary. Serve on cooked rice.

Good addition: A tablespoon of chopped preserved ginger and sirup or chopped chutney.

BARBECUED LEG OF LAMB   *Twelve* SERVINGS

Leftover slices can be heated in leftover sauce!

1 leg of lamb (about 6 pounds)
  Salt, pepper
1 cup catsup
⅓ cup honey
  Juice of 1 lemon (3 tablespoons)
1 tablespoon prepared mustard
½ teaspoon thyme
1 clove garlic
  Dash Tabasco
4 onions, sliced
  Salt, pepper

Wipe leg of lamb with damp cloth and sprinkle with salt and pepper. Place on rack in an open roasting pan and roast in slow oven, 325° F., allowing 30 to 35 minutes per pound.

In a saucepan, combine catsup, honey, lemon juice, mustard, thyme, garlic, Tabasco, sliced onions, and a little salt and pepper. Cook sauce over low heat until onions are nearly tender. Remove garlic. About an hour before lamb is done, remove from oven, take out rack, and pour off excess fat. Pour sauce over lamb in roasting pan. Return to oven and finish cooking, basting occasionally with sauce. Serve lamb on platter with barbecue sauce.

SPIT-ROASTED LAMB

*Indoors or out, lamb cooked this way is succulent and good.
Allow about ⅓ pound boneless meat per serving.*

Boned, rolled leg of lamb
Garlic
Salt, pepper
¼ cup sugar
¼ teaspoon cloves
½ teaspoon ginger
1 tablespoon lemon juice

Cut gashes here and there in the surface of the meat and insert garlic slivers. Rub into the roast a mixture of salt, pepper, sugar, spices, and lemon juice. Run spit through center of roast and anchor the clamps. Place on rotisserie. Insert a short meat thermometer in the roast (don't let it rest against the spit) and turn on the motor. Roast meat to 165° F., or allow about 25 minutes per pound, if you don't use a thermometer. If you like, brush meat occasionally with barbecue sauce as it turns.

Marinated Lamb. Instead of using the foregoing seasonings, place lamb in a small, deep dish for its size, and pour over it a combination of ⅓ cup oil, 1 cup red wine, a sliced onion, a bay leaf, a teaspoonful of peppercorns, a minced garlic clove, and some chopped parsley. Let stand overnight or for several hours. Turn once or twice in the marinade. Drain, wipe dry, rub with salt, and place on the rotisserie.

BAKED LAMB HASH   *Four* SERVINGS

Your family may enjoy this more than the original roast!

2 cups finely chopped or
    ground cooked lamb
½ cup finely diced
    raw potato
½ cup diced green pepper
1 small onion, minced
1 cup leftover lamb gravy

½ cup tomato sauce (canned)
Salt, pepper, paprika
1 teaspoon Worcestershire
    sauce
Grated Parmesan or Swiss
    cheese
Butter

Cook potatoes 10 minutes in water to cover, add pepper and onion, and cook about 5 minutes longer. Add to lamb with thick leftover gravy and tomato sauce. Adjust seasonings as necessary and add Worcestershire. Place in shallow greased platter or baking dish, cover with grated cheese and bits of butter, and broil until browned and hot. Hash can be bordered with hot mashed potatoes before going under the broiler, if you wish. Beat an egg yolk into the hot mashed potatoes and brush with butter. when you've made a border of them.

LAMB CURRY A LA MARY MEADE Six SERVINGS

"I must tell you how he proposed! I invited him over for dinner and served your lamb curry—only I put more curry powder in it than you do. He ate it to the last bite, put down his fork and said, 'Will you marry me?'" That is a true story, and this is the curry!

It is just right for the average curry lover—not too hot; not too mild.

2 pounds cubed lamb	1 tablespoon curry powder
2 teaspoons salt	3 cups hot lamb stock
1/8 teaspoon pepper	or bouillon
1/4 cup butter	Juice of 1 lemon
1 clove garlic, minced	1 slice lemon rind
3 small onions, minced	1 teaspoon sugar
1/4 cup oil or butter	1 tablespoon ginger sirup
2 medium apples, chopped	1 tablespoon chopped
1/4 cup flour	preserved ginger

Add salt and pepper to lamb. Brown in the 1/4 cup butter. In separate pan, sauté garlic and onion in oil or butter and add apples. Blend in flour and curry. Add hot stock and cook, stirring, until thickened. Add lemon juice, rind, sugar, ginger, and sirup. Blend well and pour over browned lamb in skillet. Simmer 1/2 hour. Serve with fluffy rice and curry condiments such as chutney, kumquats, chopped nuts, chopped parsley, chopped hard-cooked eggs, and pickle relish.

BARBECUED LAMB CHOPS   *Four* SERVINGS

Better yet cooked out of doors!

4 shoulder lamb chops,
   cut ½ inch thick
½ tablespoon fat
1 onion, diced
¼ cup vinegar
1 cup tomato juice
2 tablespoons brown sugar

2 tablespoons Worcestershire
   sauce
1 teaspoon dry mustard
½ cup water
¼ teaspoon chili powder
1 tablespoon paprika
⅛ teaspoon cayenne pepper
¼ cup catsup

Brown chops in hot fat. Remove chops from skillet and add all remaining ingredients to fat in skillet. Stir and cook until blended, about 2 minutes. Return lamb chops to the skillet and spoon barbecue sauce over the chops. Cover and simmer slowly, or bake at 350° F., about 1½ hours. Remove cover and cook 15 minutes more, spooning sauce over the chops. Serve hot over hot fluffy rice.

LAMB, ITALIAN STYLE   *Six* SERVINGS

It's really a delicious stew!

2 pounds lean stewing lamb,
   cubed
1 large onion, sliced thin
1 clove garlic, minced fine
¼ cup olive oil
½ cup flour

1½ teaspoons salt
½ teaspoon pepper
1 teaspoon paprika
6 ounce can tomato paste
2 cups warm water
Cooked rice

Cook onion and garlic slowly in olive oil until onion is light yellow, about five minutes. Remove from oil. Put flour, salt, pepper, and paprika into paper bag. Shake lamb cubes in flour-filled bag. Brown meat on all sides in oil. Return onion and garlic to pan and pour in tomato paste and water. Cover pan tightly; cook slowly about 1 hour. When meat is tender, serve over cooked rice.

LAMB CHOP AND FRUIT GRILL *Four* SERVINGS

To round out this dinner, serve creamed potatoes and buttered peas.

4 lamb loin or shoulder chops or 8 rib chops
4 slices canned pineapple
2 bananas, split lengthwise
  Butter, salt, paprika

Broil chops on one side, 6 or 7 minutes, season and turn. Brush pineapple slices and bananas well with butter and place on rack with chops to broil 6 or 7 minutes more. Turn fruit once during this time. Season second side of meat. Serve hot.

LAMB STEW *Twelve* SERVINGS

Make a big batch, so you can freeze some.

5 pounds lamb shoulder, boned and cut in cubes
  Flour
  Fat for browning
1 tablespoon salt
½ teaspoon pepper
½ teaspoon thyme
4 onions, sliced
12 carrots, cut in chunks

Dredge the lamb with flour and brown on all sides in fat. Season with salt, pepper, and thyme. Add onions. Add 2 cups water, cover, and simmer gently until meat is tender, adding carrots 10 or 15 minutes before you estimate the meat will be done. Don't overcook the carrots.

You may need to add more water from time to time. Turnips, peas, leeks, potatoes, celery, and cabbage are other vegetables that are suitable for a lamb stew. Whole small onions are attractive in stew of any kind

Freeze stews without potatoes.

257

NORWEGIAN LAMB AND CABBAGE

Eight SERVINGS

There's a lot of good flavor in this simple dish.

4 pounds lean lamb, in 2-inch cubes
2 medium heads cabbage, sliced
4 teaspoons salt
1 tablespoon whole black pepper
1/4 cup flour
2 cups water

Arrange alternate layers of lamb and cabbage in a lightly greased casserole, beginning and finishing with cabbage. Sprinkle seasonings and flour over each layer. Pour water over the top. Cover and cook at 325° F. for 2 hours, or at simmering on top of the range, for the same length of time. Serve with small parsley potatoes.

SHISH KEBAB

Four SERVINGS

Skewered lamb is popular indoors and out.

2 pounds boneless lamb shoulder, cut into 1 1/2-inch cubes
1/2 cup salad oil
2 tablespoons vinegar
2 tablespoons lemon juice
1 teaspoon dry mustard
1/8 teaspoon thyme
1 teaspoon salt
1/4 teaspoon pepper
1/2 grated onion
1 large tomato, quartered
2 medium green peppers, cut 1 1/2 inches square
8 large mushrooms

Blend salad oil, vinegar, lemon juice, seasonings, and grated onion. Add lamb cubes and let stand several hours or overnight in the refrigerator. Drain. Thread on each of four long metal skewers (12 inches long) a lamb cube, green pepper square, mushroom, lamb cube, tomato wedge, lamb cube, mushroom, green pepper square, lamb cube, and pepper square. Brush threaded skewers with marinade. Broil 3 inches from heat for 8 minutes. Turn and broil an additional 8 to 10 minutes, or until done. When cooking over glowing coals, brush with marinade several times and turn until brown and cooked, about 20 minutes in all.

VARIATIONS

Crush a clove of garlic with the salt in the marinade. Onions may be quartered and skewered, too. Red wine or sherry may be used in place of lemon juice and vinegar. A teaspoon of oregano could replace mustard and thyme.

BARBECUED PORK LOIN ROAST
Ten to Twelve SERVINGS

I'm in favor of this preliminary oven cooking. It simplifies the spit-roasting and gets you off to a good start.

1 6-pound rolled boneless pork loin
3 cloves garlic
7 peppercorns
1 teaspoon salt
1 teaspoon cumin seed
1 tablespoon oregano
Barbecue Sauce (see below)

Crush together the garlic, peppers, salt, cumin, and oregano and rub into the meat. Place roast on rotisserie spit and put it in a shallow roasting pan. Roast at 350° F. for 1 hour. Meanwhile, build a charcoal fire and let the coals burn down to a gray ash. When fire is ready, transfer roast to rotisserie. Turn on motor and cook about 4 hours more, basting now and then with Barbecue Sauce.

BARBECUE SAUCE: Sauté in 2 tablespoons oil 1 large chopped onion, 3 minced cloves garlic, 1 chopped green pepper. Add 2 cans tomato paste and then fill the emptied cans with water and add that. Add 2 cups canned tomatoes (1 can), 2 tablespoons chili powder, 1 teaspoon mustard, 1½ teaspoons oregano, 2 tablespoons vinegar, 2 tablespoons brown sugar or molasses, 1 teaspoon Worcestershire, ¼ teaspoon Tabasco sauce, 4 whole cloves, 4 peppercorns, and a bay leaf. Simmer over low heat for 45 minutes.

Or use a spicy, bottled barbecue sauce, or the one on page 202 or page 240.

PORK CHOP AND CORN SKILLET Six SERVINGS

Doesn't this combination sound typically mid-western? It's an Iowa-Illinois dish, and mighty good.

6 rib or loin pork chops,
   cut 1 inch thick
¼ cup hot water
1½ teaspoons salt
⅛ teaspoon pepper
½ teaspoon thyme

2 cans (1 lb. each)
   whole-kernel corn
Salt, pepper
6 tablespoons chili sauce
6 dill pickle slices

Brown chops slowly in hot skillet. Add water, salt, pepper, and thyme. Cover and simmer for 40 minutes. Remove chops from skillet and put the corn into it. Sprinkle lightly with salt and pepper. Place the chops on top of the corn and crown each chop with a tablespoonful of chili sauce and a pickle slice. Cover skillet and continue cooking for about 10 minutes.

BAKED STUFFED PORK CHOPS Six SERVINGS

There are many ways to stuff a pork chop—this is only one.

6 double thick pork chops with
   pockets cut for stuffing
2 tablespoons butter
1 onion, chopped fine
2 tablespoons celery
2 tablespoons chopped
   green pepper

1 teaspoon salt
¼ teaspoon pepper
2½ cups bread crumbs
Water or stock to
   moisten dressing

Cook onion, celery, and green pepper in butter until lightly browned. Add crumbs, and sprinkle with water to barely dampen. Season with salt and pepper. Fill pockets in chops and brown chops in hot fat. Add ¼ cup water or stock to pan and season the chops with salt and pepper. Cover and bake at 350° F. for an hour.

Glamour treatment: Put a slice or a half-slice of pineapple on each chop (maybe a slice of onion, too) and use pineapple juice instead of water in the pan.

PORK CHOP DINNER   *Four* SERVINGS

Make a batch of muffins, a salad, a pot of coffee.

    4 thick pork chops
    1 quart pared, sliced potatoes
    ½ cup diced green pepper
    1 cup diced celery
    1 cup sliced onion
    2 teaspoons salt
      Pepper
    1 can condensed tomato soup
    ½ cup water
      Dash Tabasco sauce

Brown chops in skillet and remove from pan. Arrange vegetables in layers in deep 2-quart skillet, sprinkling each layer with some of the salt and pepper. Put brown chops on top and season. Combine soup, water, and Tabasco; pour over meat, cover, and cook gently for 1–1½ hours. Or bake the same length of time at 325° F.

SPARERIBS AND SAUERKRAUT   *Six* SERVINGS

You can't beat this combination for a savory country dinner!

    4 pounds or 2 sides spareribs
    1 quart sauerkraut, or a No. 2½ can (3½ cups)
    1 apple, chopped (optional)
    2 tablespoons brown sugar (optional)
    1 tablespoon caraway seeds
    1 onion, sliced
      Salt, pepper for ribs
    2 cups water

Cut ribs into serving-size portions and brown them under the broiler. Pour off fat. Place kraut mixed with apple, sugar, caraway, and onion in a kettle. Season ribs and place on top. Pour water around the meat and kraut. Cover tight and simmer for 1¼ hours, or until ribs are very tender.

SWEET-SOUR PORK   *Six* SERVINGS

You can't make a mistake in choosing this dish for a com-
pany dinner. I don't know anyone who doesn't love it.

2 pounds lean pork shoulder,
    cut in 2 x ½-inch strips
¼ cup flour
½ teaspoon salt
¼ teaspoon pepper
2 tablespoons drippings
½ cup water
2 tablespoons cornstarch

¼ cup brown sugar
¼ cup vinegar
1 tablespoon soy sauce
1 can (1 lb. 4½ ozs.)
    pineapple chunks
1 green pepper cut in julienne
    strips
1 small onion, sliced thin

Dredge meat in seasoned flour and brown well in drippings. Add water,
cover pan, and simmer for an hour. Combine cornstarch and sugar. Add
vinegar, soy sauce, and juice drained from pineapple. Cook on low heat,
stirring constantly until mixture is thick and clear. Pour sauce over
meat. Add pineapple, green pepper, and onion. Heat through. Serve
over cooked noodles or rice.

BARBECUED SPARERIBS   *Twelve to Fourteen* SERVINGS

There are many excellent ready-made barbecue sauces which
you may use instead of this one, but I think you'll like this
sauce very much. It is good on other meats, as well.

    About 9 pounds spareribs, preferably back ribs
½ cup vinegar
2 tablespoons Worcestershire sauce
    Juice of ½ lemon (1½ tablespoons)
1 teaspoon salt
⅛ teaspoon pepper
¾ cup brown sugar

1 cup chopped onion
1 sliver garlic, minced
1 cup water or stock
1 cup chili sauce
   Paprika, Tabasco sauce

Cut the ribs into serving portions and cover with boiling, salted water. Bring to a boil, then reduce heat, cover kettle, and simmer ribs until almost tender, about 1 hour. Drain and place in baking pans or over low coals of a charcoal fire. Bake at 350° F., or grill, turning once or twice. If you bake the ribs, pour the sauce over them first; if you grill, use it to baste. Half an hour more in the oven or on the grill should brown and tenderize the ribs.

Make the sauce by mixing all ingredients and simmering 20 to 25 minutes. Thin it with water or red wine if it becomes too thick.

SQUAW CORN   *Eight* SERVINGS

There are many variations of this dish which was always a favorite in the days when I went for breakfast hikes in the early morning. It's a good indoor luncheon, but I think it tastes better around a campfire.

1 pound bacon or bulk sausage
12 eggs
2 cans cream style corn
1 or 2 onions, sliced or chopped (optional)
   Salt, pepper

Cook the bacon or sausage in a skillet over hot coals, then pour off most of the fat (not into the fire!). If you use onion, push the meat aside when partly cooked and sauté the onion in the fat. Then stir in madly the eggs and corn. Scramble well, season to taste, and serve piping hot! Diced cheese, chopped green pepper, chunks of raw tomato may be added.

PORK TENDERLOIN SUPREME   *Six* SERVINGS

Here is one of the most appealing ways to serve this delicacy which is the gourmet's choice of pork.

12 slices bacon
 6 pork tenderloin patties
    Salt, pepper
 6 thick slices tomato
 6 slices onion

Cross 2 slices bacon and place a tenderloin patty in the center. Sprinkle with salt and pepper. Place a slice of tomato on the patty, season, and top with a slice of onion. Add more salt and pepper. Bring the bacon ends up over the onion and fasten with toothpicks or skewers. Place patties in baking pan and cover. Bake 30 minutes at 350° F. Uncover and bake 30 minutes more.

PORK TENDERLOIN   *Four* SERVINGS
WITH SOUR CREAM

Fruit stuffing and cream gravy make an epicure's dream of the meat.

 2 pork tenderloins, about 1 pound each
1½ teaspoons salt
 ¼ teaspoon pepper
 6 cooked prunes, pitted
 2 tart apples, pared, cored, chopped
 2 tablespoons butter
 1 cup sour cream
 1 cup sweet cream

Cut tenderloins half through lengthwise, open and pound flat. Season with salt and pepper. Place prunes and apples on one piece of meat and top with the second. Tie with string in several places. Brown on both sides in butter in a heavy skillet. Blend sour and sweet cream and pour over meat. Cover and simmer for about 1 hour.

264

KALUA PIG

The Commodores, a Hi-Y group of lads, have twice dug a pit in our back yard in the city to roast a pig for a luau. The graduation party brought out more than sixty boys and girls. A luau on the farm would be easier, but if you don't mind having your lawn dug up, you can have one in town. It will be the most memorable party you've ever given! It takes work, but that's part of the fun. Here's how it goes.

The first step is to acquire a pig, a collection of rocks, some wood for a wood fire, chicken wire, and a dozen or so gunny sacks. You'll also need some fresh green branches, so I hope your shrubbery needs trimming. Then you'll need a crew for digging a pit 3 or more feet on a side, or wide enough and deep enough to take a lining of rocks and accommodate the pig. Dig it deep, for the pig will be covered with dirt or sand in his underground oven.

The pit should be dug the afternoon before or the early morning of the feast. Line it with rocks, then build a wood fire in the pit and keep it burning for several hours, to heat the rocks. Meanwhile, heat smaller rocks in the wood fire or in your oven, to put inside the piggy.

Rub the pig well with the seasonings you like. We used salt, pepper, and half a jar of dried powdered orange peel for one of the pigs, which weighed 35 or 40 pounds. Onions were placed in the body cavity, then small, very hot rocks. An overwrap of heavy-duty foil keeps the pig clean in his pit. When the rock oven is ready, put the pig on a length of chicken wire long enough to afford leverage for getting him out of the pit. Put some small branches or corn husks on the hot stones, place the pig on his wire bed in the pit, cover with more leaves, and pour a quart or more of water into the pit to generate steam. Cover the pig and leaves with wet gunny sacks and a tarpaulin, if you have it, then shovel dirt or sand back over the pig and forget him for at least 6 hours (if a small pig), preferably for 7 or 8 hours. If any steam comes from the pit, shovel on more dirt to keep it in. Be sure you've left the ends of the chicken wire out so that when you uncover the pig, you can lift him out easily.

Whole sweet potatoes, bananas, and corn may be cooked in the underground oven at the same time.

Opening the pit and serving the pig is the highlight of your party. What a clambake!

SAUSAGE-PINEAPPLE STACKS   *Four* SERVINGS

*Add a tomato slice and cheese to each stack, maybe a slice
of onion, too, if you'd turn a stack into a tower.*

1 pound bulk pork sausage
4 slices canned pineapple
  Prepared mustard

Form sausage into four patties a little larger than the pineapple slices.
Partly cook in a skillet, browning lightly on both sides. Spread pine-
apple with mustard and lay a sausage patty on each slice. Bake at 350°
F. for 30 minutes, basting occasionally with pineapple sirup.

JULE'S HAM LOAF AND   *Twelve* SERVINGS
NEXT-DAY CASSEROLE

*Dinner at the Wilkinsons' is always memorable, for Jule is
an excellent cook. This ham loaf is one of her specialties.*

2 pounds ham	½ cup chopped onion
2 pounds fresh pork	¼ cup salad oil
1 cup cornflake crumbs	¼ cup chili sauce
2 eggs, beaten	¼ cup light cream
¼ cup chopped green pepper	1 teaspoon prepared mustard
½ cup sliced celery	

Have meats ground together. Mix with cornflake crumbs and eggs.
Sauté the vegetables for a few minutes in the oil and add. Add remaining ingredients, mix well, and pack into two loaf pans. Bake at
350° F. for about 1½ hours.

Now for the casserole, which Jule makes out of whatever is left
of the ham loaf. "Ideally I have at least a pound of the loaf, and I break
or cut it into bite-size pieces, adding 2 packages of elbow macaroni,
cooked, a can of tomato soup, a can of mushroom soup, and a canful
of milk. Then I mix in ½ pound sharp Cheddar cheese, cut in small
chunks. The mixture may be topped with crumbs or not. Bake it 45
minutes at 350° F. It's better every time it's warmed up!"

HAM AND GREEN TOMATOES   *Four* SERVINGS

Serve plain whipped potatoes with this prize-winning combination.

1 slice ham, ¾ inch thick
1 tablespoon drippings
4 medium green tomatoes, sliced ¼ inch thick
2 medium onions, sliced ¼ inch thick
1 tablespoon Worcestershire sauce
¼ cup brown sugar
½ teaspoon salt
¼ teaspoon pepper

Brown ham in drippings on both sides. Place in casserole and top with tomatoes and onions. Sprinkle seasonings on vegetables. Cover and bake at 350° F. for 40 minutes.

HAM, GREEN BEAN, AND   *Six to Eight* SERVINGS
MUSHROOM CASSEROLE

A savory meal!

1 pound fresh mushrooms, sliced, sautéed in ¼ cup butter
⅓ cup flour
3 cups milk and cream
  Salt
⅛ teaspoon white pepper
1 pound green beans, cut in 2-inch pieces, cooked
3 cups cooked ham, cut in strips
⅓ cup pimiento, cut in strips
  Grated cheese

Add flour to sautéed mushrooms, blend and add milk and cream. Cook until thickened. Stir in seasonings. Blend sauce with beans, ham, and pimiento, and turn into a 2-quart casserole. Top with grated cheese. Bake at 350° F. for 20 minutes.

HAM, MACARONI, AND CHEESE CASSEROLE

Six to Eight SERVINGS

Together with a salad of sliced summer tomatoes, this cas-serole makes a hearty and delicious lunch or supper. Mighty nutritious, too!

7 ounces elbow macaroni
3 tablespoons chopped onion
2 tablespoons butter
1/4 cup flour
1/2 teaspoon mustard
1 teaspoon salt

1/8 teaspoon pepper
2 cups milk
1 cup shredded sharp Cheddar cheese
2 cups cooked cubed ham
Buttered crumbs

Cook macaroni according to package directions. Sauté onion lightly in butter, stir in flour, mustard, salt, and pepper; then add milk. Cook and stir to smooth sauce. Add cheese and stir until cheese melts. Add cooked macaroni and ham to sauce, turn into a buttered 2-quart cas-serole, and top with crumbs. Bake at 350° F. for 45 minutes.

HAM POLYNESIAN

Six SERVINGS

"I serve this at almost every party, and there's never been a complaint!" says Phyllis Ann Lovrien.

3 cups cooked ham, cut in pieces
2 tablespoons butter
1 can (13 ozs.) pineapple tidbits
2 medium green peppers, cut in strips

1/2 cup brown sugar
2 tablespoons cornstarch
1/2 cup vinegar
1/2 cup chicken bouillon
2 teaspoons soy sauce
3 cups cooked rice

Brown the ham pieces lightly in butter. Add pineapple with sirup and green pepper strips. Cover and simmer 15 minutes. Mix brown sugar and cornstarch, add vinegar, bouillon, and soy sauce. Add to ham mix-ture and stir until thickened. Serve over hot rice.

OLD-FASHIONED BEAN SOUP WITH HAM BONE
Three QUARTS

With fruit salad and cornbread, you'll have a fine supper.

1 pound navy beans
3 quarts water
1 ham bone
½ cup chopped green pepper
1 cup chopped celery
2 cups diced, pared potatoes

1 medium onion, chopped
3 carrots, sliced
1 tablespoon salt
¼ teaspoon pepper
1 cup tomato juice

Simmer beans in water with ham bone for 2 hours. Add other in-gredients and simmer 2 hours longer or until beans are tender.

HAM SALAD
Six SERVINGS

Radishes replace the usual celery in this salad—a pleasing variation.

3 cups cubed, cooked ham (about 1 lb. cut into ½-inch cubes)
15 radishes, sliced thin
8 sweet pickles, sliced thin
2 hard-cooked eggs, chopped
½ cup Cooked Salad Dressing (page 327)
½ cup mayonnaise
1 teaspoon prepared mustard
½ teaspoon salt,
¼ teaspoon pepper
Hard-cooked egg slices

Combine ham, radishes, pickles, and chopped hard-cooked eggs. Blend salad dressing and mayonnaise, then season with mustard, salt, and pepper. Stir salad ingredients into dressing. Pile salad into lettuce cups placed in individual bowls or large serving platter. Garnish each serving with hard-cooked egg slices.

MACARONI, CHEESE, AND BACON CASSEROLE

Four SERVINGS

This dish is a pet of niece Phyllis Ann. It has lots of flavor.

½ pound bacon
1 can (2 ozs.) mushroom
    stems and pieces
1 cup macaroni, cooked
1 cup grated Cheddar cheese
½ cup sour cream
¼ cup milk

2 tablespoons chopped
    green peppers
1 tablespoon chopped pimiento
1 teaspoon Worcestershire
    sauce
½ teaspoon onion salt
1/16 teaspoon pepper

Heat oven to 350° F. Cook bacon crisp; drain and crumble. Combine all ingredients, place in a 1½-quart casserole, and bake 30 minutes.

HOT MEAT-FILLED BUNS

Twelve SERVINGS

For picnics and teen-age parties, these meat-and-cheese-filled frankfurter buns are just great. They can be fixed ahead of time and warmed in the oven or on a grill. Use chopped left-over roast beef or other meat if you prefer it to the canned luncheon meat.

1 can (12 ozs.) luncheon meat, chopped fine
¼ cup chopped onion
1 medium green pepper, chopped fine
2 tablespoons catsup
1 cup Cheddar cheese
2 tablespoons milk
2 tablespoons chopped sweet pickle
¼ cup melted butter or margarine
12 frankfurter buns, split, buttered

Combine ingredients (it is easy to put meat, onion, and green pepper through the food grinder, if you have one). Spread between the halves of buns. Scoop out some of the bun to make room for filling, if you wish. Wrap prepared buns in foil and heat at 300° F. for about 20 minutes. Or heat over a charcoal fire, turning the wrapped buns several times.

Strays & Oddballs

THERE ARE ALWAYS LEFTOVERS and misfits in a cook book. They are recipes that don't fit into any of your main categories, but they are ones you want to include. I could have put the venison with the beef recipes, I suppose, but where would I put the egg, cheese and rice dishes that aren't meat, but are good, substantial protein food?

This handful of recipes represents the oddballs. But don't ignore them because they are few. They are also among the very best dishes in this book, or I wouldn't have found a special little section for them.

RAGOUT OF ELK or VENISON

This is a good way to cook game when you don't know the age of the animal. A ragout is just a stew, but it sounds more gourmet-ish, and this is a gourmet's dish.

2 pounds elk, venison, or moose
    meat, cut in 2-inch cubes
2 cups Burgundy or other
    red table wine
¼ cup bacon or salt pork
    or ham fat
1 onion, chopped fine
    Pinch of thyme and
    a bay leaf

½ teaspoon freshly ground
    black pepper
1 teaspoon (or more) salt
1 tablespoon finely cut bacon
1 cup beef stock
1 dozen small white onions
1 dozen medium mushrooms,
    cooked in butter
1 tablespoon minced parsley

Cover meat with wine and refrigerate 24 hours. Remove meat from wine, wipe dry, and brown in hot fat on all surfaces. Add onion, seasonings, bacon, stock, and the wine used for marinade. Cover and simmer gently until meat is tender, about 2 hours, adding onions for the last hour. Serve garnished with mushrooms and sprinkled with parsley. Liquid may be thickened with a little cornstarch mixed to a paste in cold water, if you wish.

POT ROAST OF VENISON   *Eight* SERVINGS

Somehow I never can think of cooking venison without red wine. This method is a good one for any game—elk, moose, raccoon, woodchuck, or rabbit, to name several possibilities.

4-pound round or
    shoulder roast of venison
Oil or drippings
Flour, salt, pepper
Mixed salad herbs
2 or 3 onions

1 bay leaf
    A few sprigs of parsley
2 cups Burgundy or other
    red table wine
    Bacon strips

If possible, have the roast larded. This is a process whereby strips of fat salt pork are drawn through the meat with a larding needle. It is difficult to do at home; your meat dealer may be willing to do it.

Larded or not, heat about ¼-inch of oil or drippings in a dutch oven or deep, heavy skillet. Flour, salt, and pepper the meat generously and brown it all around. Season with herbs. Add onions, bay leaf, and parsley to pan. Pour in 1 cup of the wine and cover the pot. Simmer gently 3 or 4 hours, until meat is very tender, adding the other cup of wine at some middle point of cooking. If you haven't had the meat larded, put strips of bacon over it as it cooks.

VENISON ROAST, WINE GRAVY

Cousin Clark has always been a great hunter and Helen is used to cooking venison roasts and steaks and making deer-burgers of the trimmings. But somehow the deer on our hill, who troop down through the snow to find something to eat in the orchard, are too beautiful to kill. This recipe and the others are for venison from some other hill than ours.

1 leg of venison
    Marinade: Combine 1½ cups Burgundy (California),
        1½ teaspoons ginger, 2 teaspoons salt, ½ teaspoon pepper,
        1 minced garlic clove, 1 minced medium onion.
    Strips of bacon or fat salt pork
½ glass currant jelly

Trim the venison, removing any dry pieces, skin, and fat. Wipe meat with a damp cloth. Prepare the marinade and pour over meat. Cover, and refrigerate overnight. Turn the meat in the sauce several times. Drain well, saving the marinade.

Place venison in roasting pan and cover surface with strips of bacon or salt pork. Pour ½-cup water into the pan. Roast uncovered in a hot oven, 450° F., for 20 to 30 minutes, until meat is nicely browned, then turn heat down to 400° F. and pour part of the marinade over the meat. Roast until tender, allowing about 20 minutes to the pound and basting at intervals. Skim and discard excess fat from pan juices. Add jelly to sauce and serve with meat.

RABBIT COOKED WITH BEER

Four to Six SERVINGS

This recipe works best with wild rabbit. Domestic rabbit may be cooked in any favorite way for chicken.

1 rabbit, cut in pieces
Salt, pepper
½ teaspoon oregano
2 eggs
1 cup beer

½ cup flour
1 cup fine dry crumbs
1 cup shortening or oil
    for frying

Rub each piece of rabbit with salt, pepper, and oregano. Beat eggs and stir in half the beer. Dip rabbit into flour, then into egg mixture, and roll each piece in crumbs. Heat shortening in a large heavy skillet and brown the rabbit well in the hot fat. Pour off any excess fat. Add rest of beer, turn down heat to simmering, and cover. Cook over low heat for about an hour or until rabbit is very tender.

MOTHER CHURCH'S RICE AND NUT LOAF

You'd swear there was meat in this loaf, but there isn't a smidgen!

2 cups cooked rice
1 cup chopped walnuts
1 cup thick tomato purée or tomato sauce
2 medium onions, chopped fine
1 cup cracker crumbs
2 tablespoons oil or bacon fat
½ teaspoon sage
2 tablespoons chopped celery
1 tablespoon chopped parsley
1 teaspoon salt
Pepper

Combine ingredients and bake in a 350° F. oven for 1 hour. Serve with tomato sauce.

JO'S MOM'S CHEESE SPREAD   *Two* CUPS

*This is a favorite lunch, spread on rye bread and served with
soup, says Jo Will.*

½ pound Cheddar cheese
 3 hard-cooked eggs
 1 small onion, peeled
¼ cup mayonnaise
 1 tablespoon prepared mustard
   Salt, pepper
¼ teaspoon Worcestershire sauce
   Dash of Tabasco sauce

Put cheese through food grinder, using medium fine blade. Do the
same with eggs and onion. Then put a cracker through to clean the
grinder; it goes right into the mixture. Add mayonnaise, mustard,
and seasonings. Cover and refrigerate. It improves on standing.

SPANISH RICE   *Six* SERVINGS

*Spanish Rice is a family favorite. I sometimes use the bigger
can of tomatoes.*

  2 slices bacon, diced and fried
  1 cup raw rice
  2 cups canned tomatoes (1-lb. can)
  2 medium onions, chopped
  1 green pepper, chopped
2½ cups boiling water
  1 teaspoon salt (more if needed)
 ½ teaspoon chili powder (optional)
 ¼ teaspoon pepper

Add rice to bacon and sauté until lightly browned. Add other ingredients, cover closely, and cook until rice is tender and has absorbed excess
moisture, about 45 minutes. A small can of button mushrooms may be
added.

275

WELSH RABBIT   *Four to Six* SERVINGS

The genuine rabbit is greedy with cheese!

1 pound sharp, aged Cheddar cheese
1 teaspoon butter
1 cup ale, beer, or milk or cream
1 teaspoon dry mustard
   Paprika, or few grains cayenne
6 slices hot toast or split toasted English muffins

Cut cheese into small pieces and place in top of double boiler in which butter has been melted. As cheese melts, gradually add liquid, stirring constantly. Add seasonings. As soon as cheese has melted, serve. This bunny won't wait. If rabbit and a salad compose your meal, 4 persons can eat this mixture. It's especially good over sliced tomatoes on toast.

VARIATIONS

Anchovy Rabbit. Spread anchovy paste over the toast before pouring the cheese.

Blushing Bunny or Tomato Rabbit. Use a can of condensed tomato soup for the liquid.

Bean Rabbit. Cover hot toast with hot canned or home-baked beans, and add the cheese sauce.

Golden Buck. Place a freshly poached egg on each serving of rabbit, and garnish, if desired, with crisp bacon strips or thin slices of fried ham.

Sardine Rabbit. Lay heated sardines over the toast before adding the sauce, or put the fish on top, if you'd rather.

Sauterne or Sherry Rabbit. For the liquid use equal parts cream and wine.

Oyster Rabbit. Cut-up fresh or canned oysters (drained well) are cooked right in the cheese sauce. You'll need to add a little salt.

Dried beef, shrimp, or ripe olives are some of the other things you can add to a rabbit to change its name and character.

CHEESE CUSTARD PIE   *Eight* SERVINGS

Serve this wonderfully good pie as main course for luncheon or supper.

½ pound bacon, cut into small pieces
½ pound process Swiss cheese, grated
½ pound process American cheese, grated
4 eggs, beaten slightly
2 cups milk
1 teaspoon salt
1 teaspoon Worcestershire sauce
1 tablespoon grated onion
  Speck cayenne pepper
  Pastry-lined 10-inch pie plate

Cook bacon crisp, pour off fat, and sprinkle bacon over pie shell. Sprinkle the 2 kinds of cheese over the bacon. Blend eggs with milk and seasonings, and carefully pour over cheese. Bake at 450° F. for 15 minutes; reduce heat to 300° F. and bake 35 to 40 minutes longer, or until set. Let stand 10 minutes before cutting.

CHEESE-RICE LOAF   *Eight to Ten* SERVINGS

It's a flavorsome, custardy mixture that slices neatly.

2 cups milk
¼ cup butter or margarine
6 eggs, slightly beaten
1 cup soft bread crumbs
3 cups cooked rice

3 cups grated Cheddar cheese
2 teaspoons minced onion
2 teaspoons minced parsley
1 teaspoon minced green pepper
2 teaspoons salt

Heat milk with butter until butter is melted. Combine with eggs and blend well. Add remaining ingredients and mix. Turn into large, well-greased loaf pan. Set in pan of hot water and bake at 350° F. about 1 hour or until firm. Serve with tomato sauce.

SWISS BAKED EGGS   *Four* SERVINGS

They're delightful for late Sunday breakfast or lunch.

       4 1-ounce portions process Gruyère cheese, shredded
4 or 8 eggs
            Salt, pepper, sprinkle of nutmeg
½–⅔ cup evaporated milk or cream

Sprinkle ¾ of the cheese over bottom of a well-buttered shallow baking dish or individual bakers. Break eggs, being careful not to break yolks, and place one at a time over cheese. Sprinkle with salt, pepper, and nutmeg. Pour evaporated milk or cream over eggs. Sprinkle with remaining cheese. Bake at 350° F. until egg whites are set, about 15 minutes. Serve immediately.

PARTY EGG MOLD   *Six* SERVINGS

*Attractive and delicious; it is definitely worth making for
a summer luncheon.*

       6 hard-cooked eggs
       2 tablespoons mayonnaise
       6 anchovies, minced
       1 teaspoon tarragon vinegar
     ¼ teaspoon pepper
       1 tablespoon plain gelatin
     ¼ cup cold water
1½ cups well-seasoned chicken broth
     ¼ cup dry white wine

Cut eggs lengthwise and remove yolks. Mash yolks and mix with mayonnaise, anchovies, vinegar, and pepper. Fill whites with mixture and arrange halves, cut side up, in a shallow ring mold. Soften gelatin in cold water. Dissolve in hot soup. Add wine; pour over eggs and chill until firm.

278

From GARDEN
and ORCHARD

IF IT WERE left to me to plant a garden, I confess I
would not; my gardening would consist in gathering the
bounty Nature bestows upon us—the wild asparagus, the
abundance of wild grapes, elderberries, hazel nuts, hickory
nuts, plums, and apples—and shopping in the fresh-produce
departments of the supermarket six miles away. But my family has been smiled upon by fortune: the cousins who live
within a stone's throw of our country cottage garden like
mad all summer long, and since they plant enough to feed
the Army, the Air Force, the Navy, and the Marines, they
are constantly begging us to do something with the cucumbers, the tomatoes, the watermelons, and the beans. There
are times when we think we can't look another cucumber
in the eye—and then we find a couple of bushels on our
doorstep! We've learned, however, that summer guests love
to be organized into a pickle-making crew. Some wash the

279

cucumbers, others slice. Someone (me!) gets the pickling
sirup boiling, and before we know it we have three or four
dozen quarts of pickles sitting there looking beautiful! Then
we all go for a swim to cool off and rejoice in the new
load on the basement shelves. Those pickles will taste mighty
good by Christmas!

Vegetables

ANY VEGETABLE FRESH from the garden—new peas, baby carrots, tiny beets, young snap beans, curly Swiss chard, sweet corn— is naturally sweet and tender. There is so much flavor present that the simplest form of cooking usually is the best. I remember a time when Cousin Helen came running over with a panful of hot green beans. We had not had supper; her family had eaten.

"We've devoured all the beans we could, and they tasted so de-licious we thought you ought to have the rest of them. They're straight from the garden, they're still hot, and they're *swimming* in butter!"

Whereupon we sat down and made a meal of those crisp, buttery beans. It was all we wanted. They had one hundred times the flavor of beans which have sat around in the market even for a few hours.

But the times we can eat vegetables that fresh are rare, and we need to compensate for loss of flavor by adding sundry seasonings. For-tunately there are many ways to make vegetables more appealing, and I think I have chosen some good ones for you. Begin with the freshest vegetables possible (sometimes frozen ones are the freshest!), undercook them rather than overcook them, and serve them very hot, or possibly very cold. Often the success of a meal depends upon its vegetables.

ASPARAGUS AND HAM ROLLS   *Four* SERVINGS

The O'Donnells, who go to the country with us so much, are great at spotting places where the wild asparagus grows most abundantly. In May we find enough to freeze, along the lane and at the edge of the woods. We usually just cook it and eat it with butter, salt and pepper, or cream it. But there are many other good ways to fix fresh asparagus, and we never tire of it, because good old Mom Nature shuts off the supply just it time!

      4 slices baked or boiled ham
    20 stalks cooked or canned asparagus
      1 cup Medium White Sauce (see below)
    ½ cup grated sharp cheese

Roll 5 stalks of asparagus in a slice of ham and place rolls on a heat-proof platter, side by side. Pour the hot White Sauce over the rolls, sprinkle with cheese, and broil or bake at 400° F. until hot and lightly browned. Beat into the sauce the yolk of an egg or 2 tablespoons of mayonnaise, if you'd like it to be puffy. You know, of course, that you should break off asparagus stalks at the point where they snap. The stalk below that point tends to be woody.

MEDIUM WHITE SAUCE.   Blend 2 tablespoons flour, ¼ teaspoon salt, 2 tablespoons butter. Add 1 cup milk and cook and stir to a smooth sauce.

ASPARAGUS LOAF (SOUFFLE)   *Eight* SERVINGS

Lovely when turned out to show a pattern of asparagus and pimiento.

      2 cups cooked or 1 can green asparagus tips
      1 pimiento, cut in strips
      5 eggs, separated
    1½ cups Thick White Sauce (see next page)
    ¼ teaspoon salt

282

Line greased shallow pan with asparagus tips. Garnish with pimiento strips. Beat egg yolks until thick and lemon colored, and add to White Sauce. Fold in egg whites, beaten stiff. Pour over asparagus. Set pan in another pan of hot water, and bake at 350° F. about 45 minutes. Unmold on platter and pour melted butter over loaf.

THICK WHITE SAUCE: Melt 6 tablespoons butter, add 6 tablespoons flour, ½ teaspoon salt, 1½ cups milk. Stir and cook.

ASPARAGUS CUSTARD   *Six* SERVINGS

Broccoli also is delicious prepared this way.

3 eggs, beaten	1 teaspoon grated lemon rind
2 cups milk	Dash of nutmeg
1½ cups cooked or canned	½ teaspoon salt
asparagus, cut in pieces	¼ teaspoon pepper
2 tablespoons melted butter	

Combine ingredients, pour into a greased baking dish; set in a pan of hot water. Bake at 350° F. about 50 minutes, or until set.

SCHNITZEL BEANS   *Six* SERVINGS

A favorite vegetable is delightfully different prepared thus.

4 strips bacon, chopped
2 medium onions, chopped fine
1 pound green beans, cut diagonally into 1-inch pieces
3 tomatoes, skinned and chopped
1 teaspoon salt
¼ teaspoon pepper
⅓ cup water

Fry bacon until crisp and remove from pan. Add onions and sauté 5 minutes. Add beans, tomatoes, seasonings, and water. Cover, bring to boiling point, then lower heat and cook 15 minutes. Add bacon.

GREEN BEANS IN SOUR CREAM *Four* SERVINGS

These are divine!

1 pound cooked green beans, slivered
1 medium onion, chopped
2 tablespoons parsley, chopped
2 tablespoons butter or margarine
1 tablespoon flour
1 teaspoon each, sugar, vinegar
½ teaspoon salt
⅛ teaspoon pepper
½ cup thick sour cream

Sauté onion and parsley in butter and stir in flour. Add ½ cup liquid from beans to flour paste and cook, stirring constantly, until thick-ened. Add sugar, vinegar, salt, pepper, and sour cream. Pour over beans and serve.

SWEET-SOUR GREEN BEANS   *Six* SERVINGS

An old-country favorite, and one of the most delicious ways to serve beans.

1 pound green beans
4 slices bacon, cooked crisp
1 small onion, chopped fine
¾ cup cooking water from beans, or stock
¼ cup vinegar or lemon juice
2 tablespoons sugar
  Salt, pepper

Cook beans covered in small amount of water until barely tender. Sauté onion in bacon fat after removing bacon from skillet. Add liquids, sugar, and seasonings. Add beans and crumbled bacon.

GREEN BEAN BAKE
Twelve SERVINGS

One of the most successful of all green bean dishes is this one, which has half a dozen variations, all of them enticing. This recipe is of a size to take care of an outdoor-cooking crowd. It can be doubled or tripled for a really large party, and you can substitute artichoke hearts or green lima beans for some of the green beans. Canned mushrooms will do if you don't have fresh ones. It's a recipe you can play around with successfully, in other words.

    1 pound fresh mushrooms, washed, sliced
    1 small onion, minced
    ½ cup butter
    ¼ cup flour
    3 cups scalded milk or milk and cream
    ¾ pound diced sharp Cheddar cheese
    2 teaspoons soy sauce
    1 teaspoon salt
    ½ teaspoon pepper
    2 cans (8 ozs. each) water chestnuts, drained, sliced thin
    4 packages (10 ozs. each) french-cut green beans, drained
    1 can french-fried onions, crumbled

Sauté mushrooms and onion in butter. Blend in flour and gradually add milk. Cook and stir until thickened and smooth. Add cheese and stir until melted. Add vegetables, except onions, turn into buttered casserole and top with onions. Bake 20 minutes at 375° F. Serve hot with any barbecue meal.

GREEN AND WAX BEAN CASSEROLE   *Six to Eight* SERVINGS

A dish such as this gives vegetables real importance.

1 pound green beans, frenched
   (sliced "on the bias")
1 pound wax beans, frenched
1 cup water
1 teaspoon salt
½ pound mushrooms, sliced
¼ cup butter
2 tablespoons minced onion
¼ cup butter
1 teaspoon salt

¼ teaspoon pepper
¼ cup flour
   Liquid from beans
1¼ cups milk
2 cups grated Swiss or
   sharp Cheddar cheese
   (processed)
6 hard-cooked eggs, sliced
1 2-oz. jar chopped pimiento

Place beans, water, and salt in a pan. Cover and cook to boiling. Lower the heat and steam for 10 minutes. Drain, and reserve the liquid. Sauté the mushrooms in ¼ cup butter for 5 minutes. Set aside. Sauté onions in ¼ cup butter for 5 minutes. Blend in the flour, salt, and pepper. Add milk and liquid from beans and cook, stirring constantly, until thick. Stir in 1 cup of the cheese. Add mushrooms, 4 of the sliced, hard-cooked eggs, beans, and pimiento; mix lightly. Turn into a casserole and top with remaining cheese. Bake at 350° F. for 20 minutes. Garnish with remaining 2 eggs and serve immediately.

BARBECUE BEANS   *Six* SERVINGS

A campers' or Boy Scout special. Multiply the recipe for a crowd.

1 pound ground beef
1 medium onion, chopped
2 tablespoons shortening
1 large can pork and beans

1 cup chili sauce
1 tablespoon brown sugar
1 teaspoon salt
¼ teaspoon pepper

Brown meat and onion in shortening. Add remaining ingredients. Turn mixture into a casserole and bake at 350° F. for 30 minutes. Or simmer together in a pot for the same length of time.

OLD-FASHIONED BAKED BEANS   *Six* SERVINGS

My mother, early a widow, could not often afford to buy meat. We had baked beans often, and always prepared the New England way—no tomatoes. I love to bake them the same way, even though there are so many good canned beans available. Home baked, they taste better!

   2 cups dried navy beans
 1/4 pound salt pork or bacon
 1/3 cup molasses or brown sugar
   1 tablespoon dry mustard
   2 teaspoons salt
 1/4 teaspoon pepper
   1 onion

Wash beans, cover with water, and simmer gently until tender, 2 hours or more. Add more water as necessary. Drain beans, saving cooking water. Turn beans into bean pot or casserole. Scrape pork rind until white, score fat, and bury in beans with rind exposed. Bury onion in beans. Mix molasses and seasonings with 1 1/2 cups of the cooking water and pour over beans. Cover and bake at 275° F. for 6 hours, uncovering beans during last hour. Add more cooking water from beans as necessary. Liquid remaining from cooking beans makes delicious soup.

SOME EXCELLENT VARIATIONS

Hambone Beans.   Simmer the beans with a ham bone and forget about the salt pork. Add scraps of ham from bone to bean pot.

Beans with Tomato Sauce.   Add 1 minced clove garlic, and 1 cup (8 oz. can) tomato sauce as part of liquid. Or just add 1/4 cup catsup or chili sauce to beans.

Honey or Maple Beans.   Use 1/2 cup honey or 1 cup maple sirup instead of molasses or brown sugar.

Wine or Brandy Beans.   Add 1/2 cup sherry or other wine or 1/4 cup brandy during last 1/2 hour in oven.

Hawaiian Baked Beans.   Add 2 cups crushed pineapple to the beans. Use brown sugar, not molasses.

BAKED BEAN CASSEROLE

Four SERVINGS

A little different, and very tasty.

2 small onions, finely chopped
2 green peppers, finely chopped
3 tablespoons butter or margarine
1 pound can baked beans
¾ cup grated sharp cheese
½ cup fine, fresh bread crumbs

Cook onions and green peppers in 2 tablespoons butter until tender, add beans, and mix. Arrange beans in alternate layers with the cheese in a greased casserole, having beans on top. Top with the crumbs mixed with remaining butter or margarine and bake at 375° F. for 30 minutes.

KIDNEY BEANS WITH FRANKFURTERS

Six to Eight SERVINGS

Here's a good camping-out dish. It's easy and filling, and boys and girls like it.

2 large onions, chopped
¼ cup diced celery
1½ cups diced green pepper
1 pound frankfurters (usually 10), sliced 1 inch thick
¼ cup oil
1 teaspoon prepared mustard
1 can tomato soup, undiluted
2 cans (1 lb. size) kidney beans

Brown the vegetables and frankfurters lightly in the oil. Add everything else and let the mixture simmer for 10 minutes.

BEETS AND BEET GREENS   *Two or Three* SERVINGS

Beet greens are succulent when they are young. If you have a garden and can gather the beets while they aren't more than an inch in diameter, the tops will be delicious. Beets and tops together are a dish to drool over.

12 small beets with tops
   Salt, pepper
   Sour cream flavored with horseradish, or lemon juice or
      vinegar for a sauce

Top the beets, wash them, and boil or bake (at 325° F., covered) until tender. Wash tops well and cook in just the water clinging to them after washing, in a covered pot, only long enough to wilt them. Chop and season with salt and pepper. Skin the baby beets, season them, too, and mix with the greens, whole or sliced. Serve hot with the sour cream sauce, lemon juice, or vinegar.

BEETS WITH ORANGE SAUCE   *Four* SERVINGS

Everybody will like these! Yes, even the beet haters, if they'll try them.

6 fresh beets, cooked, peeled, and sliced or diced,
      or 1 can (1 lb.) sliced beets
1 tablespoon cornstarch
2 tablespoons water
3 tablespoons grated orange rind
1/4 teaspoon salt
3 tablespoons lemon juice
1/2 cup orange juice
1/4 cup butter

Blend cornstarch and water, add remaining ingredients, except beets. Bring to boiling point and cook, stirring constantly, until thick and smooth. Add beets and heat through.

289

SCALLOPED BROCCOLI   *Six* SERVINGS

A flavorsome, attractive casserole, and just try the same method with the midribs of Swiss chard or kale!

1 large bunch broccoli, trimmed, cooked barely tender
1/4 cup melted butter
1/4 cup minced onion
1/4 cup flour
1 teaspoon salt
1/8 teaspoon pepper
2 cups milk
1 1/2 cups grated Cheddar cheese
1/2 cup buttered bread crumbs

Cook onion in butter until tender, add flour and seasonings, and blend. Add milk and cook until thickened, stirring constantly. Remove from heat and stir in cheese. Arrange alternate layers of broccoli and sauce in greased 1-quart casserole. Top with crumbs and brown in 350° F. oven 20 minutes.

Note on substituting Swiss chard or kale: Sometimes the stalks of these greens are cooked as a separate vegetable from the rest of the leaf, since they take longer to cook. This is an excellent way to prepare them.

Actually, any vegetable—asparagus, cauliflower, green beans, Brussels sprouts, summer squash, and others—may be prepared with this sauce, which is simply a good oniony cheese sauce.

BROCCOLI WITH SOUR-CREAM SAUCE   *Six* SERVINGS

Pure white on deep green—beautiful and inviting!

2 bunches broccoli or 2 packages frozen, cooked
2 tablespoons minced onion
2 tablespoons butter
1 1/2 cups dairy sour cream
2 teaspoons sugar
1 teaspoon vinegar
1/8 teaspoon pepper
1/4 cup chopped nuts

Sauté onion in butter for 5 minutes. Mix with remaining ingredients, except nuts, in top of double boiler. Heat through. Serve piping hot over seasoned broccoli, and top with nuts.

BRUSSELS SPROUTS WITH SAVORY SAUCE

Four SERVINGS

A sharp sauce really peps up the little fellows.

    1 quart Brussels sprouts, cooked barely tender
    1 tablespoon flour
    2 tablespoons butter or margarine
    ½ cup meat stock
      Juice of 1 lemon
      Salt and pepper

Blend flour and butter in a saucepan; stir in stock and lemon juice. Cook until smooth and thickened, stirring constantly. Season with salt and pepper and pour over the hot drained sprouts. Serve immediately.

RED CABBAGE WITH CURRANT JELLY

Four SERVINGS

Sweet, tart and fruity, a most delicious vegetable.

    4 cups shredded red cabbage
    2½ tablespoons butter or margarine
    1 tablespoon vinegar
    2 tart cooking apples, pared and chopped
    ½ cup chopped onion
    2 tablespoons currant jelly
    ½ teaspoon salt
    ¼ teaspoon pepper

Add butter, vinegar, apples, and onion to cabbage and steam until tender, 5 to 8 minutes. Add jelly, salt, and pepper, and serve hot.

HUNGARIAN HOT SLAW   *Five* SERVINGS

Use red or white cabbage or a mixture of the two for this tasty dish.

1 medium onion, chopped	Salt, pepper
½ green pepper, chopped	3 tablespoons vinegar
3 tablespoons oil or butter	1 tablespoon sugar
4 cups thin-sliced cabbage	1 cup dairy sour cream

Cook onion and green pepper until soft in oil and add cabbage. Season with salt and pepper, add vinegar and sugar, cover, and cook 6 minutes. Stir in sour cream and serve at once.

SCALLOPED CABBAGE   *Six* SERVINGS

My favorite cabbage dish.

1 medium head cabbage, shredded
2 cups Medium White Sauce (see below)
1 cup grated cheese or buttered crumbs

Cook cabbage until barely tender, 5 minutes, in a small amount of boiling, salted water. Cooking water may be used as part of liquid in sauce. Place cabbage in greased baking dish, cover with sauce, and top with cheese or buttered crumbs. Bake at 400° F. 10 minutes or until hot and browned.

MEDIUM WHITE SAUCE: Blend ¼ cup flour with ¼ cup melted butter. Add ½ teaspoon salt, a little pepper, 2 cups milk. Cook and stir until smooth and thickened.

SOME EXCELLENT VARIATIONS OF SCALLOPED CABBAGE

With dill and thyme. Add a pinch of thyme, ¼ teaspoon finely chopped dill or dill seeds, 1 tablespoon minced green onion tops.

With green pepper and pimiento. Add 2 tablespoons chopped green pepper and 2 tablespoons chopped pimiento or sweet red pepper to the cabbage.

BUTTER-BROWNED SAUERKRAUT

Four SERVINGS

Smells up the house, but it's worth it!

2 cups packed sauerkraut
3 tablespoons butter
3 tablespoons brown sugar
   Caraway seeds, if you like

Heat kraut gently in butter, stirring in sugar as it cooks. When blended, turn up heat slightly to brown. Add caraway.

CARROTS PIQUANT

Six SERVINGS

Sweet-sour and tomato sauced—here's an interesting blend of flavors.

12 medium carrots, cooked, drained, and diced,
      or 2 cans diced carrots, heated and drained
 1 tablespoon sugar
 2 tablespoons cornstarch
 ½ teaspoon salt
 1 tablespoon grated onion
 1 tablespoon grated lemon rind
 2 tablespoons lemon juice
 1 cup carrot liquid or water
 1 can (8 ozs.) tomato sauce

Mix sugar and cornstarch in saucepan. Add salt, onion, grated lemon rind, and lemon juice, then stir in water and tomato sauce and blend. Cook, stirring constantly, until smooth and thickened. Add hot cooked carrots, blend, and serve.

FRIED CARROTS AND APPLES   *Six* SERVINGS

Very simple, very good.

6 medium carrots, sliced
   lengthwise
6 tart apples, sliced crosswise

2 tablespoons butter or
   drippings
1 tablespoon brown sugar
A sprinkle of salt

Place apples and carrots in a single layer in a large skillet with the butter, cover tightly, and cook until browned on one side. Turn with
spatula and brown other side. Sprinkle with sugar and salt after turning.

PANNED CARROTS   *Four* SERVINGS

Try panning carrots and cabbage in equal parts.

4 cups shredded carrots
2 tablespoons minced green
   pepper
2 tablespoons chopped parsley

Salt, pepper
3 tablespoons melted butter
   or margarine

Combine ingredients in heavy saucepan with a tight cover and cook
over low heat until carrots are tender, stirring occasionally. Trade green
pepper for onion, if you like, or use both. If you have sweet teeth, add a
tablespoon of brown sugar.

SPANISH CARROTS   *Six* SERVINGS

This is a fine way to dress up carrots!

12 medium carrots, cooked,
   diced
½ clove garlic
2 tablespoons butter or
   margarine

¾ teaspoon salt
⅛ teaspoon pepper
1 4-ounce can pimientos,
   drained and chopped
1 tablespoon chili sauce

Cook garlic in butter for 3 minutes. Remove garlic, add carrots, salt,
pepper, pimientos and chili sauce. Heat thoroughly.

CAULIFLOWER IN CHEESE-WINE SAUCE

Six SERVINGS

Such elegance for cauliflower! Delicious!

1 large head cauliflower, broken apart	2 tablespoons flour
1 cup process nippy cheese, diced	½ teaspoon salt
	¼ teaspoon dry mustard
1 egg, well beaten	¼ teaspoon pepper
1 tablespoon butter	1 cup dry white wine
	Buttered toast

Cook cauliflower in boiling salted water until barely tender. Combine cheese, egg, butter, flour, and seasonings and place over hot water or low heat. Stir until smooth and blended, then gradually stir in wine. Continue to cook until smooth and thickened, stirring constantly. Arrange drained, cooked cauliflower on toast and cover with hot sauce.

BRAISED CELERY or CELERY CABBAGE

Four SERVINGS

This is a delicious method for endive, too.

2 strips bacon	½ cup boiling water
4 sprigs parsley	1 bouillon cube
2 teaspoons chopped chives or ½ onion, sliced	1 cup soft bread crumbs, sautéed in 1 tablespoon butter or margarine
2 cups crisp celery cut into 3-inch lengths, or 2 cups sliced celery cabbage	

Lay bacon strips in bottom of an oval baking dish. Top with parsley and chives or onion. Arrange celery on top. Dissolve bouillon cube in water and pour over the celery. Cover dish tightly and bake at 350° F. for 30 minutes. Remove cover, top with crumbs, and brown 30 minutes longer.

COMPANY CORN FONDUE   *Twelve* SERVINGS

*A wonderful buffet dish. The recipe divides easily if you
don't want so much.*

6 eggs, separated
2 cups milk, scalded
2 tablespoons butter or mar-
    garine
2 cans cream style corn, or
    whole kernel corn, drained

1 cup grated cheese
2 cups soft bread cubes
1 teaspoon dry mustard
1½ teaspoons salt
¼ teaspoon pepper
¼ teaspoon Tabasco sauce

Beat egg yolks. Add milk, stirring constantly. Mix in butter, corn,
cheese, bread, mustard, salt, pepper and tabasco. Beat egg whites until
stiff; fold into mixture. Bake in a 3-quart casserole at 325° F. for 1 hour
or until firm.

CORN FRITTERS   *Four to Six* SERVINGS

These are so good we should have them more often!

1½ cups fresh or canned whole kernel corn (12 oz. can)
        drained
1 cup flour
½ teaspoon salt
1 teaspoon baking powder
½ teaspoon sugar
2 eggs
¼ cup milk
1 tablespoon melted butter

Sift dry ingredients, add eggs beaten with milk, and stir in corn and fat.
Drop by spoonfuls into hot fat, 365° to 375° F. Fry golden brown, drain
on paper toweling, and serve hot with maple sirup or as an accompaniment for fried chicken.

CORN ROAST

I don't believe that anyone who has ever attended one of our country corn roasts will ever forget it. This is Cousin Clark Lovrien's own show, and he runs it with his usual FBI kind of thoroughness. In the first place, he may plant as many as five varieties of sweet corn (all yellow, of course) in order to have them ripening in succession all summer.

On the first Saturday when enough corn for our customary weekend crowd has reached the peak for succulent maturity, Clark gathers a few bushels, and whichever child or adult is handiest lends a hand at stripping off some of the outer husks, leaving enough to protect the corn on the grill. Then under the pump in pails go the garden-warm ears. A half hour's cold-water bath will leave enough moisture to create steam on the grill. Meanwhile, charcoal fires are being built in several grills. The coals must burn down so that they look gray all over before the cooking can begin. Tongs for turning the corn are brought out and someone may speak up for a little hamburger space on the grills. There *are* people who like something more than corn for supper, although this is hard to understand!

Onto the grill go the dampened ears, with room left for turning and re-arranging as necessary. Twenty to 25 minutes cooks the corn to a turn. Sometimes an ear gets a little hot on one side and the kernels caramelize and turn brown. This is an eating bonus, making the ear even more delicious. Then it is every man, woman, and child for himself, with husks falling all over the grass, butter dripping in rivulets, and cries of joy rising to the roof (the sagging roof) of the ancient barn. There's nothing in the world more delicious than tender young corn not more than an hour from the garden!

There are other ways to roast corn, and some are neater. You can strip off all the husks, remove the silks, lay the corn on a piece of heavy duty foil, add salt, pepper, butter or barbecue sauce, then wrap it tight and roast it on the grill or in burned-down ashes. About 20 to 25 minutes should do it.

FRESH SWEET CORN IN CREAM   *Six* SERVINGS

This is almost as delicious as roasted corn, and it is easier for
many people to eat. Neater, too, of course.

12 ears of tender corn, cooked or not
¼ cup butter
½ cup cream
   Salt and black pepper

Cut the kernels from the corn raw or after boiling or steaming, and
scrape cobs with back of knife to get the milky residue of the kernel.
Add other ingredients and heat to a simmer. Don't cook more than 5
minutes if you start with cooked corn, 10 minutes if uncooked.

The corn is better if you start it fresh, but this is also a great way
to use leftover corn on the cob.

Some cooks add a pinch of sugar. Others sauté a little onion and
green pepper in the butter and add that. You could also add chopped
pimiento.

CORN PUDDING   *Six* SERVINGS

I always think of this dish as Iowan, but I believe it may be
just midwestern. It was favorite family fare when I was
growing up, and is an indispensable accompaniment for the
turkey dinner at Thanksgiving, even now. It's a filling and
nutritious dish, good any time.

2 cans cream style corn
3 eggs, slightly beaten
½ teaspoon salt
¼ teaspoon pepper

1 cup milk
1 cup coarse cracker crumbs
¼ cup melted butter

Mix eggs, salt, pepper, and milk with corn. Place in buttered (or teflon
lined) casserole and top with cracker crumbs. Drip the butter over the
crumbs. Bake for an hour at 350° F.

CORN SOUFFLE   *Six to Eight* SERVINGS

This, like all soufflés, must go direct from oven to table.

¼ cup butter or margarine
¼ cup flour
1½ cups milk
 1 teaspoon salt
 1 teaspoon grated onion
 4 eggs, separated
 1 can cream-style corn

Melt butter and add flour, blending well. Stir in milk and cook, stirring constantly, until smooth and thick. Add seasonings. Pour over well beaten egg yolks. Cool; add corn and fold in stiffly beaten egg whites. Pour into buttered baking pan and bake at 300° F. until firm, about 1½ hours. Serve immediately.

EGGPLANT BROILED   *Four* SERVINGS
WITH CHEESE AND BACON

My favorite eggplant combination is a simple one.

 1 small eggplant, pared
   Flour, salt, paprika
   Melted butter
 4 slices American cheese
 4 slices tomato
 4 slices bacon

Cut eggplant into ½-inch thick slices. Dredge in flour seasoned with salt and paprika. Sauté in butter until almost tender. Place eggplant slices on broiler rack; cover each with a thin slice of cheese, then a slice of tomato. Top with strip of bacon, cut in half. Broil until cheese is melted and bacon is crisp. Serve immediately.

MEAT-STUFFED GREEN PEPPERS *Four* SERVINGS

Serve with more of the sauce used to moisten filling.

4 nicely shaped, squatty green peppers
1 cup cooked rice
1 cup cooked ground ham, lamb, beef or other meat
1 teaspoon minced onion
    Tomato sauce, mushroom soup, or gravy to moisten
    Grated cheese

Cut off a slice from the top of each pepper, remove seeds and parboil peppers 5 minutes and drain. Combine other ingredients except cheese, fill peppers, and top with cheese. Place in pan with ½-inch water in bottom. Bake at 350° F. for 40 minutes.

MUSHROOMS IN SOUR CREAM *Six* SERVINGS

I'm sure you'll think this one of the most delicious ways to serve mushrooms.

1 pound fresh mushrooms, washed and sliced
1 medium onion, finely chopped
2 tablespoons butter
1 teaspoon flour
1 teaspoon Worcestershire sauce
1 cup dairy sour cream
    Toast
    Bacon curls

Cook onion in butter until delicately browned. Add mushrooms and cook for 10 minutes on low heat. Sprinkle flour over mushrooms and mix well. Add Worcestershire and sour cream and heat through on low heat or in a double boiler. Serve on toast and top with bacon.

STUFFED MUSHROOMS   *Six* SERVINGS

Don't pass these up if you love mushrooms!

12 large fresh mushrooms
 1 cup toasted fine bread crumbs
½ cup minced parsley
 1 teaspoon poultry seasoning
 2 tablespoons minced onion
 1 teaspoon salt
 3 tablespoons butter

Wash mushrooms and remove stems. Place mushroom caps hollow side up in a shallow buttered baking dish in which you have put 2 table-spoons water. Mix fine-chopped mushroom stems with remaining in-gredients, except butter. Knead butter into mixture with hands, until it will hold together. Form into peaked mounds, and place firmly in mush-room caps. Bake in a hot oven (450° F.) 10 minutes.

OKRA CREOLE   *Five or Six* SERVINGS

Onions and tomatoes are okra's favorite companions.

 2 dozen young, tender okra pods (1-1½ lbs.)
 1 small onion, minced
 1 sliver garlic, minced
½ small green pepper, minced
 2 tablespoons butter or bacon drippings
 2 fresh tomatoes, cut in pieces
   Salt, pepper

Wash okra and remove ends. Sauté onion, garlic, green pepper in butter for about 6 minutes. Add tomatoes, okra, and seasonings and simmer until okra is tender, about 10 minutes.

BATTER-FRIED ONION RINGS   *Six* SERVINGS

There's no better dressing for a good steak or even a hamburger.

6 large sweet Spanish onions,
    peeled, sliced 1/4-inch
    thick
  Milk and water (optional)
1/2 cup flour

3/4 teaspoon salt
1/4 teaspoon pepper
1/2 teaspoon baking powder
1 egg, beaten
1/2 cup milk

Separate sliced onions into rings and soak 1/2 hour in milk and water, if very mild flavor is wanted. Drain, and dip into batter made by sifting dry ingredients and stirring in egg and milk. Drain rings and drop into deep fat at 375° F. Fry golden brown, turning once. Drain on soft paper. Sprinkle with salt. Keep hot until served.

Onion Rings Fried Without Batter. Rings may be dipped in flour, potato meal, or into a mixture of cornmeal and flour, then into a slightly beaten egg diluted with 1/4 cup milk, again into the covering mixture, then fried.

CREAMED ONIONS   *Four to Six* SERVINGS

Our most popular seasoner makes an amazingly good hot vegetable dish. I usually make double this amount for a barbecue meal.

1 1/2 pounds (about 24) small
    onions
1/4 cup butter
3 tablespoons flour
1/2 teaspoon salt
1/8 teaspoon pepper

1/4 teaspoon dry mustard
2 cups milk, scalded
1/2 green pepper, cut julienne
    style (optional)
1 cup buttered bread crumbs

Cook onions covered with 1 teaspoon of salt in 1 cup water for 20 minutes. Drain. Melt butter, blend in flour, salt, and other seasonings. Add milk and cook, stirring constantly, until thick and smooth. Add onions and turn mixture into a casserole. Add green pepper strips. Top with buttered crumbs and bake at 350° F. for 20 minutes.

CURRIED BAKED ONIONS   *Six* SERVINGS

This dish can be assembled ahead of time, ready for last-minute baking.

2 pounds small white onions	1 teaspoon salt
1/3 cup butter	1/4 teaspoon pepper
1/4 cup flour	1 cup beef bouillon
Speck cayenne	1 cup milk
1/2 teaspoon curry powder	1/2 cup grated cheese
1/2 teaspoon paprika	

Peel onions and cook in rapidly boiling salted water for 15 minutes. Drain and place in a buttered casserole. Melt butter in a saucepan. Add flour and seasonings and blend. Add liquid and cook, stirring constantly, until thick and smooth. Add cheese and stir until melted. Pour over onions and bake at 350° F. for 30 minutes.

ORANGE-GLAZED PARSNIPS   *Six* SERVINGS

Didn't know "snips" could be such a delicacy, did you?

6–12 young parsnips, cooked whole
1 cup brown sugar, packed
1 cup orange juice
1/2 teaspoon salt
1/4 teaspoon each, pepper, paprika
1/4 cup butter or margarine

Mix ingredients for sauce and boil 5 minutes. Glaze parsnips in the sauce by cooking over low heat, turning from time to time until they are well coated. If you buy parsnips of uneven size, or big ones, slice them lengthwise into strips.

PEAS WITH LETTUCE   *Six* SERVINGS

Serve this combination with fried chicken or roast beef.

2 strips bacon, diced
3 green onions and tops, sliced thin
¼ cup butter
1 tablespoon flour
½ teaspoon salt
2 cups shredded lettuce
3 pounds fresh peas or 2 packages (10 ozs. each) frozen
     peas, thawed
½ cup chicken broth
1 jar (2 ozs.) pimiento, chopped

Fry bacon until crisp. Drain on absorbent paper. Sauté onions in butter for 5 minutes; blend in flour and salt. Add lettuce, peas, and chicken broth. Cover pan and heat to boiling. Lower heat and cook 5 minutes more. Top with pimiento and crisp bacon before serving.

SPINACH SQUARES   *Six* SERVINGS

With crisp bacon and a slice of tomato, you'll have a fine lunch.

1 package frozen chopped spinach, thawed
3 tablespoons butter, melted
1 teaspoon Worcestershire sauce
3 tablespoons vinegar
1½ teaspoons salt
3 eggs, slightly beaten

Mix ingredients. Turn into buttered baking dish about 7x11 inches. Place in another pan containing hot water. Bake at 325° F. for 1 hour. Cut into squares and serve immediately.

304

SPINACH SUPREME   *Six to Eight* SERVINGS

Keep this in mind for guest dinners, for it can be baked during last-minute dinner preparations.

> 2 packages frozen spinach or 2 pounds fresh,
>   cooked and drained
> 1/2 cup milk
> 1 cup grated sharp cheese
> 1/2 teaspoon salt
> 3 hard-cooked eggs, sliced
> 1 cup fresh buttered bread crumbs

Place spinach in a buttered casserole. Heat milk, cheese, and salt in top of a double boiler until cheese is melted. Blend. Arrange eggs on top of spinach, and cover with cheese sauce. Top with crumbs. Bake at 375° F. about 20 minutes.

Deviled Spinach. Add 1/2 teaspoon dry mustard, 2 tablespoons lemon juice to sauce.

CANDIED SWEET POTATOES   *Six* SERVINGS
WITH PINEAPPLE

If you're entertaining, the potatoes and other ingredients may be prepared early and baked just before serving.

1/2 cup brown sugar	1 cup orange juice
1/2 teaspoon salt	1/4 cup butter
1 tablespoon cornstarch	6 to 8 cooked sweet potatoes
1 can (9 ozs.) crushed pine-apple, not drained	1/2 cup salted pecans

Mix sugar, salt, and cornstarch in heavy pan. Add pineapple, orange juice, and butter. Cook, stirring constantly, until sauce is thick and clear. Peel potatoes and cut them into halves. Place in a casserole and cover with sauce. Bake at 350° F. for 20 minutes. Top with nuts and serve. If the potatoes are hot, there's no need to bake the preparation. Simply mix hot potatoes with sauce and serve.

SWEET POTATO-APPLE CASSEROLE

Four SERVINGS

Maple sirup is delicious with potatoes or apples, doubly delicious with a combination of the two.

3 medium sweet potatoes, cooked, peeled, sliced
2 tart apples, pared, cored, sliced
　Salt
⅓ cup brown sugar
3 tablespoons butter
¼ cup maple sirup
⅓ cup chopped pecans

Arrange half the potatoes in the bottom of a greased baking dish and sprinkle lightly with salt. Add a layer of apple slices, sprinkle with brown sugar, and dot with butter. Add half the pecans. Repeat the process, then pour maple sirup over the mixture, and bake 20 minutes at 350° F.

SWEET POTATOES IN ORANGE SHELLS

Six to Eight SERVINGS

Surround the roast turkey with these decorative filled oranges. All the preliminary preparation may be done early in the day.

3 or 4 medium oranges
6 to 8 medium sweet potatoes cooked and skinned
½ cup butter
½ teaspoon salt
¼ to ½ cup orange juice

Grated rind of 1 orange
⅓ cup brown sugar
½ cup broken pecans
¼ to ⅓ cup sherry
½ cup tiny marshmallows

Cut oranges into halves and extract juice. Remove pulp and scallop edges of shells. Mash potatoes with electric mixer until smooth and fluffy. Add butter, salt, orange juice, rind, and sugar to potatoes and beat until blended. Add nuts and sherry. Place orange shells on a heatproof platter and fill with sweet potato mixture. Dot with marshmallows. Bake at 350° F. for about 20 minutes.

MAPLE-CANDIED SWEETS   *Four* SERVINGS

Sweet, simple, superb!

   4 cooked sweet potatoes, peeled, cut in halves
½ cup maple sirup
    Salt
¼ cup butter

Put potatoes in a casserole, pour sirup over them, and sprinkle lightly with salt. Dot with butter and bake 20 minutes at 375° F.

TWICE-BAKED POTATOES   *Four* SERVINGS

These freeze well, and are a joy to have ready for company occasions.

   4 hot baked potatoes
½ cup cream, scalded
¼ cup butter or margarine
½ teaspoon salt; dash pepper
   2 eggs, slightly beaten
   1 tablespoon chopped chives or 1 teaspoon grated onion
       (optional)
½ cup grated Cheddar cheese

Bake potatoes at 425° F. about 45 minutes or until tender.

Slice off top of each hot potato, lengthwise. If potatoes are huge, use just 2, and cut each in half, lengthwise. Scoop out pulp, leaving shells unbroken. Mash potato, adding cream, butter, seasonings, and eggs and beating until fluffy with electric mixer. Taste and add salt, if needed. Pile into potato shells, top with cheese, and brown at 425° F. for 10 minutes. These may be prepared in the afternoon and reheated for 20 minutes before serving.

To freeze, first cool the potatoes, then freeze in a shallow pan. Wrap in foil or place in plastic bags and seal airtight; return to the freezer. Do your thawing, heating, and browning of frozen stuffed spuds at 375° F. Takes 30 to 40 minutes.

NEW-FASHIONED SCALLOPED POTATOES

Eight SERVINGS

The inexperienced cook will find this recipe easier to use than that for old-fashioned scalloped potatoes, I think.

6 medium potatoes, pared and
   sliced thin
⅓ cup butter
⅓ cup flour
1 teaspoon salt
¼ teaspoon pepper
3 cups milk, scalded

1 jar (2 ozs.) pimento,
   chopped
4 green onions and tops, sliced
   thin
½ pound sharp cheese, diced
1 cup buttered soft bread
   crumbs

Place potatoes, ½ cup water, and 1 teaspoon salt in a pan. Cover, cook to boiling. Lower heat and cook for 10 minutes. Drain. Melt butter, blend in flour, salt, and pepper. Add milk and cook, stirring constantly, until thick and smooth. Stir in pimiento, onions, cheese and potatoes. Turn mixture into a casserole and top with crumbs. Bake at 350° F. for 30 minutes.

OLD-FASHIONED SCALLOPED POTATOES

Eight SERVINGS

They're always good reheated, so have plenty!

8 medium potatoes, sliced thin
   Salt, pepper, flour
2 tablespoons butter or margarine
2½ cups hot milk

Place a layer of the thin-sliced potatoes in a buttered baking dish, sprinkle with salt and pepper, and dredge with flour. Repeat with another layer. Add butter or margarine to hot milk and pour over the potatoes. Bake covered at 350° F. for ½ hour, then uncover and bake about 20 minutes longer, or until a delicate brown crust has formed on top.

SOME VARIATIONS OF SCALLOPED POTATOES

With Cheese.   Add 1 to 2 cups shredded cheese to potato layers.

With Onions.   Strew 2 to 4 thin-sliced onions among the potato slices.

With Sausage or Ham.   Cooked sausage, crumbled, or diced ham may be sprinkled over the potato layers in any amount you like—say 1 cup of either meat.

COUNTRY BREAKFAST POTATOES Six SERVINGS

There have been and continue to be many all-boy weekends in the country. We've had as many as sixteen starving high school lads for a skiing or canoeing weekend, and I always wish their mothers could see them devouring breakfast. Fruit, cereal, four or five eggs apiece, and the bacon can't be cooked fast enough to keep up. Pancakes always go over with smashing success, new batters having to be constantly mixed. But what the boys really love is fried potatoes. Yes, country-fried potatoes and this variation of them.

        6 medium cooked potatoes, diced or sliced
        1 onion, chopped
        1 small green pepper, chopped
          Salt, pepper
        4 eggs
        ½ cup milk
          Bacon drippings

Melt bacon drippings in a large skillet and add the potatoes, onion, green pepper, salt, and pepper. Cook until well browned, turning occasionally with a spatula for even cooking. Beat the eggs lightly with the milk, and pour them over the potato mixture. Stir and turn until eggs have coagulated. Add more salt and pepper, and serve hot. Crumbled bacon may be added to the mixture.

Cooking could be done in ham or sausage fat, and bits of meat might be added.

POTATOES AU GRATIN   *Twenty-four* SERVINGS

During the Mary Meade staff excursions to the farm, Helen Dickinson, ordinarily a gourmet-type cook (she loves elaborate, winey, be-truffled concoctions which take half a day to put together and taste divine!) usually takes on the responsibility for the hot potato dishes. She's especially famous for her potatoes au gratin in crowd-sized proportions, and is lucky enough to have four blonde little daughters who are handy helpers for jobs such as peeling and dicing the spuds.

7 pounds potatoes (about 20 medium)
1 medium onion, chopped
¾ cup butter (1½ sticks)
⅔ cup flour
2 quarts (8 cups or ½ gal.) milk, scalded
5 teaspoons salt

1 teaspoon freshly ground black pepper
1 tablespoon Worcestershire sauce
¼ teaspoon Tabasco sauce
1 pound Cheddar cheese, grated
6 green onions and tops, sliced thin

Cook potatoes covered in a small amount of water until just tender, usually about 35 minutes (depends upon size). Drain and strip the skins when potatoes are cool enough to handle. Cut in ¼-inch dice. Cook onion in butter gently for 5 minutes and blend in flour. Add 3 cups of the scalded milk; cook, stirring constantly, until thickened and smooth. Smooth in electric blender or with egg beater if you need to. Return to pan and add rest of milk, the seasonings and about two-thirds of the cheese. Cook and stir to smooth sauce. Add half the chopped onions. Turn potatoes into two buttered shallow casseroles. Pour sauce over potatoes, mixing lightly. Top with remaining cheese and onions. Bake at 350° F. for about 30 minutes, or until hot and lightly browned.

NEW POTATOES
WITH CHEESE-PEA SAUCE

Ten SERVINGS

Sliced new green onions might be added to the sauce with the peas. This is a Helen Dickinson favorite.

20 small new potatoes
½ cup butter
½ cup flour
6 cups milk, scalded
½ pound sharp Cheddar cheese, grated
2½ teaspoons salt

½ teaspoon freshly ground pepper
¼ teaspoon oregano
2 teaspoons Worcestershire sauce
2 packages (10 ozs. ea.) frozen peas, partly thawed

Pare potatoes and cook, covered, in boiling water with 1 teaspoon salt, for 20 to 25 minutes or until tender. While potatoes cook, prepare sauce. Melt butter; blend in flour and add milk, cheese, and seasonings gradually, while cooking and stirring. When sauce is thickened and smooth, add peas and cook until peas are hot, 4 or 5 minutes. Don't overcook them. Pour sauce over hot drained potatoes and serve in vegetable dishes, allowing 2 potatoes apiece.

ZUCCHINI CASSEROLE

Six SERVINGS

Chopped fresh tomatoes in season are perfection in this delightful dish.

4 large zucchini squash
½ cup flour
1 teaspoon salt
2 eggs, slightly beaten
¼ cup drippings, or oil

2 cups canned tomatoes (No. 303)
½ teaspoon salt
2 cloves garlic, minced
2 teaspoons chopped parsley
½ cup grated sharp cheese

Cut squash in half and then into thin lengthwise slices. Dip into seasoned flour and then eggs. Sauté in drippings until brown on both sides. Cook tomatoes, salt, garlic, and parsley together for 10 minutes. Place half of squash in a casserole, then half of cheese, and half of sauce. Repeat, finishing with cheese. Bake at 350° F. for 30 minutes.

BAKED SUMMER SQUASH   *Six* SERVINGS

Crookneck, patty-pan, banana squash, zucchini—use any kind at all!

2–3 pounds summer squash	¼ teaspoon pepper
½ cup boiling water	1 small onion, minced
1 teaspoon salt	1 teaspoon rosemary

Wash squash and cut into thin slices without paring. Place in saucepan with water, salt, pepper, onion, and rosemary. Cover and cook to boiling; lower heat and simmer about 15 minutes or until squash is tender. Drain.

SAUCE

¼ cup butter	1½ cups coffee cream
2 tablespoons flour	2 egg yolks, slightly beaten
1 teaspoon salt	1 cup grated Swiss cheese
Speck cayenne	1 cup buttered bread crumbs

Melt butter, blend in flour, salt, and cayenne. Add cream and cook, stirring constantly, until mixture is thick and smooth. Add a small amount of hot mixture to egg yolks; blend with ingredients in pan. Add ½ of the grated cheese and cook about 3 minutes longer. Add cooked squash to the sauce and place in a casserole. Top with remaining cheese and crumbs. Bake at 300° F. for about 20 minutes.

STUFFED ACORN SQUASH   *Six* SERVINGS

This is a tasty combination of flavors—quite intriguing!

3 acorn squash, cut in halves, seeded
¼ cup butter or margarine
⅔ cup diced celery
1½ cups diced apple, unpeeled
1½ cups soft bread crumbs
1 cup grated American cheese
½ teaspoon salt
⅛ teaspoon pepper

312

Super Burgers, page 245

Bake squash, cut side down, at 400° F. for 20 to 30 minutes, or until nearly tender. Sauté celery and apple in butter for 5 minutes. Add remaining ingredients and blend. Fill partially baked squash halves with mixture. Bake about 10 to 15 minutes longer.

BROILED TOMATOES   *Six* SERVINGS

This is a delicious accompaniment for a broiled steak or chops.

6 firm, medium-size tomatoes	¼ teaspoon freshly ground
½ cup butter, melted	black pepper
2 cups coarse fresh bread crumbs	½ teaspoon sweet basil
½ teaspoon salt	1 tablespoon grated onion

Cut tomatoes crosswise into halves. Place them, cut side up, in a shallow pan. Mix remaining ingredients and sprinkle over tomato halves. Broil 3 inches from heat source for about 15 minutes, or until topping is delicately browned.

PENNSYLVANIA DUTCH   *Four* SERVINGS
FRIED TOMATOES

Gentle cooking is necessary as the sugar scorches easily.

4 firm red or green tomatoes, in thick slices
    Flour, salt, pepper
¼ cup butter or margarine
    Brown sugar
⅓ cup heavy cream

Dredge tomatoes with flour and sprinkle with salt and pepper. Cook very slowly in a skillet with butter or margarine. Sprinkle each slice with brown sugar before and after turning. When tomatoes are lightly browned, add cream and cook until cream is heated and slightly thickened. Pour over tomatoes when serving.

313

TOP – *Beef, Veal, and Lamb Stews, pages* 232, 257
BOTTOM – *Country-Fried Chicken, page* 192

TURNIP CROQUETTES   *Eight* SERVINGS

These patties are both appetizing and good.

2 cups mashed turnips or rutabagas
3 tablespoons fine bread crumbs
3 tablespoons chopped peanuts (optional, but nice!)
2 eggs, beaten
3 tablespoons grated cheese
3 tablespoons butter or margarine, melted
Salt and pepper to taste
Flour

Combine turnips, bread crumbs, peanuts, eggs, cheese, and 1 tablespoon of melted butter or margarine. Mix well and shape into patties. Dip in flour. Brown in remaining butter or margarine, about 5 minutes on each side. Or fry in deep fat at 375° F.

VEGETABLE CHOP SUEY   *Three or Four* SERVINGS

Simple, attractive, flavorful—the nuts add a nice crunch.

¼ cup butter or margarine
½ cup thin green pepper strips
½ cup sliced onion
1 cup sliced fresh mushrooms
1½ cups sliced celery, with tops
2 tablespoons flour
½ cup bouillon or liquid from
    bean sprouts

1 can bean sprouts
½ cup shredded
    toasted almonds
¼ cup soy sauce
Salt, pepper
Hot cooked rice or
    fried noodles

Sauté green pepper, onion, mushrooms and celery in butter or margarine 2 or 3 minutes. Sprinkle flour over vegetables. Add bouillon and cook until thickened, stirring constantly. Add bean sprouts, soy sauce, almonds, salt and pepper to taste. Heat through and serve on hot rice or noodles.

Salads & Soups

ON MOST SUMMER Saturday evenings the two sets of "country cousins" take potluck under our willow tree; or in mosquito and fly season, on one or the other of our new, spacious, screened-in porches. Helen Lovrien goes to the garden, gathers lettuce, radishes, onions, spinach, baby carrots, and any other handy vegetables, and makes a bowlful of the most delicious, crispy salad you ever ate!

Nobody needs a recipe for such a salad. You use what the garden yields, drenching it with oil and vinegar, sprinkling it with salt and pepper. Other salads require recipes, yes. But not that one!

Here is a little group of *other* salads—bean salads and slaws, marinated tomatoes, potato salads, and a summer squash mousse. You'll find the heartier salads tucked in with the chicken dishes and the meats and fish in Part III (The Main Course).

Here too is a group of ever-popular soups—the easy, simple kind.

MOLDED ASPARAGUS AND EGG SALAD

Six SERVINGS

A perfect Sunday supper salad, with cold cuts and hot French bread.

1 tablespoon (envelope) plain gelatin
¼ cup cold water
1 cup boiling vegetable liquid
½ teaspoon salt
1 tablespoon each, minced onion, pimiento, lemon juice

2 cups coarsely chopped cooked asparagus
3 hard-cooked eggs, chopped
½ cup chopped celery
1 cup mayonnaise
Lettuce
2 tomatoes, sliced
French dressing

Soften gelatin in water and dissolve in boiling liquid from asparagus plus water to make 1 cup. Add salt, onion, pimiento, and lemon juice. When mixture begins to thicken, fold in asparagus, eggs, celery, and mayonnaise. Pour mixture into a large oiled mold. Chill until firm and unmold on large plate. Garnish with lettuce and tomatoes. Serve with French dressing.

HOT GREEN BEAN SALAD

Six SERVINGS

Tender home-grown beans are especially good served this way. Wonderful for a buffet supper.

1½ pounds green beans, cut diagonally into 1-inch pieces, cooked
3 slices bacon, diced
1 small onion, chopped fine

¼ cup vinegar
1 tablespoon sugar
1 teaspoon salt
⅛ teaspoon pepper

Fry bacon until crisp. Remove from pan. Sauté onion in drippings for 3 minutes. Add bacon, and remaining ingredients and heat through. Pour over warm beans. You could use fewer beans and add some shredded lettuce.

316

KIDNEY BEAN SALAD   *Eight* SERVINGS

This is the kind of salad you may never make twice the same. You'll make substitutions and additions, but the chances are you'll still have a delicious bean salad.

    2 cans (1 lb. 4 ozs. each) kidney beans, well drained
    1 cup pickle relish or chopped sweet or dill pickles
    2 cups chopped celery
    ¼ cup chopped onion
    ¼ cup chopped green pepper
    1½ teaspoon salt (about)
      Mayonnaise (⅔ to 1 cup)

Combine ingredients and chill for several hours. Serve in a bowl or in lettuce cups. Add 6 hard-cooked eggs, diced, if you wish.

COLE SLAW WITH   *Six* SERVINGS
BUTTERMILK DRESSING

Just as good as it sounds, too!

    4 cups finely shredded cabbage
    1 cup grated Cheddar or Swiss cheese
    2 teaspoons sugar
    2 teaspoons salt
    ½ teaspoon paprika
    2 tablespoons each, vinegar, prepared mustard
      Dash cayenne
    1 cup buttermilk
    6 thin green pepper rings

Toss cabbage and cheese; chill. Mix remaining ingredients, except green pepper, and chill. Just before serving add dressing to cabbage and mix lightly. Garnish with green pepper rings.

Variation.   Add 1 cup drained crushed pineapple.

GARDEN SLAW

Eight to Ten SERVINGS

There are slaws and slaws, but none better than this. It is my choice for a country weekend crowd.

6 cups finely shredded cab-
    bage
4 carrots, shredded
½ green pepper, shredded
4–6 green onions with tops,
    sliced thin
1 cucumber, pared and
    chopped

½–1 cup thinly sliced radishes
1½ teaspoons salt
¼ teaspoon coarsely ground
    pepper
3 tablespoons sugar
¾ cup salad oil
¾ cup white vinegar
¾ cup ice water

Prepare vegetables and chill well. Just before serving add remaining ingredients and mix lightly. If cabbage is not crisp, chill it in ice water and drain well. The soaking removes some of the nutrients, but given a choice between palate appeal and nutrition, who wouldn't pick what tastes best?

SOUR-CREAM SLAW
WITH WATERCRESS

Eight SERVINGS

Fix it early in the day, because the flavor develops in the refrigerator.

6 cups finely shredded cabbage
    (part red, if you wish)
1 cup sour cream
2 tablespoons sugar
2 tablespoons vinegar

1 teaspoon celery seed
2 tablespoons minced onion
1½ teaspoons salt
½ teaspoon pepper
½ bunch watercress, chopped

Mix cream, sugar, vinegar, celery seed, onion and seasonings. Add to cold cabbage and mix lightly. Chill. Mix in cress shortly before serving.

CORN RELISH SALAD   *Four* SERVINGS

Serve this delightful combination in little wooden bowls.

1 cup canned or cooked corn
2 tablespoons diced
    green pepper
1 tablespoon minced pimiento
1/4 cup chopped celery
2 tablespoons diced onions

1/2 teaspoon salt
1/8 teaspoon pepper
1 tablespoon vinegar
1/4 cup French dressing
1 bunch watercress, coarsely cut

Combine ingredients except watercress and chill. Add watercress just before serving.

HOLIDAY CRANBERRY SALAD *Twelve* SERVINGS

Makes a hit at Thanksgiving and Christmas dinner, and at church suppers.

1 pound cranberries
1 3/4 cups water
2 packages cherry gelatin
1/2 cup sugar
1 cup Tokay grapes, cut in
    half, seeded
1 cup finely chopped celery

1 can (1 lb. 4 ozs.) crushed
    pineapple
1 3-ounce package cream cheese
16 marshmallows, quartered
1 cup whipping cream
Crisp salad greens

Wash cranberries, add water, and cook until they start to pop. Boil for 5 minutes. Beat with a rotary beater to break up berries. Add gelatin and sugar, and stir until dissolved. Place over ice water, and stir frequently until thick. Fold grapes into jellied mixture with celery and undrained pineapple. Pour into pan about 12x8x2 inches. Chill overnight. Mash cheese slightly in a bowl. Add marshmallows and cream, and place in refrigerator overnight, or for several hours. Beat with electric mixer or rotary beater until stiff. Cut salad into squares, and serve on crisp salad greens topped with whipped-cream mixture.

WILTED LETTUCE or SPINACH

Four to Six SERVINGS

For one of our first dinners, as a bride, I fixed a huge bowl of wilted spinach. My new husband ate it with gusto, to the last bite. "Let's have this again. It's really good. What is it?" said he.

"It's spinach," said I, flattered.

"SPINACH!" he roared. "I HATE SPINACH!"

Try mixing your greens: lettuce, spinach, dandelion, curly endive.

    Bowlful (about 2 quarts) leaf lettuce, spinach,
        or other greens, torn in shreds
6 slices bacon, diced, cooked crisp
2 green onions, with tops, sliced
1 teaspoon sugar
½ teaspoon salt
    Plenty of freshly ground black pepper
¼ cup vinegar
2 tablespoons cream or sour cream (optional)
2 hard-cooked eggs, chopped

To hot bacon and 3 tablespoons drippings add onions, sugar, salt, pepper, and vinegar. Add cream, if you use it. Pour while hot over greens, tossing lightly. Sprinkle with egg. Sliced radishes may be mixed with the greens.

SWEDISH CUCUMBERS

Six SERVINGS

They're crisp, cold and sharp—just sharp enough to make a perfect relish to accompany a casserole.

2 cucumbers, pared, sliced
Salt
1 cup white vinegar
⅓ cup sugar

2 bay leaves
6 whole allspice
Black pepper
Chopped parsley

320

Sprinkle cucumbers with salt and put a weight on them for an hour. Pour off juice. Mix remaining ingredients and pour over cucumbers. When ready to serve, sprinkle with parsley.

CUCUMBERS IN SOUR CREAM   *Six* SERVINGS

Cucumber skins once were thought to be poisonous. They aren't but if they're waxed, I'd peel the cukes.

2 medium cucumbers, sliced thin (pared or not)	2 tablespoons wine vinegar
1 teaspoon salt	2 tablespoons minced parsley
1 teaspoon celery seed	2 green onions and tops, sliced thin
1/4 teaspoon freshly ground black pepper	1 cup dairy sour cream
1 tablespoon sugar	1 or 2 tomatoes, cut in sixths

Mix cucumbers with seasonings, sugar, vinegar, parsley, green onions, and sour cream. Cover and refrigerate for several hours. Turn mixture into serving dish. Garnish with tomato wedges and additional minced parsley. Serve plain or over wedges of crisp head lettuce.

PICNIC SALAD BOWL   *Six* SERVINGS

The kind of salad you can alter, extend, and play around with as you please.

1 cup cold cooked peas	2 tablespoons each, chopped onion, sweet pickle
1/2 cup diced cooked carrots	1/4 teaspoon paprika
1/2 cup sliced cucumbers	1/2 teaspoon salt
1/4 cup diced celery	1/3 cup mayonnaise
2 hard-cooked eggs, sliced	2 tablespoons French dressing

Combine vegetables, eggs, pickle, and onion. Sprinkle on seasonings. Toss lightly and mix with combined mayonnaise and French dressing. Turn into salad bowl with crisp greens.

SOUR-CREAM POTATO SALAD   *Eight* SERVINGS

This takes lots of sour cream, but oh-h, the flavor!

4 cups diced cooked potatoes
½ cup diced cucumber
1 tablespoon minced onion
¾ teaspoon celery seed
1½ teaspoons salt
½ teaspoon pepper

3 hard-cooked eggs
1½ cups dairy sour cream
½ cup mayonnaise or salad
   dressing
¼ cup vinegar
1 teaspoon prepared mustard

Toss together lightly potatoes, cucumber, onion, celery seed, salt, and pepper. Separate yolks from whites of eggs. Dice whites and add to potato mixture. Mash yolks and combine with sour cream, mayonnaise, vinegar, and mustard. Add to potatoes and toss together lightly. Chill. Garnish with crisp salad greens.

HOT POTATO SALAD   *Six* SERVINGS

Frankfurters are the usual accompaniment, but this is wonderful all by itself.

6 strips bacon, chopped, cooked crisp
1 tablespoon flour
1 small onion, minced, or 6 green onions with tops, sliced
¼ cup vinegar
1½ teaspoons salt
½ teaspoon pepper
1 tablespoon sugar
½ cup water
4 cups hot sliced cooked potatoes

Blend flour with bacon and fat. Add onion, vinegar, salt, pepper, sugar, and water; cook for 5 minutes. Pour over hot potatoes and mix lightly. Serve while still warm. If potatoes are cooked ahead of time; they may be re-heated slowly in the sauce in top of a double boiler.

MARIE KEES' FAMOUS GERMAN POTATO SALAD

Fifty SERVINGS

Marie Kees, our right-hand helper in the Mary Meade Kitchen, has made about seven tons of her famous German potato salad in thirty years' time, she thinks. Marie caters for German weddings, on weekends, and thinks nothing of making 150 pounds of her wonderful salad at a time. It is absolutely the best I've ever eaten, and maybe you think it was easy to pry the secret out of Marie! Even when she gave it, we found she really hadn't a recipe. Assistant Margaret Piont worked out proportions by following Marie around while she made a batch. There are two success secrets, Marie tells me—red potatoes, and that last-minute soup-stock bath.

15 pounds potatoes
½ cup finely chopped onions
1 cup finely cut green onions
¼ cup salt
1½ teaspoons pepper
2 tablespoons sugar

2 cups oil
2¼ cups white vinegar
1 quart well-seasoned soup stock (chicken, beef, or veal)

Scrub potatoes. Cook in salted water until just tender. Drain well. Cover and cool. Peel and slice thin. Add onions. Sprinkle on salt, pepper, and sugar. Then add oil and vinegar. Last, add stock. Mix carefully.

MARINATED TOMATOES

Twelve SERVINGS

Add a clove of garlic, cut very fine, if you wish.

12–16 ripe tomatoes, peeled and cut in chunks
1 large sweet onion, peeled and cut in chunks
1 green pepper, seeded and cut in pieces
1 bottle Italian style dressing
Salt; freshly ground pepper
Minced chives or parsley (be generous)
Sprinkle of sugar

Combine ingredients in a bowl and chill for several hours. Stir carefully once or twice during storage. This mixture is best if the tomatoes are home-grown.

SUMMER SQUASH MOUSSE   *Six* SERVINGS

Appealing and unusual. A queenly salad for a summer buffet.

1 tablespoon each, minced
    onions, chopped green
    pepper
2 tablespoons butter or marga-
    rine
2 tablespoons flour
1 teaspoon salt
⅛ teaspoon pepper
1 cup milk

1 egg, beaten
1 tablespoon (envelope)
    plain gelatin
2 tablespoons cold water
2 cups sieved, cooked summer
    squash
1 pimiento, chopped
1 cup heavy cream, whipped

Sauté onion and green pepper in butter until tender but not brown. Stir in flour, salt, and pepper; stir in milk and cook, stirring constantly, until smooth and thickened. Add a small amount of hot mixture to beaten egg and blend; return to pan and cook and stir 2 minutes longer. Add gelatin which has been softened in cold water; stir to dissolve. Add squash and pimiento and mix well. Cool, stirring occasionally. When mixture begins to congeal, fold in whipped cream. Chill in a mold until firm. Serve with mayonnaise.

FRUITS IN A MELON BOWL   *Twelve* SERVINGS

The more kinds of fruit, the merrier. Here's the perfect finish for a clambake or a barbecue.

1 shapely watermelon
    All kinds of fruit: cantaloupe, peaches, pineapple, blue-
        berries, strawberries, oranges, grapefruit, bananas,
        sweet cherries, several kinds of grapes

Cut off the upper third of the melon, lengthwise, leaving a boat shape. Remove the pink flesh and scallop the rim of the melon bowl. Cut up the watermelon, removing as many seeds as possible, and replace it in the bowl with a mixture of sliced, diced, and whole fruits and their juices. Pile the fruit high in the melon bowl and scatter berries over the top.

When I prepare a melon bowl I combine the fruit in the hydrator of my refrigerator and keep it cold and ready for filling the shell shortly before serving. Strawberries and bananas soften unattractively on standing, so if they are used, they should be added last. For a sophisticated adult party, a sweet wine such as cointreau, kirsch, or crème de menthe may be poured over the fruit. However, I believe that most guests enjoy summer fruits in their natural state.

FROZEN PARTY SALAD   *Ten to Twelve* SERVINGS

This is the kind everybody likes!

1 tablespoon plain gelatin
2 tablespoons cold water
¼ cup boiling water
2 tablespoons sugar
½ cup lemon juice
1 cup heavy cream, whipped
1 cup mayonnaise

1 cup each, drained, crushed pineapple, finely cut or-ange sections, halved grapes
½ cup finely cut grapefruit sections
1 cup marshmallows, cut in pieces
½ cup coconut
¼ cup sliced maraschino cherries

Soften gelatin in cold water, add boiling water and sugar and stir until dissolved. Cool slightly and add lemon juice. Chill until thickened. Fold whipped cream lightly into mayonnaise. Fold the remaining ingredients into this dressing quickly and gently. When the gelatin mixture is thick, but not congealed, fold the 2 mixtures together and place in refrigerator tray. Freeze several hours without stirring. Cut into squares and serve on crisp greens. No dressing is needed.

WITH CANNED FRUIT: Use a No. 2½ can of fruit cocktail (3½ cups) instead of the pineapple, orange, grapefruit, and grapes, if you wish.

24 HOUR SALAD   *Ten to Twelve* SERVINGS

*It doesn't take 24 hours to make this salad; it takes that
long for it to ripen. The recipe has been around a long,
long time. Purists call the salad dessert, because it is sweet.
But everybody loves it, and every hostess should know about
it.*

 3 egg yolks, well beaten
½ cup cream
¼ cup lemon juice
⅛ teaspoon salt
 1 can (about 1 lb.) Royal Anne cherries, pitted,
    (or seedless grapes)
 1 can (1 lb. 4 ozs.) pineapple, cut in small pieces
 1 cup almonds, blanched and slivered
½ pound marshmallows, cut in pieces
 1 cup heavy cream, whipped

First you make your dressing. Combine egg yolks, ½ cup cream, lemon
juice, and salt in top of double boiler. Cook and stir over boiling water
until thick. Cool. Fold in fruit, nuts, and marshmallows. Fold in
whipped cream. Pour into a large, shallow pan or bowl and chill for
several hours or overnight. Serve on lettuce with a cherry garnish. And,
yes, you may serve it for dessert.

MINT VINEGAR   *One* PINT

If you have a bed of mint, make yourself some mint vinegar to use in seasoning sauces for lamb, and for fruit salad dressings.

1 pint fresh mint leaves
1 pint white wine vinegar
1 peeled garlic clove
2 whole cloves

Wash mint and dry it on paper towels. Bruise the leaves and stems. Heat vinegar and pour it over mint, garlic, and cloves. Store in a covered jar. Remove garlic after a few hours. Let mint stand in vinegar for a week, then strain it out and put the vinegar in a bottle for use.

OLD-FASHIONED COOKED DRESSING *One* PINT

Much sharper than mayonnaise, this is excellent for potato salad, meat and seafood salads, and to blend with sour cream or whipped cream for all kinds of other salads.

2 tablespoons flour
1½ teaspoons salt
1 teaspoon dry mustard
1 tablespoon sugar
¼ teaspoon paprika
2 egg yolks, or 1 egg
1¼ cups milk, scalded
⅓ cup vinegar
1 tablespoon butter

Mix flour and seasonings in top of a double boiler. Add beaten egg and mix well. Add hot milk gradually, stirring constantly. Cook over hot water until smooth and thick, 12 to 15 minutes. Remove from heat, add vinegar and butter, beat until smooth, and chill. Dressing may be thinned with cream, milk, or French dressing.

BEEF-VEGETABLE SOUP   *Eight* SERVINGS

How about a batch of dumplings with this?

2½ pounds beef shank bone, with some meat, cracked
 1 tablespoon salt
 1 onion, sliced
 1 carrot, sliced
   Bay leaf
12 peppercorns
 1 quart mixed cut vegetables (potatoes, onions, green
      beans, carrots, turnips—whatever you like)

Simmer meaty bones in 2½ quarts water with salt and seasonings 3 to 4 hours. Remove bones, skim fat (chill stock if you have time, and remove fat in hardened layer). Add mixed vegetables and the diced meat from the soup bone to stock and cook tender. Adjust seasonings. Serve hot. It's just as good reheated.

I like to add a can of tomatoes or two or three fresh, peeled tomatoes cut in wedges to a batch of this soup, for color as well as flavor. A package of frozen peas added at 5 minutes before serving time is great, too.

FRENCH ONION SOUP   *Four* SERVINGS

A universal favorite, easy to make.

2 large mild onions, sliced thin
3 tablespoons butter or margarine
4 cups beef stock, bouillon cube broth, or canned bouillon
    or consommé, diluted as directed
4 slices toasted hard roll, covered with grated Parmesan
    cheese

Sauté onions in butter until yellow, add stock or consommé (salt and pepper if you need it). Heat thoroughly and serve in earthenware bowls if you have them, with a cheesed roll slice on each.

Added glamour: ¼ cup sherry, if you like.

CREAM OF PEA SOUP   *Four* SERVINGS

This soup is a pale green velvet aristocrat.

2 pounds (2 cups shelled) fresh peas; or 1 package frozen
      peas, cooked; or 1 No. 303 can (2 cups) peas
1 cup water or stock (except for canned peas)
1 small onion, minced
1 tablespoon butter
2 tablespoons flour
2 cups milk or milk and cream or evaporated milk
    Salt, pepper

Cook fresh or frozen peas tender in water or stock. Put through a
sieve or purée in an electric blender. Sauté onion in butter; add flour.
Blend and add milk. Stir and cook smooth, then add puréed peas and
salt and pepper to taste. Serve very hot.

Minted Pea Soup: Add 2 tablespoons chopped mint.

FRESH TOMATO SOUP   *Four* SERVINGS

*In the season of red-ripe tomatoes, nothing could be more
delicious!*

3½ cups chopped fresh tomatoes   3 slices onion
  3 sprigs parsley   1 teaspoon sugar
  6 whole cloves   1 teaspoon salt
  1 bay leaf   ·2 cups Thin White Sauce
  ¾ teaspoon whole
      black peppers

Simmer tomatoes, parsley, cloves, bay leaf, peppers, onion, sugar, and
salt, about 5 minutes, or until tomatoes are mushy. Rub through a
sieve or food mill. You should have 2 cups of purée; add boiling water
if necessary. Pour hot purée slowly into hot white sauce. Stir well
and serve.

CREAM OF CORN SOUP   *Six* SERVINGS

Almost my favorite soup. Garnish it with popcorn.

1 teaspoon minced onion
1 tablespoon minced green pepper (optional)
¼ cup butter or margarine
¼ cup flour
1 quart milk
1 can cream-style corn
Salt, pepper, paprika

Sauté onion (and green pepper) in butter a few minutes; add flour and blend. Add milk and stir until thickened. Add corn and seasonings. The flavor improves if you keep it hot 15 to 20 minutes in a double boiler.

Pickles & Relishes

CAN YOU FIND Grenadine Pears in your grocery? Or Red Pepper Jam? How about Cherry Dill Pickles, Minted Watermelon Cubes, or Pickled Plums?

All of these appetite-perkers are unusual, but they're all easy to make, and what fun they are to show off at special dinners!

Having your own corn relish to serve or give as gifts, being able to open a jar of your own homemade sauerkraut, and making pie from green tomato mincemeat you put up yourself are unique little thrills you may enjoy as you explore the field of pickle-making. What was fun for Grandma is even more fun for you. You don't *have* to make pickles; she did.

BREAD-AND-BUTTER PICKLES   *Five* QUARTS

This is the top-favorite pickle at our house—crisp and full of flavor.

25 medium cucumbers, sliced	2 teaspoons mustard seed
12 onions, sliced	2 teaspoons turmeric
½ cup salt	2 teaspoons celery seed
1 quart vinegar	2 teaspoons cassia buds or
2 cups sugar	1 stick cinnamon

Soak cucumbers and onion slices in ice water with salt for 3 hours. Heat pickling mixture to boiling, add cucumbers and onion, and heat for 2 minutes. Do not let pickles boil. Fill clean jars and seal at once.

It may be necessary to make twice the pickling mix, if cucumbers are bigger than medium size. Some cooks add a few sliced green and red peppers, just for color.

CHERRY DILL PICKLES   (*As many as you like*)

A delectable, sweet, crisp pickle. Better make a big batch.

Rinsed cucumbers, 4 to 5 inches long
Cherry leaves (grape leaves are good, too)
Dill
Brine (1 cup salt to 5 qts. water)
Mixed pickling spices
Sirup (3 cups sugar to 1 cup vinegar), boiled 10 minutes

Line bottom of a big stone crock with cherry leaves and dill, add a layer of cucumbers, then more dill and cherry leaves, more cucumbers, etc., until crock is three-fourths full. Dill and cherry leaves should be on top. Cover with brine. Weight down with plate and stone, cover with clean cloth, and let cure for 10 days at room temperature. Take cucumbers from brine, wash, dry, and slice into chunks, ½ to ¾ inch thick.

Pack in clean jars, add 1 teaspoon pickling spices to each jar, and cover with hot sirup. Seal and store 4 to 6 weeks.

DILL PICKLES MADE IN A CROCK

*This method takes from 2 to 3 weeks as a rule and pro-
duces a firm, crisp, flavorsome pickle.*

¼ bushel (12 lbs.) very fresh young cucumbers
2 gallons soft water
2 cups cooking salt
2 cups vinegar
    Grape or cherry leaves, if you have them
       or can get them
  Dill

Wash and scald a 4- or 5-gallon crock and cover the bottom with a
layer of well-washed grape or cherry leaves and dill. The leaves aren't
necessary, but they're awfully nice, for the sake of flavor as well as
for keeping color in the pickles.

Wash the cucumbers very well and pack half of them into the
crock. Add another layer of dill and leaves. Put in rest of pickles and
top with a final layer of leaves and dill. Boil water, salt, and vinegar
for 5 minutes and cool. Pour over cucumbers. Place a cover or plate
with a weight on it over them so that the cucumbers will be kept below
the brine during fermentation. Cover the crock with a clean cloth and
let it sit in a fairly warm place, 80° to 86° F., if possible. At a lower
temperature the process is slower. Remove scum from the top of the
pickles two or three times a week, and replace brine that evaporates
with more made in the same proportions of salt, water, and vinegar.

When pickles have stopped bubbling and are firm and flavorsome,
remove them from the brine and pack into clean jars with a sprig of
dill in each. Bring the strained brine to a boil and boil it 5 minutes,
then pour it over pickles and seal the jars. Label and store the pickles
in a cool place.

Kosher Dills. These are made in the same way, but a few cloves of
garlic and some small hot peppers are packed in the crock during fermentation. Two tablespoons of mixed pickling spices may be added to
the crock.

Green Tomato Dills. These may also be prepared by this recipe. Use
12 pounds small green tomatoes, and add ¼ cup mixed pickling spice
to the crock.

QUICK DILL PICKLES   *Eight* QUARTS

Unbelievably easy, and very, very good!

> 6–7 dozen cucumbers of even size (medium small)
> 1 head dill for each quart
> 3 quarts water
> 1 quart vinegar
> 1 cup salt

Scrub firm cucumbers thoroughly; rinse and pack closely into quart jars. Place a head of dill in the top of each jar. Mix water, vinegar, and salt; bring to a boil, and pour at once over the cucumbers. Seal the jars and store in a cool, dark place for at least six weeks before opening. Cucumbers will not be properly brined before that time. Use these pickles within 6 to 8 months.

Quick Garlic Dills. Put a peeled garlic clove in each jar.

Green Tomato Dill Pickles. Use the same recipe, with 6 quarts small green tomatoes. Put a garlic clove or two in each jar.

EASY PICKLED BEETS   *Two* QUARTS

A popular and excellent recipe.

> 2 quarts cooked or canned beets, cut with ridged cutter
> 2 cups vinegar
> ½ cup sugar
> 1 teaspoon salt
> 2 4-inch sticks cinnamon
> 16 whole cloves
> 1 bay leaf

Boil vinegar, sugar, salt, and spices 10 minutes. Heat beets in pickling mixture, let stand half an hour, drain and serve. Or bring to boil and seal in hot jars.

Purple Eggs. Chill hard-cooked eggs in beet pickle juice.

CHOW CHOW   Six PINTS

A mixed mustard pickle—the sauce is wonderful in potato and other vegetable salads.

1 quart tiny white onions, peeled
1 quart small cucumbers, sliced, or gherkins
2 heads cauliflower, broken into florets
2 green peppers, sliced thin

½ cup dry mustard
¼ cup flour
2 tablespoons curry powder
1½ cups sugar
½ cup cold vinegar
3½ cups hot vinegar

Cover vegetables with cold water and salt, allowing 1½ cups salt to 2 quarts water. Let stand overnight. Drain, add fresh water, and simmer until vegetables are barely tender. Drain again. Add dressing made by mixing mustard, flour, curry powder, and sugar to a paste with cold vinegar, stirring in hot vinegar, and stirring over moderate heat until thick. Simmer vegetables in dressing 10 minutes. Seal in hot, sterilized jars.

PICKLED SNAP BEANS   Two QUARTS

These are really delicious; you can't stop eating them!

2 pounds green beans (young, tender, stringless)
3 cups vinegar
2 cups water
2 cups sugar

2 tablespoons mustard seed
2 teaspoons peppercorns
2 teaspoons salt
2 cinnamon sticks
2 cloves garlic, chopped

Boil vinegar, water, sugar, and seasonings 10 minutes. Strain and keep hot. Remove ends from beans and cook in boiling water until almost tender. Drain well, pack into hot, clean jars, and pour the hot pickling mixture over them. Seal.

PICKLED BANANA PEPPERS   One QUART

Excellent—crisp and just bitey enough.

1–1½ dozen banana peppers
   3 cups vinegar
1½ cups sugar

Wash enough peppers to fill a quart jar when prepared. Cut off tops, remove seeds, cut into rings. Cover with boiling water, and let stand for 5 minutes. Drain, add cold water, and let stand for 10 minutes. Drain, pack into sterilized jar, and cover with sirup made by boiling vinegar and sugar for 15 minutes.

PICKLED CRAB APPLES   Three QUARTS

Use the prettiest of your apples for pickling, the others for jelly or jam.

3 quarts crab apples, firm and ripe, with stems
1 quart vinegar
5 cups sugar
1 stick cinnamon
1 tablespoon each, whole cloves, allspice, blade mace

Wash apples. Boil vinegar, sugar, and spices tied in a bag for 5 minutes. Add apples, and heat slowly to keep them from bursting. Simmer apples just until tender. Pack in clean, hot jars and fill with sirup. Seal.

PICKLED PEACHES   Four QUARTS

An excellent product. Honey may replace half the sugar.

4 quarts, whole, firm peaches, scalded, peeled
1 pint cider or white vinegar
4 cups sugar
2 sticks cinnamon
  Whole cloves

Boil vinegar, sugar, and cinnamon 5 minutes. Press 3 or 4 whole cloves into each peach. Drop peaches a few at a time into the hot pickling sirup and simmer until barely tender. Do not overcook. Pack in steril-ized jars, cover with boiling sirup, and seal.

Pickled Apricots. Use the same recipe, but don't peel the fruit.

GRENADINE PEARS
Six PINTS

The recipe divides easily—but they're so lovely and luscious, you'll want pints and pints of these pears!

8 pounds pears
6 cups vinegar
2 bottles grenadine (⅘ qt. each)
2 teaspoons cloves, heads removed
1 3-inch stick cinnamon

Pare, halve, and core pears. Bring other ingredients to a boil and drop in the pear halves, not too many at a time. Do not crowd them. Sim-mer until tender and place in jars. Fill with boiling sirup and seal.

PICKLED PLUMS
Six PINTS

Use the same recipe for green gages or red plums—equally delicious, but very different.

2 quarts large, firm-meated plums
3½ cups sugar
2 cups distilled white vinegar
1 stick cinnamon
1 teaspoon whole cloves
1 teaspoon allspice

Cook sirup and spices (in bag) 5 minutes. Add plums and cook gently until tender. Avoiding overcooking. Seal in hot jars.

OLD-FASHIONED WATERMELON PICKLES

Aftermath of a watermelon feast—a little pickling spree.

4 pounds (about 2 qts.) prepared watermelon rind
10 2-inch pieces cinnamon
2 tablespoons whole allspice
2 tablespoons whole cloves

1½ quarts white vinegar
1 lemon, sliced thin
1 quart water
10 cups sugar
2 tablespoons preserved ginger in thin slices (optional)

Cut off green and pink parts of rind; slice or cut into strips 2 inches long and an inch wide. Soak for about 2½ hours in 2 quarts water with 2 tablespoons salt. Drain, cover with fresh water, and cook until tender, adding more water as needed. Let stand in cooking water several hours.

Tie whole spices in a bag and add to vinegar, lemon, water, sugar, and ginger (if used). Boil 5 minutes, add watermelon rind, and simmer for 2 hours or until sirup is fairly thick and rind transparent. Remove spice bag, pack pickles into jars, and fill with boiling sirup to within ¼ inch of top. Seal.

MINTED WATERMELON CUBES *Six* HALF-PINTS

A firm, attractive pickle, delicious with roast lamb.

6 cups cubed watermelon rind
1 cup fresh mint sprigs, tightly packed
2 teaspoons whole cloves
2 sticks cinnamon

3½ cups water
6 cups sugar
1 cup vinegar
1 lemon, sliced thin
Green food coloring

Soak melon overnight in salt water to cover (2 tablespoons salt to 1 quart water) in refrigerator. Drain, cover with clear water, and boil for 30 minutes. Drain again. Tie mint leaves, cloves, and cinnamon in small cloth bag. Boil with water 2 minutes. Add sugar, vinegar, lemon and drained melon. Boil gently 50 minutes until cubes are transparent and sirup is slightly thickened. Tint the pickles with a few drops of food coloring. Remove spice bag and seal in hot jars.

CHILI SAUCE

Six PINTS

Just a good old-fashioned recipe for a good old-fashioned relish.

25 large ripe tomatoes, scalded, peeled,
      chopped, then drained
 3 small green peppers, chopped fine
 2 hot red peppers, chopped (optional)
 6 medium-size onions, chopped fine
 2 cups vinegar
 2 cups sugar
 2 tablespoons salt
 1 teaspoon ginger
 2 teaspoons cinnamon

Combine ingredients and boil until thick, about 2 hours. Seal in sterilized jars.

CRANBERRY CHUTNEY

One QUART

Excellent with the holiday turkey; pretty, pleasing.

2 cups fresh cranberries,
    coarsely chopped
3 slices fresh or canned
    pineapple, diced
6 dried apricots, diced
½ cup crystalized ginger,
    chopped
½ cup raisins
½ cup slivered blanched
    almonds

1 orange, seeded (peel on),
    ground
1 cup sugar
1 cup wine vinegar
1 teaspoon each of curry
    powder, dry mustard,
    cinnamon
½ teaspoon cloves
1 teaspoon salt

Combine ingredients in a saucepan and simmer for ½ hour. Let stand several hours to blend flavors before using. Keeps well.

EAST INDIAN CHUTNEY   Three QUARTS

A reader of my column gave me this recipe and it's terrific!

1 pint vinegar
1 pound brown sugar
2 pounds green tomatoes, sliced
    thin
1 mango, cut in pieces
3 large green apples, pared and
    sliced thin

3 small white onions, sliced thin
½ cup seedless raisins
½ cup seeded raisins
¼ cup sliced preserved ginger
½ teaspoon chili powder

Boil vinegar and sugar together until sugar is dissolved. Add remaining ingredients and cook until thick and dark like jam. Seal in sterilized jars. This is so good you can eat it right out of the jar.

BEET-AND-CABBAGE RELISH   Four PINTS

No cooking for this sweet-sour and peppery mixture.

1 quart cooked chopped beets
1 quart shredded cabbage
2 cups sugar
1 cup horseradish

1 tablespoon salt
1 teaspoon pepper
1½ cups vinegar
1 cup water

Mix beets, cabbage, sugar, horseradish, salt, and pepper and place in jars. Cover with vinegar and water and seal cold.

CHERRY RELISH   Three HALF-PINTS

A small batch of an unusual meat accompaniment.

3 cups pitted tart cherries
1 cup seedless raisins
1 teaspoon cinnamon
½ cup brown sugar
¼ teaspoon cloves

½ cup honey
½ cup vinegar
1 cup chopped walnuts or
    pecans

Simmer all ingredients except nuts for 45 minutes. Add nuts and cook 3 minutes longer. Seal in clean, hot jars.

CELERY RELISH   *Three* PINTS

A kitchenette recipe I predict you'll like. Make a double recipe, if you wish. Proportions are easy to multiply.

1 quart chopped celery
1 cup chopped white onions
2 large green peppers, chopped
2 large red peppers, chopped
2 cups vinegar
½ cup sugar
1 teaspoon salt
1 teaspoon dry mustard

Cook celery and onions in small amount of salted water for 10 minutes. Drain and mix with other ingredients. Boil until all vegetables are tender. Seal in clean, hot jars.

COUNTY FAIR CORN RELISH   *Five* PINTS

Here's the best corn relish ever made, for my money!

6 cups corn, cut from cob
3 cups cabbage, chopped fine
1 cup onions, chopped fine
1 cup celery, chopped fine
1 cup green pepper, chopped fine
3 tablespoons salt
1 quart cider vinegar
1 cup water

2 cups sugar
2 tablespoons dry mustard
4 teaspoons turmeric
½ teaspoon white pepper
½ cup flour
1 can pimiento (12 ozs.)
   chopped fine

Mix raw vegetables and salt. Add 2 cups vinegar and bring to boiling point. Boil gently for 20 minutes, stirring occasionally. Mix sugar, mustard, turmeric, white pepper, and flour together. Add remaining 2 cups vinegar and stir until smooth. Cook until thickened, stirring constantly. Add to vegetables and cook slowly for 30 minutes. Add pimiento last 5 minutes. Pour into hot, sterilized jars and seal.

CUCUMBER RELISH   *Five* PINTS

Everybody who samples it says, "Wonderful!"

12 large cucumbers	1 cup sugar
4 green peppers	1 tablespoon mustard seed
4 large onions	1 tablespoon celery seed
½ cup salt	White vinegar
1 cup horseradish	

Peel cucumbers, quarter, and remove seeds. Put all vegetables through food chopper. Add salt, mix well, and let stand overnight. In the morning drain, and add horseradish and other seasonings. Pack tightly in clean jars, add vinegar to cover, and seal.

PEPPER RELISH   *Seven* PINTS

This is prettier with both red and green peppers, but all green may be used.

12 sweet red peppers, chopped	2 cups sugar
12 green peppers, chopped	3 tablespoons salt
12 onions, chopped	1 tablespoon mustard seed
2 cups vinegar	

Cover peppers and onions with boiling water and let stand 5 minutes. Drain, add vinegar, sugar, and salt. Boil mixture for 5 minutes. Pour into clean hot jars and seal.

RED PEPPER JAM   *Five* SIX-OUNCE GLASSES

Really a relish of jam consistency, this is mighty tasty.

12 large red peppers, ground	2 cups vinegar
1 tablespoon salt	3 cups sugar

Sprinkle peppers with salt and let stand 3 to 4 hours. Drain, add vinegar and sugar. Boil to the consistency of jam, about 1 hour. Pour into hot glasses and cover with paraffin. Delicious with any kind of meat.

MIXED PICKLE RELISH   *Three to Four* PINTS

A very fine relish—you keep taking another spoonful!

1 green pepper, seeds removed	1 cup vinegar
1 red pepper, seeds removed	1 cup sugar
3 green tomatoes	½ teaspoon each, cinnamon,
1 large red tomato	turmeric
6 medium cucumbers	¼ teaspoon each, cloves, all-
1 onion	spice (ground)
2 tablespoons salt	1½ tablespoons mixed pickling
½ cup water	spices

Put vegetables through coarse blade of meat grinder, add salt, and let stand 24 hours. Drain. Combine with remaining ingredients (mixed pickling spices should be tied in a bag), and boil gently for 20 minutes. Stir frequently. Pour into clean, hot jars and seal.

TOMATO RELISH   *One* QUART

Flavor and color are excellent. The relish is sweet rather than sharp.

6 large ripe tomatoes, peeled and quartered	2 cups seedless raisins
6 large green tomatoes, ground	2 cloves garlic, mashed with salt
½ cup water	2 teaspoons salt
1 pound brown sugar	1 small red pepper, chopped (optional)
1 teaspoon ground ginger	2 cups slivered almonds
1 cup white vinegar	

Mix together all ingredients except almonds in a heavy saucepan. Bring to boiling point, lower heat, and cook until mixture is thick, stirring frequently about 1 hour. Add almonds, turn into hot, sterilized jars and seal immediately.

EASY PICCALILLI   *Seven* PINTS

Not too many ingredients, nor too much work.

1 dozen green tomatoes, medium size	1 cup brown sugar
	1 teaspoon dry mustard
1 dozen green peppers	1 teaspoon allspice
1 dozen onions, medium size	1¼ teaspoons red pepper (not cayenne)
1 cup salt	
1 quart vinegar	

Grind tomatoes, peppers, and onions in food chopper. Sprinkle with salt and let stand 4 hours, then drain. Place vinegar and sugar in saucepan and bring to a boil. Add chopped vegetables and spices. Boil 10 minutes. Seal in clean, hot jars.

SAUERKRAUT   *Sixteen to Eighteen* QUARTS

This is a Department of Agriculture method, with some modern refinements such as the use of a plastic bag of water to hold the kraut under its brine. Just be sure it is a strong bag!

About 50 pounds cabbage
1 pound (1½ cups) canning and pickling salt. (Table salt has a starchy filler to prevent caking. Try to get pure salt. Above all, do not use iodized salt, which may darken the kraut.)

Wash, quarter, and core mature heads of cabbage, discarding outer leaves. Shred fine, evenly. Work with 5-pound batches of the shredded cabbage, adding 3 tablespoons salt and packing into a clean crock. Let stand while you prepare the next batch. Cabbage wilts slightly and begins to form brine. Repeat shredding, salting, and packing, pressing cabbage down firmly until crock is filled to within 3 or 4 inches of top.

Cover cabbage with a clean muslin cloth, then with a plate or round paraffined board that fits just inside the container so that cabbage is not

344

Wild Grape Jelly, page 350, and Crabapple Jelly, page 348

exposed to air. Put a weight on the cover to keep brine over kraut. Or try this new method: Fill a heavy plastic bag (or use two, one inside the other) with water and place on top of the fermenting cabbage. The bag seals the surface of the sauerkraut, keeping out air, and serves as a weight. Let cabbage ferment for 5 or 6 weeks, until it ceases bubbling. Then heat to simmering (do not boil), pack hot in clean hot jars, covering with hot juice to within 1/2 inch of top of jar. Seal and process in boiling-water bath 20 minutes. Cool on racks, then store in a cool place.

HOW TO MAKE SAUERKRAUT IN JARS

When I was a child we ate a lot of sauerkraut, which we bought from a farmer who had a truck garden. I didn't know for years that anybody ever cooked kraut. We always ate it cold, juicy, and crisp. I still prefer it that way, although I have also learned to enjoy it cooked a long time with ribs or frankfurters. I am so glad for the country house, when it comes to kraut cookery. In the city on any evening when we'd have sauerkraut, the minister would come to call, or friends we hadn't seen in a long time would drop in, and I'd have to explain with some embarrassment why the house stank. In the country, with all that fresh air around, it doesn't matter.

Choose nice firm, mature heads of cabbage, remove outer leaves, quarter, and shred fine. To each 2 quarts shredded cabbage add 1 tablespoon salt and 1 tablespoon sugar. Mix well, put a weight on the cabbage and let stand overnight until a brine forms. Pack as tightly as possible into sterilized 2-quart jars (or 1-quart, if you haven't the bigger ones), screw on the lids, and place the jars in a shallow pan in a warm room until fermentation stops; about 2 weeks. During fermentation it is normal for the juice to run out and down the sides of the jars. If liquid doesn't cover the kraut at the end of fermentation, make a hot weak brine (2 tablespoons salt in a quart of water) and fill the jars. Tighten the covers when bubbling has ceased, wipe the jars, and dip tops in paraffin to prevent entry of air. Eat the kraut any time after 2 weeks. Store in a cool place.

345

TOP – *Sour-Cream Potato Salad, page 322*
BOTTOM – *Old-Fashioned Baked Beans, page 287*

BRANDIED MINCEMEAT   *Five* QUARTS

Very little trouble for so many fine pies!

2 pounds boneless beef, sim-
    mered tender and ground
½ pound suet, ground
6 tart apples, chopped
5 cups sugar
2 teaspoons salt
1 tablespoon cinnamon
1 tablespoon nutmeg
1½ teaspoons allspice
1½ teaspoons mace

1 pound raisins
1 pound currants
¼ pound candied orange peel,
    chopped fine
¼ pound candied lemon peel,
    chopped fine
1 pint cider or fruit juice
3 cups sherry or port
1 cup brandy

Combine all ingredients but brandy. Simmer 30 minutes. Cool, add brandy, and store covered in a cool place.

GREEN TOMATO MINCEMEAT   *Five or Six* PIES

*Here's a good reason for not caring when frost threatens be-
fore your tomatoes are all ripe.*

1 gallon sliced green tomatoes,
    chopped and drained
2 quarts quartered apples, cored
    and chopped
1 orange with peel, ground
1 cup ground suet
1 pound raisins

1 teaspoon salt
2 pounds brown sugar
2 cups cider or grape juice
2 teaspoons cinnamon
1 teaspoon cloves
1 teaspoon nutmeg
½ teaspoon ginger

Combine ingredients, cook slowly until thick, stirring occasionally. Pack in sterilized jars and process in pressure cooker at 10 pounds for 25 minutes.

Jellies & Preserves

THERE'S NOT MUCH REASON for making your own jellies and jams any more.

Except when strawberries in the market are exceptionally bright and juicy, and inexpensive.

And when the family has gone blackberrying.

And when your neighbor has given you a basket of plums.

And when you feel like doing something with all that fresh fruit, knowing it's going to be fun!

APPLE or CRAB APPLE JELLY

Six to Eight GLASSES

Rosy crab apples make the most beautiful and delicious jelly of all, but any crisp, fresh summer apple will do.

1 quart apple juice (see below)
3 cups sugar (4 cups for under-ripe apples and crab apples)

Boil juice and sugar in a large, heavy saucepan until sirup "sheets" from the edge of a spoon. At this point, sirup is thick, and two or three drops will run together at the edge of your spoon, hang for a second or two, and fall together. A candy thermometer is helpful, but only the sheet test tells you exactly when to skim and pour. Don't leave the boiling sirup for a moment, as the test comes fast with tart apples. Jelly point on a thermometer is indicated at around 220° F. At this stage, watch for the jelly point. Skim foam from sirup quickly and ladle it into clean jelly glasses. Cover at once with a thin layer of paraffin, and later put a lid on the glass or cover it with foil.

To Obtain Juice: Wash firm tart apples, quarter and place in a kettle with water to cover. Cover kettle and cook until fruit is very soft. Drain overnight in a jelly bag. Measure juice and cook it in 4-cup batches for perfect results.

Apple Butter. Pulp in the bag may be made into Apple Butter. Put it through a food mill, add ⅔ cup sugar for each cup of pulp (plus cinnamon, cloves, and nutmeg, if you wish, or a little bottle of hot cinnamon candies). Cook the mixture until thick, and seal in clean canning jars. Or make a second extraction of juice for jelly by adding water, reboiling, and straining again. Add only enough water to make a juicy mixture.

VARIATIONS

Thorn Apple Jelly. The bright little apples also known as red haws make beautiful jelly. Wash them, cook them soft in water to cover, and proceed as for apple jelly.

Rose Geranium Jelly. Put a washed, carefully dried (with paper towel) rose geranium leaf in each glass before pouring jelly.

Mint Jelly. Tie a cup of bruised mint leaves and stems in cheesecloth and boil 10 minutes with the apple juice before adding sugar. Put a mint leaf in each glass. A few drops of green food coloring usually are added to the boiling sirup, but aren't necessary unless you insist that mint must be green.

Fruit Combinations. You can make jelly from apple juice in combination with another fruit, half and half. Beautiful and delicious combinations include raspberry, elderberry, apricot, or nectarine.

CIDER AND SAGE JELLY   *Ten to Twelve* GLASSES

Delicious with roast pork, chicken, or turkey!

3 tablespoons dried sage leaves	7½ cups sugar
½ cup boiling water	1 bottle pectin
3½ cups cider	

Prepare a sage infusion by pouring the boiling water over the sage and letting it stand 15 minutes. Strain. Mix sugar, cider, and sage infusion in a large saucepan. Bring to boil over hottest heat, and at once add pectin, stirring constantly. Then bring to a full rolling boil and boil hard 1 minute. Remove from heat, skim, and pour quickly. Paraffin while hot.

Fresh Sage. Crush a cupful of packed leaves and bring to boiling point in 2 cups water. Let stand 20 minutes, strain, and add 2 cups cider. Proceed as directed. Total amount of liquid—4 cups—is the same.

CRANBERRY JELLY   *Four* SMALL GLASSES

Jewel-toned and very delicious, this goes a step beyond jellied cranberry sauce.

4 cups cranberries (1 pound)
3 cups water
  Sugar (¾ cup per cup of juice)

Cook berries in water until soft. Strain juice through jelly bag, or simply strain it. Measure juice and allow ¾ cup sugar for each cup of juice. Heat juice to boiling, add sugar and stir until dissolved. Cook rapidly to jelly point (see page 348), 10 minutes or so. Pour into sterilized glasses and seal with paraffin.

CURRANT JELLY or   *Six* SMALL GLASSES
CURRANT AND RASPBERRY JELLY

The queen of all jellies is currant, which you'll want to serve with duck and pheasant and all kinds of game. The color is deep ruby and the flavor just a little tart, but fruity.

2 quarts currants
1 cup sugar for each cup of juice

Wash and drain currants without removing stems, and place them in a kettle. Crush them as they heat for 2 or 3 minutes, until very juicy. Drain in a jelly bag, measure the juice, and add an equal amount of sugar. Stir to dissolve and bring to boiling. Boil rapidly until sirup gives the jelly test (page 348). Skim quickly and pour into clean, hot glasses. Seal with a thin layer of paraffin.

Wild Grape Jelly: Use same method; cook grapes with about an inch of water in the kettle, until very juicy before straining.

Raspberry and Currant Jelly. Equal parts raspberries and currants produce one of the most beautiful and delicious jellies you've ever seen or tasted. Here is a breakfast spread beyond comparison. My family laps it up all too fast!

DAMSON PLUM JELLY   *Four to Six* GLASSES

Damsons are first choice, but any bright-colored, tart plum can be used.

1 quart plum juice
3 cups sugar

Boil juice and sugar until sirup sheets from a spoon. Skim, pour, and seal with paraffin. Double the recipe if you like, but don't triple it.

To OBTAIN JUICE: Cover your washed plums with water in the preserving kettle, and cook them until very soft. Turn them into a jelly bag and let the juice drip overnight. You can then make jelly from the juice, put the pulp left in the bag through a food mill, and make a plum butter of that.

TO MAKE THE BUTTER: Add ⅔ cup sugar for each cup of pulp and cook down to a thick mixture. Be careful not to scorch. Spices may be added as for apple butter. Seal the butter in clean pint canning jars.

UNCOOKED GRAPE JELLY   *Four to Six* GLASSES

Surprisingly easy! Blackberries and apples make this kind of jelly too, which has fresh fruit flavor.

2½ cups grape juice (see below)
3¾ cups sugar

Combine 2 quarts Concord grapes, washed and with coarser stems removed, with ½ cup water, crush slightly, and cook about 10 minutes or until seeds are free and fruit is soft. Turn into a dampened jelly bag and let the juice drip. Measure 2½ cups into a preserving kettle. Bring to a full rolling boil; add sugar, and remove from heat at once. Stir for 2 minutes or until all sugar is dissolved. Pour into sterilized glasses and seal at once. This kind of jelly keeps better in the refrigerator or freezer than on the pantry shelf.

LEMON-HONEY JELLY   *Five* GLASSES

This is an unusual product. If you like honey, you'll love it. The texture is softer than usual.

2½ cups honey
¼ cup shredded outer yellow peel of lemon
¾ cup lemon juice
2 cardamom capsules, crushed
½ bottle liquid pectin (½ cup)

Add lemon peel to honey. Add lemon juice, and cardamom tied in a bag. Bring to a full boil, add pectin, and boil hard for 1 minute. Remove from heat, remove spice bag, skim, and pour into hot sterilized glasses. Seal with paraffin.

ELDERBERRY JELLY   *Eight to Ten* GLASSES

Late in August we gather elderberries at the farm. There are scads of bushes along the lane and down near the pond. We've tried making wine, of course, but elderberry jelly is better, and we like to keep on hand quart jars of elderberry sirup to pour over pancakes.

Elderberries won't jell of themselves. You have to use pectin, or combine the juice with apple juice.

3 cups elderberry juice   ½ cup lemon juice
7½ cups sugar   1 bottle fruit pectin

Stem about 4 pounds washed, ripe elderberries, crush in a large pre-serving kettle, and heat until juicy. Simmer uncovered for 15 minutes, strain through a jelly bag, squeezing out the juice. Measure sugar and juice back into kettle. Add lemon juice and mix well. Bring to a brisk boil and at once pour in the pectin, stirring constantly. Boil hard ½ minute, remove from heat, skim, and pour at once. Seal with paraffin.

PARADISE JELLY   *Six* GLASSES

Here's a beautiful jelly to accompany the Thanksgiving tur-key or the Christmas goose.

6 quinces, cut in pieces
10 apples, cut in quarters
2 cups cranberries
  Sugar (1 cup for each cup juice)

Cover quinces with water and cook 20 minutes. Add other fruit and more water if necessary, to just cover it. Boil until soft and let drain overnight in a jelly bag. Measure juice, bring to boiling point, and add sugar. Boil until sirup sheets from the edge of a spoon. A few drops may be tested on a cold plate to help determine jellying point. Beware of over-cooking this pectin-rich jelly, or flavor and texture will be spoiled. Pour and seal as soon as jelly test has been reached. A second extraction can be made.

PARSLEY HONEY
Four SMALL GLASSES

An old-fashioned, soft-textured jelly with a parsley bouquet —serve it with a chicken dinner.

2 quarts parsley, well washed and firmly packed
6 cups water
¾ cup sugar for each cup juice
   Juice of 1 lemon
   Few drops green coloring

Boil parsley in water for 10 minutes and squeeze out juice through 2 layers of cheesecloth. Add sugar, lemon juice, and coloring, bring to boil, and boil 15 minutes. Skim well. Pour into sterilized glasses and seal.

ROSE GERANIUM ORANGE JELLY
Six to Eight GLASSES

An unusual, delightful treat for your favorite guests.

2½ cups orange and lemon juice, strained
          (6 oranges, 4 lemons)
4½ cups sugar
½ bottle liquid fruit pectin
7 rose geranium leaves

Measure combined juices into a large saucepan. Add sugar and mix well. Place over high heat, bring to a boil, stirring constantly, and at once stir in pectin. Bring to a full, rolling boil, and boil hard 1 minute, stirring constantly. Remove from heat and skim off foam with a metal spoon. Place one washed, towel-dried rose geranium leaf in each of 7 jelly glasses. Pour jelly and cover at once with a ⅛-inch layer of paraffin.

Nasturtium Orange Jelly. Use nasturtium instead of geranium leaves.

BLACKBERRY JAM   *Eight to Ten* GLASSES

It's easy to overcook blackberry jam if you don't use pectin.
This way, you're sure.

  4 cups prepared fruit (2 quarts ripe blackberries)
  7 cups sugar
  ½ bottle liquid fruit pectin

Crush completely, one layer at a time, about 2 quarts fully ripe blackberries. (If desired, sieve half of pulp to remove some of the seeds.)
Measure 4 cups pulp into a very large saucepan. Add sugar to fruit in
saucepan and mix well. Place over high heat, bring to a full rolling boil,
and boil hard 1 minute, stirring constantly. Remove from heat and stir
in pectin. Then stir and skim by turns for 5 minutes to cool slightly, to
prevent floating fruit. Ladle quickly into glasses. Seal with paraffin.

QUICK GRAPE JAM   *Six* PINTS

My Aunt Addie, years ago, gave my mother the recipe for
the most wonderful-tasting grape jam I've ever eaten. It has
the true flavor of the fresh Concord grape, and is ridiculous-
ly simple to make.

    Don't try to double the recipe. This is as large a quantity
as will work successfully without the kettle boiling over,
or the jam becoming overcooked. Half this recipe is even
better, if you don't have bushels of grapes to put up.

  12 cups ripe Concord grapes, stripped from stems
  12 cups sugar

Combine grapes and sugar in a big preserving kettle. Place over high
heat and bring to a boil. Boil, stirring frequently for 20 minutes. Put
mixture through a food mill to remove seeds, then pour into clean, hot
pint jars and seal.

    (During World War II when sugar was hard to come by, we cut
the proportion to ¾ cup per cup of juice. Result: same marvelous fresh
grape flavor, but a thinner jam.)

BLUEBERRY or HUCKLEBERRY JAM

Twelve GLASSES

By either name, it's a colorful, delicious spread.

4½ cups crushed blueberries or huckleberries
    Juice of 1 lemon
    Grated rind of ½ lemon
  7 cups sugar
  1 bottle fruit pectin

Add lemon juice and rind to fruit. Add sugar and mix well. Bring to full rolling boil over high heat, stirring constantly. Boil hard 2 minutes, remove from heat, and stir in pectin. Skim and pour quickly. Seal with paraffin at once.

PEACH JAM

Ten to Twelve GLASSES

Everybody loves peach jam!

  4 cups prepared fruit (about 3 pounds ripe peaches)
¼ cup lemon juice
7½ cups sugar
  1 bottle liquid fruit pectin

Peel, pit, and grind or chop peaches. Measure 4 cups into a very large saucepan. Add lemon juice. Add sugar to fruit, mixing well, and place over high heat. Bring to a full rolling boil, and boil hard 1 minute, stirring constantly. Remove from heat and at once stir in liquid pectin. Skim off foam with spoon. Then stir and skim by turns 5 minutes to cool slightly. Pour quickly into glasses. Seal with paraffin.

    Crack a peach pit or two, blanch the "almond" therein, and boil it with the jam for an almond flavor.

CHERRY-CURRANT-RASPBERRY JAM
Six GLASSES

What a handsome and happy combination!

2 cups pitted sweet or sour cherries
2 cups stemmed currants
2 cups red or black raspberries
5 cups sugar

Combine prepared fruits and sugar in preserving kettle and bring to a boil. Boil as rapidly as possible without scorching, until a little of the juice dropped on a cold saucer seems fairly thick. Seal with paraffin.

PINECOT JAM
Ten HALF-PINTS

Add a cup of chopped nuts to make a conserve, if you wish.

1 pound dried apricots soaked overnight
2 large pineapples sliced, pared, cored, chopped fine
7 cups sugar

Cook chopped pineapple in 2 cups of the water used to soak apricots. When tender, add drained apricots and sugar. Cook, stirring occasionally, until thick, about 45 minutes. Seal with paraffin in hot jars.

PLUM JAM
Five PINTS

Thick, clear red, and delicious with meats or as a spread.

5 pounds (3 qts.) red plums, pitted and cut in pieces
9 cups sugar

Cook plums with ½ cup water until soft, add sugar and cook, stirring frequently, until thickened (make jelly test, page 348), about 20 minutes. Seal with paraffin in hot jars.

Plums can be cooked without seeding and put through a food mill to remove seeds.

RASPBERRY JAM
Six GLASSES

Color and flavor are superb and the recipe is foolproof, if directions are followed.

3 cups red raspberries
Juice of 1 lemon
3 cups sugar

Place raspberries in pan and mash slightly. Add lemon juice. Bring to boiling point and boil hard 1 minute. Add sugar and bring to boiling point again. Boil hard, stirring constantly, for 3 minutes. Pour into hot sterilized glasses and seal with paraffin.

FREE'S ROSE-PETAL JAM
Four to Six GLASSES

My husband amused himself and fellow Navy officers during some of his leisure time in the days of World War II by concocting unusual jams and jellies to present as gifts. Rose-petal Jam was the favorite of the Navy wives who were recipients. I believe that some of the husbands preferred the bourbon jelly, which is not in this book. Athens, Ga., the site of all this preserve-making, was bountifully supplied with both roses and bourbon.

Use fresh petals from your most fragrant roses. It may break your heart to tear the flowers apart—but later, you'll be glad!

2 cups ripe strawberries, cut in halves
2 cups rhubarb, diced and scalded
2 cups rose petals
4 cups sugar

Cover fruits and petals with sugar and let stand overnight. Cook until sirup sheets from a spoon, stirring frequently to prevent floating fruit. Pour into sterilized glasses and seal with paraffin.

357

STRAWBERRY JAM   *Five* HALF-PINTS

A popular and beautiful spread.

>   4 cups washed, drained, hulled strawberries
>   5 cups sugar
>   ½ cup lemon juice

Combine sugar and berries and let stand a few minutes, stirring occasionally, but being careful not to crush fruit. Bring to boiling point, then remove from heat and let stand overnight. In the morning bring to boil again, boil 10 minutes, stirring constantly, then add lemon juice and boil 2 minutes longer. Pour into clean hot glasses and seal.

OLD-FASHIONED   *Six* PINTS
CIDER APPLE BUTTER

The kind Grandma used to make, on the farm.

>   20 pounds tart summer apples   1 tablespoon cinnamon
>   1 quart cider   1 teaspoon cloves
>   Sugar (½ cup per cup fruit   1½ teaspoons allspice
>   pulp)

Wash apples, quarter, and cook with water to half cover them, until very soft. Put through colander or food mill, measure the pulp, and add half as much sugar, the cider, and the spices. Cook in a large, heavy kettle on top of the range, or spread in a dripping pan and bake in a slow oven, 250° to 300° F., stirring frequently, until thick and dark. Seal in hot, sterile canning jars.

SPICED PEACH BUTTER   *Three* PINTS

Try this with equal parts peaches and plums, too.

>   4 pounds peaches, quartered, not peeled
>   1 cup water
>   Juice 1 lemon

⅔ cup sugar per cup pulp
2 teaspoons cinnamon
½ teaspoon each, cloves, allspice

Cook peaches with water until soft, put through food mill, and measure. Add lemon juice, sugar, spices. Cook rapidly until thick and clear, stirring occasionally. Seal in clean, hot jars.

SWEET CHERRY PRESERVES *Four or Five* GLASSES

Nice trick: Add the shredded peel of an orange to this.

4 cups pitted sweet cherries and juice
½ cup lemon juice
3 cups sugar

Add enough water to cherries to keep them from scorching. Add lemon juice, and bring to the boiling point. Add sugar, and cook as rapidly as possible until preserves are clear and sirup is thick. Let cherries stand several hours in the sirup to "plump." Skim out fruit and place in clean jars. Bring sirup to a boil and pour over cherries. Seal at once.

Tart Cherry Preserves. Skip the lemon juice.

GREEN TOMATO PRESERVES *Two* PINTS

They're spiced with lemon, cinnamon, and ginger.

2 pounds tomatoes (1⅓ quarts small green ones)
2 cups brown sugar
1½ cups water
1 lemon
1 stick cinnamon
2 pieces ginger root

Combine sugar, water, thinly sliced lemon, cinnamon, and ginger and simmer 20 minutes. Remove spices. Add small green tomatoes and boil gently until they are bright and clear. Cover and let stand overnight. Drain off sirup, boil until thick as honey, add tomatoes, reheat to boiling, and seal in sterilized jars.

RED WATERMELON PRESERVES

Four HALF-PINTS

This time you use the meat of the melon, not the rind. A pretty and piquant relish.

    4 quarts diced red part of watermelon
    5 cups sugar
    ¼ teaspoon salt
    ½ cup vinegar
    2 slices lemon
    1 stick cinnamon
    1 teaspoon whole cloves

Use only red meat of watermelon. Place in colander, and with hands squeeze out as much juice as possible. (Drink it!) Then let drain for at least an hour. Combine melon with sugar, salt, vinegar, and lemon in large kettle. Add the spices tied in a small bag. Cook rapidly for 50 to 60 minutes, until thickened, stirring occasionally. Fill hot, sterilized jars and seal.

BLUE PLUM AND WALNUT CONSERVE

Eighteen GLASSES

Delightfully different.

    5 pounds blue plums, seeded, quartered
    5 oranges, quartered and ground (peel, too)
    1 pound seedless raisins
    6 cups sugar
    1 pound walnuts, chopped

Mix fruit and sugar and let stand for several hours. Bring to boiling point and then cook on low heat until thick, stirring frequently. Add nuts. Pour into sterilized glasses or jars and seal with paraffin.

GOLDEN MARMALADE   *Two* PINTS

Beautiful color, perfect flavor!

    2 medium-size oranges
 5½ cups water
    1 lemon, juice and grated rind
    2 cups dried apricots
    3 cups sugar

Slice one unpeeled orange very thin. Add 2½ cups water and grated rind from the lemon. Boil 1 hour. Rinse apricots and cover with the other 3 cups of water. Boil until tender, about 45 minutes. Beat to a pulp. Add sugar, cooked orange slices, juice from second orange, and the lemon juice. Boil slowly until very thick, about 1 hour. Stir frequently to prevent scorching. Seal in hot sterilized jars.

SPICY TOMATO MARMALADE   *Five* PINTS

Use red, yellow, or even green tomatoes for this delicious, spicy spread.

    4 quarts whole tomatoes (3 qts., sliced)
    2 oranges, sliced very thin
    2 lemons, sliced very thin
    4 pounds sugar
    1 large stick cinnamon
 1½ tablespoons whole cloves

Pour off half the juice from the peeled, sliced tomatoes (save juice for soup). Add oranges, lemons, and spices tied loosely in cheesecloth bag. Bring to boiling point, boil rapidly, stirring frequently, until thick and clear. Seal in hot sterile jars. Good with meats.

INDEX

373

374